235 STATUTE MILES————————————————————▶ ○
SAN FRAI

MIDWAY

PEARL HARBOR ○

HAWAII

C   I   F   I   C

O   C   E   A

PACIFIC
THEATER,
1942

Black areas indicate territories
occupied by the Japanese

OUR JUNGLE ROAD TO TOKYO

OUR JUNGLE ROAD
TO TOKYO

ROBERT L. EICHELBERGER

IN COLLABORATION WITH MILTON MACKAYE

NEW YORK · 1950

THE VIKING PRESS

I had intended to dedicate this book to my wife, who suffered through four years of separation and uncertainty. She has asked me, instead, to dedicate it to the lads who never came home.

CONTENTS

General Eichelberger at Buna, late December 1942.

Colonel Grose and General Eichelberger at Buna, December 1942, in The Triangle which had just been captured. A hundred yards farther on they came under heavy fire and shot four men out of a large tree.

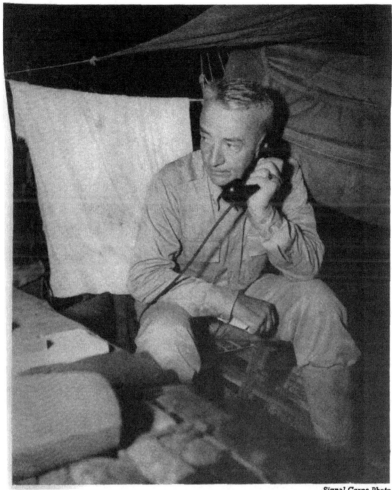

Headquarters at Buna after the end of the fighting, January 1943.

General Eichelberger and his staff go ashore in an LCV at Zamboanga on D-day.

Later the same day on the beach with General C. E. Byers, chief of staff, and Sergeant Thaddeus Dombrowski (at right).

General Eichelberger listens while interpreter questions Jap prisoner.

Looking over situation map at command post, Mindanao.

Crossing a makeshift bridge into a small town recently fallen, Zamboanga,
March 1945.

General Eichelberger inspects trophies from a banzai attack at Maramag Airstrip, central Mindanao, May 1945. At left, General Clarence A. Martin.

Last-minute instructions to members of the staff en route to Mindoro.

General Joseph Swing points out the first view of Manila to General Eichelberger and Colonel Frank S. Bowen, Jr., February 1945.

Colonel Bowen, General Eichelberger, and Colonel McGowan on two-thousand-foot Tagaytay Ridge thirty miles from Manila, February 1945.

Signal Corps Photo

En route to Manila with General Swing, February 1945.

Signal Corps Photo

**Taking cover behind old Spanish Barracks wall near Manila, February 1945.
Colonel Schimmelpfennig, chief of staff of 11th Airborne (to the general's right),
was killed a few hours later.**

Signal Corps Photo

General Eichelberger and President Osmeña of the Philippines.

General Eichelberger talks with Filipinos on Luzon after the liberation.

With the Sultan of Sulu on the Island of Jolo, May 1945.

General Eichelberger and General Swing talk to General Seizo Arisuye on
Atsugi Airstrip, Japan, August 1945, just before the arrival of General MacArthur.

Signal Corps Photo

Five minutes after the arrival of the Supreme Commander, August 1945.

With Admiral Halsey on board the *Missouri* on Surrender Day.

General Eichelberger and the crew of his plane, the *Miss Em*, November 1945.

The *Miss Em* over Fujiyama, November 1945.

U.S. Army Photograph

Robert S. Eichelberger

A PERSONAL NOTE

Every story has a beginning, and I suppose mine began when a certain Philip Frederick Eichelberger emigrated to the American colonies in 1728. The Eichelbergers had lived for several generations near Heidelberg, but they were originally German Swiss from Basle. They were honest and good people who fought in the American Revolution and lived in Pennsylvania and Maryland before moving to Ohio. The German blood, through intermarriage with other stocks, grew a little thin, but the name stayed long and rotund. I honor my ancestors—but their legacy to my three brothers and me was a name more often spelled against than spelled.

The Eichelbergers, when my father first knew them, had shifted from Lutheranism to Methodism. My father, who was graduated from Ohio Wesleyan University, interrupted his education to serve several short enlistments during the Civil War. In later years, when complacent memory and just plain lying elevated the rank of most of his G.A.R. brethren, Father maintained that he was the only noncommissioned officer ever to serve in the Union Army.

My mother was a Southern girl. Mother's family lived in Port Gibson, Mississippi, and she told me many stories of the fighting around Vicksburg. She had personal knowledge of the horrors of war because, as a young girl, she had held the basin while Confederate Army doctors in the field amputated arms and legs. And Gen-

eral McClernand of the Union forces subsequently made his headquarters in the family home. With a Northern father and a Southern
mother, to say nothing of a Southern wife, I can only settle gracefully this long after for a position of absolute neutrality in the War
between the States.

My grandfather's farm was about a mile east of the public square
in Urbana, Ohio. The old homestead, which was built in 1843, still
stands. My father was a lawyer, and a good one. His partner was
Judge William Warnock, who as a Republican member of Congress
gave me my appointment to West Point. I was the youngest of the
surviving children. I had one sister, Susan (now Mrs. J. B. Zerbe),
and my brothers were George, Fred, and Frank. No one, I believe,
could have had a happier childhood than ours.

When I was four my father bought a carload of ponies. It would
be difficult to explain to modern youngsters the very splendor and
expansiveness of this enterprise. Every child in my day wanted a
pony; my father bought a *carload*. The result, of course, was that the
old homeplace became the assembly area for most of the boys in
Urbana. For a period of years our stables had a distinct resemblance
to Grand Central Station. My brothers and I and assorted local volunteers trained those ponies, and they won many prizes in local
competitions and at county fairs.

I was graduated from Urbana High School and went on to Ohio
State University. In 1905 I entered West Point, and four years later
I was graduated. My first assignment as an officer was with the 10th
Infantry. Much of this tour of duty was spent in Panama, and it was
there I met my wife. She was Emma Gudger, daughter of Federal
Judge H. A. Gudger of Asheville, North Carolina, who was then
Chief Justice of the Panama Canal Zone. We were married in April
of 1913. Those Panama years were memorable ones. Although an
obscure lieutenant, I came to know many of the men who were per-
forming an engineering and sanitation miracle; they included General Gorgas, who defeated yellow fever there, and General Sibert,
who built the Gatun Dam. I saw the construction of the Culebra Cut
and was a passenger on the first ship which made its way through
the locks from the Atlantic to the Pacific.

I had my first glimpse of military combat when I was assigned to the 22nd Infantry in 1915 and spent a year in a tent on the Mexican border. The town of Douglas, Arizona, was jammed with American troops. Mexico was ablaze with revolution, and in our particular section General Obregón and Pancho Villa were engaged in a fight to the death. The official view was that General Obregón represented the Mexican government and that Villa was a bandit—a view that was colored by American sympathies and a view which was, perhaps, not inexact. Our troops were quartered there because no one knew what outrages Villa might attempt. This was the period which President Wilson called "watchful waiting."

Villa attacked Agua Prieta, just across the border from Douglas, in what turned out to be a three-day fight. I recall seeing on a chill moonless night just before the attack the hundreds of campfires which indicated Villa's men were there in force. And hearing from the surrounding barren hills the eerie clamor of coyotes. When daylight came I watched Villa's army of Indian youngsters straggle by with seventeen field pieces—which in those days, it might be added, was a not inconsiderable amount of artillery.

We Americans could see much of the fighting because in many places only a barbed wire fence separated us from Mexico. We were neutral, but stray bullets know no international law, and there were casualties on our side. (The camp was later called Camp Harry Jones for one of the American soldiers who was killed.) It was a bitter battle without quarter. On one occasion I stood in the door of a slaughterhouse, which was exactly on the international border, and watched the struggle in the parched Sonora sunlight. There was a water hydrant in the slaughterhouse and wounded and dying Mexicans came there to beg for a drink. As neutrals we were under strict orders not to give them water—but we did.

Villa had the edge in the battle for Agua Prieta. There were no east-west railroads in northern Mexico, but there were railroads on the American side. The *Obregonista* reinforcements which turned the tide at Agua Prieta came in over the El Paso & Southwestern, an American line. Pancho Villa took this kind of neutrality in bad part and paid off his grudge the following spring when he made his

celebrated raid on Columbus, New Mexico. This incident led in turn to Pershing's difficult punitive expedition into our neighboring republic.

I spent the next year in the uneventful environs of Kemper Military School at Booneville, Missouri, where I served as professor of military science and tactics and augmented my meager lieutenant's pay by teaching several classes in mathematics. I was restless, like most Army officers, as the thunder of the great war in Europe came always nearer. When the lightning at last struck in April of 1917 I was sent to Salt Lake City to command a battalion of the 20th Infantry. Later I went to the 43rd Infantry and then to the General Staff in Washington.

There I served under Major General William S. Graves, the Executive Assistant Chief of Staff, a highly trained, self-reliant soldier with a self-effacing sense of duty. In the summer of 1918 General Graves was sent to command the 8th Division at Palo Alto, California, and I went along. Offered his choice of combat divisions, my superior chose the 8th because it was scheduled to go to Europe within thirty days. Two weeks after our arrival in California, General Graves was summoned by code message to meet Newton D. Baker, Secretary of War, in Kansas City. This highly secret meeting completely rearranged my immediate future.

On August 15 General Graves sailed—not for Europe but for distant Vladivostok. I accompanied him as assistant chief of staff. By President Wilson's direct order, Graves had been made commander of the American Expeditionary Forces in Siberia. Some ten thousand American troops took part in the strange and unlikely military adventure of 1918–20, but to this day most of the public is unfamiliar with the historical details. Our intervention in the confused Russian situation was accomplished in cooperation with the Japanese, British, French, and Chinese. It is a complicated story from which the British and French emerge with no particular credit. The Japanese High Command, however, managed to achieve for itself a record of complete perfidy, of the blackest and most heinous double-dealing.

President Wilson had announced in effect that the purpose of the mission was the protection of Siberian railroads and the prevention of anarchy, and that there was no intention of interfering with Russian internal affairs. It was soon clear to me (I was operations officer and later head of military intelligence) that the British and French had the clear-cut purpose of overthrowing the infant Soviet republic and had perpetuated various fictions to persuade President Wilson to commit American troops and American reputation to a dubious expedition. Various representatives of our own State Department urged that large forces of American soldiers be thrown into Siberia to assist the cause of Admiral Kolchak, the White Russian commander.

Looking backward, I now feel that it would have been a blessing if the Soviet republic had been crushed in its cradle. The fact is, however, that President Wilson's orders to General Graves called upon him to bring economic relief to the Russian people and to maintain a position of neutrality between Russian factions—and Graves courageously and adamantly did so in the face of tremendous pressures. Support of Kolchak by the British and French proved to be a bankrupt and futile enterprise by late 1919. The peasants from Lake Baikal to Vladivostok had no particular interest in the Communists, but they developed an active hatred of the ancient czarist methods of the Whites, and the brutalities and cruelties of the Kalmikoffs, Semeonoffs, and Rosanoffs—the murderous wretches who were supported principally by the Japanese military.

There is not room here to comment further on my Siberian experiences, but I was young enough and adventurous enough at the time to find pleasure in a variety of hairbreadth adventures. I was in Siberia for a little less than two years and traveled thousands of miles to find out what was going on. Sometimes, in order to do so, it was necessary to be a gravedigger. On more than one occasion I directed the disinterments which established legal proof of White Russian massacres.

The full account of Japanese perfidy must wait. Suffice it to say that when I departed the Japanese were in full control of eastern Siberia. They had entered the country on the pretext of preserving law and order—and had created disorder. They had agreed solemnly to send in 12,000 troops and had sent in 120,000. They intended to

stay. Out of my Siberian experiences came a conviction that pursued me for the next twenty years: I knew that Japanese militarism had as its firm purpose the conquest of all Asia.

I left Vladivostok on April 16, 1920, and went on to Tokyo. After a few weeks' vacation my wife, who had recently come over by military transport, and I went on to the Philippines, where I became chief of military intelligence for that section of the Orient. I set up G-2 offices in Tientsin and other cities and spent a good deal of my time in China.

When I returned to Washington I remained in the military intelligence section of the General Staff, concerning myself principally with Russia and the Far East. Probably the most interesting single event of that 1921–24 tour of duty in Washington was the Limitation of Armaments Conference. Few youngsters who found themselves in uniform in the recent conflict were of sufficient years to remember the taffy-warm hopes of 1922. President Harding had invited the major nations of the world to convene here and to arrive at, through their delegates, a scheme by which an armament-weary world might shed itself of its heavy burden. Americans, then as now, were hungry for the promise of peace—and I shared the hope that a gathering of nations around a table might bring it about.

It was a spectacular conference, with the panoply of rank and full-dress uniforms. There was more gold braid than Washington had seen in all its history, and there was a formal ball almost every night. Looking back, it seems to me like the delayed sunset of a nineteenth-century Europe. But it did not seem to me that way at the time. I was the military aide to the Chinese delegation, and I enjoyed every minute of my participation. I sat in Constitution Hall when Secretary of State Hughes announced that the United States would destroy part of its fleet to meet the 5-5-3 naval apportionment to which Britain and Japan had agreed. That night, at the White House party for foreign delegates, I felt my first doubts when I observed Prince Tokugawa's happiness. But there was a considerable satisfaction for old Vladivostok hands when Japan, as part of the bargain, moved out of Tsingtao and Siberia. The Japanese had been there, despite solemn pledges, ever since our regiments had left.

There is not much about a peacetime military life which is interesting to the general public, but mine was interesting to me. I kept being sent back to school. In 1925—at the age of thirty-nine—I became a student at the Command and General Staff School at Fort Leavenworth. I learned more at thirty-nine than I ever learned at twenty-one. Business executives sometimes criticize the military services for their handling of personnel problems and their short-sighted policies, but how many corporations take a thirty-nine-year-old officer out of the production line and order him to continue his education? That year I sat next to another officer who was not in knickerbockers. The roll call was alphabetical and our names were similar. Dwight D. Eisenhower came out top scholar in our class. This was my earliest association with Ike; in subsequent years we were to meet often and pleasantly.

I spent four years at Leavenworth, Kansas. After my student year I became an instructor, and then adjutant general. Through this postgraduate school, in peace times, passed many of the Army officers who were to make their mark when the storm signal was flying. One of them was General George Kenney, who subsequently was air commander in the South Pacific. The commandant at Leavenworth at the time was Brigadier General Edward L. King, who accepted the Prohibition law with grim seriousness. Anyone on the post who took a drink was personally disloyal (in his view), and anyone bringing in liquor was subject to court-martial. George Kenney was stopped by military police as he came into camp one night and six bottles of liquor were taken from his automobile. He appeared before me, as adjutant general, next day and assumed despairingly that his military career was ruined. It wasn't. I had no recollection of the incident until years later George Kenney told me about it in the very hot and moist climate of New Guinea. He told me I had made him happy by tearing up his summons.

After Leavenworth I went to school again, this time to the Army War College in Washington, and during this year of postgraduate inquiry into military strategy I worked very hard. Caesar, Napoleon, Wellington, Sherman—a clear understanding of their military tactics has never handicapped a green officer in the field. I am still proud of the fact that at graduation I was given a superior rating and that my class of 1930 (or so I am told) turned out more generals than any class in history. Of course, the fact that a war came along later had something to do with it.

In 1931 I was sent to West Point and served there for four years as adjutant general and secretary of the Academic Board. In the spring of 1935 I was appointed Secretary, General Staff. It would be silly for me to pretend that I took this appointment calmly in my stride; I was vastly pleased, and my ego, if not my hatband, had to be let out several inches. It was a key job in the War Department, where one, by the very nature of the duties, became familiar with the most intricate and intimate problems of Army planning and administration.

There are problems of advancement in a peacetime army upon which I might comment here. There are problems of income too. In 1920 I was a temporary lieutenant colonel and reverted to the permanent grade of major. It was not until fourteen years later that I rose to lieutenant colonel and a lieutenant colonel's pay again. And I was luckier than most. There are ampler ways of making a living than a professional military career. But I guess it must have its satisfactions; despite business offers I never seriously considered getting out of the Army.

When I went to Washington, General Douglas MacArthur was Chief of Staff (he had held the post for four and a half years), and Major General G. S. Simonds, one of the most beloved officers of his generation, was Deputy Chief of Staff. During the next few months I saw General MacArthur many times each day in line of duty and became familiar with his methods of administration and his interesting personal quirks. Major Eisenhower was then his senior aide and confidant; Ike received me with friendship and the utmost cordiality. Another firm friend of the period was General "Pa" Watson, who occupied an office next to mine and was military aide to President Roosevelt.

When General MacArthur went to Manila to become military adviser to the new Philippine Commonwealth, General Malin Craig became Chief of Staff. Thus began for me a close personal association which was to last until General Craig's death in July of 1945. He had a reputation as a strict disciplinarian; to me he was a wise and understanding mentor. For three years I lunched almost daily with him in his office and heard at first hand the troubles of a Chief of Staff. I always sat facing a large portrait of William Tecumseh Sherman, and soon I felt I knew what made the grim-faced Sherman grim. Long after our ways parted General Craig and I kept up a faithful correspondence, and during the dark days of the Pacific conflict his wise, sane letters helped sustain my spirit.

The fires which were to burst into the blaze of World War II were already burning slowly in Europe. Believing that trouble might not be too far away, I transferred back to the infantry (I had been in the Adjutant General's department for some years), and late in 1938 my wife and I sailed from Charleston through the Panama Canal to San Francisco. There I took command of the 30th Infantry.

This was an old Regular Army regiment which soon became a gypsy outfit constantly on the move between San Francisco, Fort Lewis, Washington, and Fort Ord near Monterey. There were maneuvers and more maneuvers, command-post exercises over new and varied terrain. During the two years I served as colonel of the 30th I gained experience which proved invaluable to me when I assumed greater responsibilities. Taking part in many of these maneuvers were the 40th and 41st Divisions of the National Guard—divisions which I was to know well later and to soldier with in jungle combat.

During part of this period on the West Coast I also served as assistant division commander of the 3rd Division, to which my regiment belonged. It was a busy life, and I was seldom in one place very long. Our permanent home was at the Presidio in San Francisco; from our windows we could see both the Golden Gate and beautiful Treasure Island where, in 1940, a World's Fair was in progress. And from my office windows I could also see the heavily laden ships of the Japanese merchant fleet as they steamed through the Golden Gate and out to sea—carrying to the Japanese homeland war matériel and American scrap iron.

During October of that year I was back from the field and was enjoying a little home life in that (to my mind) most handsome of

all Army posts. One morning Miss Em, my wife, came home with a telegram in her hand. She was weeping. I tried to find out who had died. Finally she told me I had been promoted. My name had been on the first list of colonels to be advanced to the grade of temporary brigadier general. A day or so later I received a wire from an exuberant West Point classmate who shared my good fortune and who was to go on to great fame. This was the message:

> At last they have had sense enough to promote
> the two best damn officers in the U.S. Army.

The message was signed—George H. Patton.

From then on events moved at a fast and furious pace—fast and furious almost to the point of confusion. In only a few days, and in quick succession, I was assigned to three different posts. General Joe Stilwell was organizing the 7th Division and, as a result of a telephone call from Washington, I reported to Uncle Joe at Monterey to be assistant division commander. When I returned to San Francisco to collect my belongings I found awaiting me a superseding order which directed me to go to Columbus, Ohio, to command the VII Corps Area. Hardly had I purchased railroad tickets when there was further news. I had been appointed Superintendent of the Military Academy at West Point.

I am so constituted that I approach any new job with enthusiasm and an accelerated pulse, but I felt a particular delight in returning to West Point. There was a job to be done in the modernization of training. The cadets put on fatigue uniforms, and there were maneuvers in the New Jersey farm lands in cooperation with National Guard units. The hours given over to training were increased, at some expense to academic work and with a great reduction of the time previously devoted to riding horses. It was a gasoline age. I changed publicity methods too. There were no more polite newspaper photographs of cadets jumping horses over hurdles. Photographs of cadets smiling at pretty young women were held to a minimum. Instead there were pictures of cadets making river crossings under smoke barrages.

I also made every effort to tighten the ties between West Point and the Air Forces. I increased the emphasis on flying, and ultimately a plan permitting those students who so elected to obtain their wings before graduation was accepted by the War Department. George Catlett Marshall, whom I had known when he was Deputy to General Craig, was now Chief of Staff, and he gave me strong and friendly backing in all my enterprises, as did General Watson from his vantage point in the White House.

During the First World War the West Point period of training had been temporarily reduced to one year. This is insufficient education for officers who are to become permanent members of the military establishment, and it was a long time before the Academy could entirely recover from the blow. When I became Superintendent there were again strong pressures for reducing training to a short course. With the backing of the Academic Board, I fought vigorously to retain the full course, and eventually the clamor died down. During the war the course was reduced to three years, but I had put off the evil day.

There was a lighter side to my tour of duty. My first afternoon as Superintendent was spent at Franklin Field, where I saw the University of Pennsylvania football team demolish Army 48-0. The cadets were wonderful losers; they continued to cheer their team to the opponent's last touchdown. But I felt they deserved a team which would teach them to be good winners. I still think, insofar as Army officers are concerned, that the concept of graceful losing can be overdone; in combat warfare there may be no game next week.

I knew West Point had had two disastrous football seasons, and I believed the explanation lay, first, in cadet weight limits set by the Surgeon General's Office, and, second, in uninspired coaching. Academy tradition required that the head coach be an Army officer on active duty. I wrote Earl Blaik, successful coach at Dartmouth, and asked him not to sign a contract there until he talked to me. Then I attacked the problem of weight limits. The standard cadet, six feet tall, was supposed to heft the scales at only a hundred and sixty pounds, with a ten per cent swing either way as a limit. The Surgeon General's Office had been steadfastly refusing waivers for overweight on the theory that life expectancy is greater for a slender man. This may be true from an actuarial viewpoint, but it is a hell of a way to run a football team. And the fact that an athlete by his mere size and appearance may make a compelling combat leader apparently had been lost sight of by the yardstick experts; life expectancy in battle for big or little men is just about the same.

I made several trips to Washington, but in the end it was necessary to enlist the assistance of Pa Watson, a loyal football fan. Eventually the Surgeon General agreed to instruct examination boards throughout the country that waivers could be granted "when overweight was due to an athletic build and not to obesity." This was exactly what we wanted.

I had tremendous admiration for Red Blaik. A graduate of West Point who subsequently resigned from the Army to enter business, he had served as a civilian assistant coach back in the early 1930's before going to Dartmouth. I knew him well and thought he was the finest football strategist in the country. I still think so. He is also an honorable gentleman and an inspiration to team and cadet corps. When Red Blaik yielded to my persuasions in December of 1940 and agreed to return as head coach, the long victory drought on the highlands above the Hudson came to an end.

Colonel Blaik will forgive me for telling one story on him. In view of Academy tradition (which we were about to violate), he wondered just what his standing would be on the West Point reservation as a professional coach. I suggested he go over to the Officers' Club barbershop and have his hair cut by Tom Impel, widely known raconteur and wielder of scissors. A haircut for a second lieutenant took five minutes, for the Superintendent forty-five minutes. When Red came back with a sworn record of a thirty-five-minute shearing, we agreed he would rank second on the post.

Some readers may regard this preoccupation with football as frivolous and inconsequential, but I do not apologize. I like football. After I left West Point, I still kept track of the teams. The Army-Navy game most memorable to me took place in the late fall of 1944. It was two-thirty in the morning, and I sat by the short-wave radio in a shack on the island of Leyte in the Philippines. There were several sounds: dry rustling palm fronds, the pound of the Pacific

Ocean on the nearby shore—and static. And then came a Japanese air raid. We blacked out in a hurry, but no one turned off the broadcast. It was only the third quarter.

General Watson told me on one occasion that President Roosevelt regarded the responsibility for appointments to three Army jobs to be exclusively his: Chief of Staff, Chief of Engineers, and Superintendent of the Military Academy. As a result, Pa Watson took upon himself a large measure of responsibility for the West Point operation. I heard several times during those months that General Lesley J. McNair, boss of the Ground Forces, and Colonel Mark Wayne Clark, his chief of staff, were trying to get me away from the Academy to command a division in the new army. Whenever the wishes of the War Department were conveyed to Pa Watson, he always said, "No, he's needed there."

In July of 1941 during a luncheon I was giving at West Point for Carl Van Doren, the biographer and historian, Earl Blaik, Lawrence Perry, the sportswriter, and Perry's sportswriting son, an orderly came to say that the White House was calling. When I reached the telephone General Watson said, "Bob, are you a major general?"

"Pa, you would know better than I would."

"Well, you have been since eleven thirty-five A.M. Marshall told me I was ruining your record by not allowing you to earn your two stars by going to command of a division. On my desk was a War Department list of proposed promotions to the grade of major general. I couldn't find any room at the bottom, so I put your name at the top and took it to the President for approval. It's approved."

The times were moving fast. Some people refused to see the stormclouds. Congress reinvoked the draft law by a margin of only one vote. On the Thursday before Pearl Harbor I spoke in New York at a banquet given by Phi Gamma Delta, my college fraternity at Ohio State. Talking off the record, I told the assemblage I believed that war with Japan would come within a few days and that it would start with a surprise attack on us by the Japanese. This statement created, after the dire event, a startled correspondence. Many brethren wrote to ask how I had come into possession of advance knowledge of the Pearl Harbor assault.

The truth was, of course, that I had no inside military information. My prediction was based on the steadily disintegrating international situation, my experience with the Japanese militarists in Siberia, and a certain familiarity with the pattern of Japanese history. I remembered the surprise attack on Port Arthur in the Russo-Japanese war, the Mukden and Peking incidents, and the treacherous attack on Vladivostok which I had personally witnessed in 1920, and drew my own conclusions.

Shortly after Pearl Harbor I asked for my release from West Point. I was fifty-five years old, but I felt I would be useful to my country in a combat assignment. Three experimental divisions of a new type were being formed at that time, and, given my choice, I selected the 77th Division, which was to be activated in March at Fort Jackson, South Carolina. Commanders of the other two divisions were General Omar Bradley and General Henry (Chick) Terrell. After orientation in Washington, Bradley, Terrell, and I accompanied our principal staff officers to Leavenworth for a brief course while our artillery officers were trained at Fort Sill and our infantry officers at Fort Benning. Then we were ready for work.

When I took the 77th I requested that Clovis E. Byers, then a lieutenant colonel on duty with the General Staff, be assigned as my chief of staff. Despite promises, there was some difficulty about the matter; Byers was junior to many officers who wanted the job, and the personnel section of the Army was in a state of confusion. It was true that Byers was guilty of being young, but he had served under me at West Point, I knew his qualities, and I wanted him. I never regretted that red-tape tussle. Byers served as my chief of staff throughout the war—progressing from a division to an army—and I hereby acknowledge heavy indebtedness to him; he was resourceful, loyal, and energetic.

The 77th Division troops came mostly from New England and the metropolitan New York area. The average age of the enlisted men was thirty-two—many of them had previously been deferred in the draft because of marital responsibilities—and the ranks were full of specialists. There were mechanics, electricians, expert stenographers, and craftsmen of all sorts.

Contrary to general belief, it is much easier to teach a group of serious and intelligent men to become soldiers than it is to pound discipline into a group of careless and rowdy juveniles. And they may perform better in battle when matters of judgment come up. The troops of the 77th quickly became smart and well disciplined. An unkind order of mine was partially responsible for the speed of their progress. At that time many of the officers, working at the camp by day, were going home to their wives and families in Columbia by night. Such domesticity is admirable under ordinary circumstances, but in my opinion it had no place in war. We had night schools for our troops and early morning drills. I directed that officers sleep in camp three nights a week, and I slept there nearly every night. We drilled troops by day and educated them after sunset.

When it became known that I was out before reveille, the regimental and battalion commanders waked earlier too, and the captains and lieutenants had no choice. Sunup saw them on the job. There was a new job every day, and I was always there on what the soldiers called the "dawn patrol." This made me very unpopular among Army wives. Later General Ben Lear, commander of Second Army area, improved on my plan by an order that all officers must sleep four nights of the seven in camp. He then succeeded me as the area's least popular man.

One of the incidents of this training-camp period was a visit of Prime Minister Winston Churchill. In late June of 1942 I was called to Washington and told I had been assigned to command I Corps. My first job was to play host to Churchill. Lord Louis Mountbatten was also in the United States at the time; he had looked over the 77th Division and informed Churchill that he was tremendously impressed by the division's progress after only a few weeks of training. Churchill wanted to see the 77th in action.

My assignment was to put on a corps demonstration (we had three divisions at Fort Jackson) for our British guest. Generals Marshall, Eisenhower, and McNair impressed on me, in turn, the importance of making a good military showing; at the moment I did not know just why. What I did know was that I had only three days for preparations which in ordinary circumstances would have taken

a month. I gave preliminary orders by long-distance telephone and then high-tailed it back to South Carolina.

Forty-eight hours of concentrated effort followed. I decided that the 8th Division would be used for the firing problem. I was given seventy-four tanks for the field maneuvers and promised a drop of six hundred parachute troops. The 77th was burnished and polished for the official inspection.

The Prime Minister arrived on June 22 by special train. With him was a heavy concentration of the military brains of the Allied nations. Secretary of War Stimson and many American senior commanders were there, as were Field Marshal Sir John Dill and Sir Alan Brooke, Chief of the Imperial General Staff.

Nothing had been left to chance. A printing plant in Columbia had clanked all night to provide programs for the demonstration. Chemicals had been applied to the road leading to the demonstration area to keep down the dust. I had been warned that Churchill's health was such that he should be spared the spinal rigors of a jeep ride; and a kindly automobile dealer in Columbia gave us without charge the use of a convertible coupé.

The honor guard at the train was from the 77th Division, and it looked really smart. When Churchill stepped off the train, General Marshall introduced me as host for the day, and I remained with the Prime Minister from then on. If there was anything shaky about his health I was never able to observe it. As we toured through the 30th, 8th, and 77th Divisions, he hopped in and out of the car and walked at such a tremendous pace that most of the faithfully following entourage had to run to catch up.

The day was infernally hot, hot almost beyond belief. At noon we returned to the brief comfort of the air-conditioned train. I sat alone with the Prime Minister while official dispatches were brought to him. There was no good news; Tobruk had fallen the day before and the British were retreating toward Egypt. He discussed the dispatches with me as he read them. He talked about his commanders and said he wished he had a field general the caliber of Rommel. I asked him whether the Germans could be stopped at Halfaya Pass, and he said, "No, the line will have to be stabilized just outside

Cairo in the neighborhood of El Alamein." It was from El Alamein that Montgomery later drove triumphantly back.

At luncheon the Prime Minister tossed off several Martinis and then made great headway on a salad plate of celery hearts, remarking that he didn't get those things in England. When luncheon was finished he offered me an enormous black cigar from an oblong gold case which held only two cigars. The gold case—he told me it was a present from Lord Beaverbrook—was refilled from time to time during the day by the Scotland Yard operative who rode always with the Prime Minister.

General Marshall had insisted there be air-ground communication with the planes which were to drop the paratroopers. We did not have the modern equipment at Jackson, and it was flown in from Fort Benning. That afternoon Churchill clamped on the earphones as the airborne maneuver was about to begin. Some commander was impatient. The first words that came through were: "God damn it, I told you what to do!" Secretary Stimson, who sat on the platform in a tropical helmet, looked shocked. The Prime Minister merely laughed; he could take both profanity and perspiration in his stride.

The whole demonstration, almost providentially, went off without a hitch. Churchill saw recruits perform like veterans. These were not demonstration troops; these were hasty draft organizations, but the individual members gave a magnificent account of themselves that day.

(Many years later General Marshall spent the night with me in Yokohama and told me for the first time why that successful demonstration had been so important to him. Up until that time Churchill had refused to believe the Americans capable of raising an army of sufficient size or excellence to manage a cross-channel invasion in the foreseeable future.)

I was informed at about this time that I was to command an amphibious corps which would land in North Africa. The 9th Division was already getting amphibious training on Chesapeake Bay under Admiral Hewitt, and I went north to observe. I spent a good deal of time with Admiral Hewitt on his yacht, and he went very thoroughly into his plans with me. One Sunday early in August I was

called to Washington and informed that my divisions for the North African venture would be the 9th and 3rd of the Regular Army and one National Guard outfit. It was definite, and I was as excited as a schoolboy.

But, in wartime, generals and enlisted men are alike in that they never know their luck. That same day I was summoned abruptly to General Marshall's office. It was a curious interview. The Chief of Staff said that a shift in military assignments had come up within twenty-four hours; he wondered if I had been in touch with the Operations Division. Of course I hadn't. Puzzled, I went down immediately to the office of General Handy and learned the news: I was headed for Australia and my I Corps staff was to go along.

I know now that another high-ranking general had been designated for the post, and, for reasons the powers at the Pentagon felt to be good and sufficient, there had been an abrupt change of plans. I had ten days to prepare myself for the long and unexpected journey. Even then I did not realize the finality of the assignment. I was to be in the Pacific for six long years.

Robert L. Eichelberger

Lieutenant General, Ret.

OUR JUNGLE ROAD TO TOKYO

ON OUR WAY

America's war in the Pacific began in defeat and humiliation. Every American knows that. I have set myself, and I hope without immodesty, the task of telling, in some part at least, the story of the fight of the Army Ground Forces from Australia to Japan. It is a story well worth telling, and a great deal of it has never been told at all. There is glory enough in it for everyone—a great Navy, a gallant Marine Corps, an Air Force that flew in everything from fabric first cousins of box-kites to B-29s. It was amphibious warfare—and a new kind of amphibious warfare; every military arm was important and interdependent.

Some of the Pacific history has been written, but little of it has been concerned with the men I commanded—the ordinary, muddy, malarial, embattled, and weighed-down-by-too-heavy-packs GIs. They waded through the surf, they struggled through the swamp mud, they pushed the trucks out of quagmires with their shoulders, they cut the tracks which ultimately became roads leading to the airfields they constructed. They were the true artisans of the island-hopping campaign in the Pacific which led ultimately to the Philippines and Tokyo. They called it—The Hard Way Back.

In late August of 1942 I found myself flying the ocean to Australia, a passenger for the Great Unknown. I was fifty-six years old, a major general, a professional soldier, and not unused to the unexpected; during the First World War, supposedly headed for France, I had ended up as assistant chief of staff to an American expeditionary force in the bleakness of Siberia.

Army wives must be heroines, and they earn no ribbons for it. Husbands are here today and gone tomorrow, and the decisions of the High Command sometimes must seem capricious as a crystal ball. After thirty-one years of married life, my wife showed the first signs of incipient revolt when I kissed her good-by near a misty and overcast airfield outside San Francisco. It was a difficult parting for us both.

"When there is a war," said Miss Em in a masterly bit of understatement, "you always seem to go to the queerest places."

There were twenty-two members of my I Corps staff with me as we swept out over the Golden Gate in a B-24 bomber. A few benches in the bomb bay had converted it into a transport plane; with each bench went a guarantee of personal discomfort which was paid off in part when we arrived in Honolulu next morning, stiff and sore but glad to get there. From Honolulu it is a four-hour jump to tiny Palmyra Island. As we landed at Palmyra another plane came in from the south with General Pat Hurley, former Secretary of War, and Prime Minister Peter Fraser of New Zealand as passengers. I spent an interesting and profitable evening with them. My Southwest Pacific education had begun.

The next morning we were off for Fiji. After a long over-water hop we came down at Nandi Airfield. Here it was decided to by-pass the usual stop at Nouméa and strike straight for Australia. It was rough going. At one time we went to eighteen thousand feet to pass over a storm; we had no oxygen, and the temperature in the plane dropped below zero. Nevertheless we landed at a field eighty miles north of Sydney without ill effects, and then we were shuttled by another plane to Brisbane. There we went to Lennon's Hotel, and to bed.

General MacArthur and his family, as well as the senior members of his staff, lived at Lennon's Hotel, and next day I called to pay my respects to him and to renew my acquaintance with Major General Richard K. Sutherland, his chief of staff. I had known Sutherland at Fort Leavenworth and as a General Staff officer in Washington. Both my chief and Sutherland greeted me cordially.

My knowledge of the Australian situation was, of necessity, slight. I had had only a few days of orientation at the War Department after receiving my surprise orders. I did know there were 110,000 American soldiers in Australia, and that most of them were supply or engineering troops of one sort or another. There were only two combat divisions. The 32nd Division was at Camp Cable, thirty miles south of Brisbane. The 41st Division was at Rockhampton, three hundred miles to the north. Rockhampton had within easy access ideal training areas: hills, jungles, open country, beaches. When Generals MacArthur and Sutherland asked me where I wanted to be stationed, I chose Rockhampton.

While the Rockhampton headquarters was being set up, the senior members of my staff and I flew to Sydney and Melbourne to familiarize ourselves with the Australian and American organizations and personnel with whom we would work in the future. The Services of Supply commander at Melbourne was Major General Richard Marshall, who later became Deputy Chief of Staff; he is today president of Virginia Military Institute. Everywhere we were received warmly, but only a completely insensitive person could have failed to detect the rivalries and animosities and mutual suspicions which hid behind the clasped hands of Allied military friendship in both Melbourne and Brisbane.

This was understandable. No one had a toehold on right or wrong. Unkind Australians pointed out that the Americans had lost the Philippines. Unkind Americans pointed out that the British and Australians had lost Singapore. General MacArthur was not there by choice. The Australian government had directly requested the American government to assign him to the post of Allied Commander-in-Chief and he had left the Philippines by the order of President Roosevelt himself.

The truth was that both Australian troops in Australia and American troops in Australia were orphans of the storm. The Joint Chiefs of Staff had decided that the all-out effort must be made in Europe, and the realization of that fact tended to make the two nationalities poorer instead of better friends. The Allied agreement for integration of forces, I quickly found out, was laudable in purpose but difficult in practice.

Under the agreement Americans commanded Allied Naval Forces and Allied Air Forces. At the time of my arrival these Americans were Admiral Herbert F. Leary and General George Kenney, newly arrived. Allied Ground Forces commander was Sir Thomas Blamey, who was also Australian Army commander. On most of the Allied staffs some effort had been made to achieve a paper balance by the alternating of Australian and American officers. Because of diplomatic necessity everyone professed fealty to the unified command, but it was evident even to a newcomer that both Yanks and Aussies were restive in the fraternal bonds.

I had received a rather oblique warning about the explosive Australian situation when I had a last talk in Washington with General McNair. Up until that time he had been my boss. Both of us knew that several senior American Army officers had abruptly returned from Australia. Lesley McNair was not a very communicative man, but it was always well to listen when he talked. He said only, "Don't bounce back."

One of my predecessors had the title of Commanding General of U.S. Armed Forces in Australia, or (briefly) USAFIA. This resounding title struck me as inexact and likely to create misunderstandings. When General George C. Marshall back in Washington told me I was the heir apparent, I inquired, "Actually, isn't General MacArthur in command of American troops out there?" Marshall laughed and said, "Yes, as a matter of fact, he is."

A short time after my arrival in Brisbane I received a letter from the War Department addressed to me as Commanding General, U.S. Army Forces in Australia. I returned it through channels asking that I be addressed by my correct title: "Commanding General, I Corps."

As my staff and I made the customary courtesy calls in Australia, we found the chain of command both odd and interesting. The 32nd and 41st Divisions and assorted auxiliary troops belonged to I Corps. In turn, I Corps became part of the Australian First Army, commanded by Sir John Lavarak. I reported to Sir John at Toowomba and was received courteously by that offensive-minded professional soldier. He told me that many Australians were gravely concerned about the possibility of Japanese invasion at a time when he believed they should be organizing their resources and morale to mount an offensive against the Japs. He was highly critical of some of his own country's officials and contemptuous of any strategic plans which called for gradual abandonment of northern Australia and concentration of effort on the defense and protection of the great cities and populous areas of the south.

The attempted integration of Australian and American troops at times produced curious results. Sir John laughed about the fact that he had an American officer at Toowomba who was supposed to be his operations officer. I had been told before leaving Washington that General MacArthur had asked for key American officers to assist the Australians with their staff work. The Australians didn't think they needed much help from anyone. Many of the commanders I met had already been in combat with the British in North Africa, and, though they were usually too polite to say so, considered the Americans to be—at best—inexperienced theorists.

At Camp Cable I encountered a situation that was little less than fantastic. The 32nd Division was assigned to the American I Corps for offensive training and to the Australian II Corps for defensive training. This was a military conception entirely new to me and, of course, quite impracticable. On a day when I paid a visit to observe artillery firing, Australian staff officers arrived to look over defensive techniques. The 32nd went through its paces for them too. Out of the recollections of a Sunday school boyhood there came to me a cogent bit of Scriptural wisdom: "Man cannot serve two masters."

When I took up housekeeping at I Corps headquarters at Rockhampton I realized at once how fortunate had been the decision to locate there. Although I did not know it then, it was to be my home for many months—a home to leave for the bloody and difficult New Guinea campaign, and a home to come back to when victory had been achieved. There friendships were formed that still surmount the barrier of distance and the passage of time.

Rockhampton is a city of about thirty-five thousand in the valley

of the Fitzroy River. Located midway between Brisbane and Townsville, it is almost exactly on the Tropic of Capricorn, and the climate
is admirable. During the Australian winter (our summer), temperatures may drop on the coldest days to forty degrees Fahrenheit.
There is hot weather in summer, but I recall only two nights when
I chose to sleep on the veranda of my house. Australian beaches are
the most beautiful in the world, and Yeppoon Beach, only a few
miles away from Rockhampton, is one of the finest. Lonely, yes, but
beautiful.

Rockhampton is in a cattle and sheep country, and the town's
largest industry then was a packing plant. I quickly discovered it
was a wide-awake, enterprising community which had been settled
by people of Scottish descent. Distrustful of Commonwealth officials,
fearful of a Japanese invasion, many of the leading citizens had
evacuated their families and their possessions to the south or to the
interior. When the 41st Division moved into camp nearby it received
a warm welcome. Americans were popular as the community's pro-
tectors. Not long ago I received notice of services to be held in a
chapel built by the Yanks; this ceremony commemorates annually
the help and friendship of American troops during the war. Rockhampton remembers.

At that time Rockhampton turned over to I Corps most of the first
floor of the modern City Hall to use as offices. The city fathers also
permitted us to put up two temporary office buildings nearby. A
house of tropical construction atop a jutting ridge was rented as
living quarters for me and some members of my staff. It was a ram-
bling one-story structure built on stilts, and it had a veranda ninety
feet long. We outraged our Australian landlord by screening all the
windows, and were prevented from screening the veranda only by
his obvious distress. There are flies and mosquitoes in Australia, but
Mr. Grant, like many Australians, was unalterably convinced that
"fly-screens" keep out the air.

At the time I reached Australia the Japanese were at the peak of
their power. Except for setbacks in two naval battles, their movement southward had been a procession of triumphs, truly one of the
most astonishing advances of history. In a period of months they had

sunk a large section of our fleet at Pearl Harbor (I had seen the dead hulks as I passed through Hawaii), taken Singapore, captured the Philippines, overrun Java and Indo-China and oil-rich Borneo. They owned everything above tidal reef from Yokohama to Rabaul, and they had invaded the north coast of New Guinea with the idea of seizing Port Moresby, the Australian outpost there. They had superiority in the air and on the sea.

It can be said without fear of challenge that military and naval aggression never before achieved control of so many thousands of miles of land and ocean in so short a time. Eastward the Japanese controlled half the Pacific, southward they were halted just above Australia, and westward they had gone overland to the mountain barriers of the Burma front. They were in possession of the wealth of the Indies, areas rich beyond imagination in oil, rubber, rice, and all the natural resources necessary to the prosecution of modern war. China, an ancient enemy, was effectively isolated from Occidental allies. It must have seemed to the cold, patient dreamers in Tokyo that the long vision was almost at hand—Japan would become Asia.

It is not surprising that, as the Japanese enveloped a thousand bays and sea channels and marched down the island steps of the Solomons, Australians decided that the next step would be an invasion of their mainland. Documents captured after the end of the war, however, seem to indicate that an Australian invasion was never part of the Japanese plan; the aim, instead, was to separate Australia and New Zealand and to cut the supply line from the United States. Airfields were to be built from which land-based Jap planes could sink and harry our transports.

This is the situation the American Navy met and dealt with in the South Pacific area. The Battle of the Coral Sea in May of 1942 was a battle of planes and carriers. In addition to heavy casualties among other craft, the enemy lost the carrier *Shoho*. We lost the carrier *Lexington*, which could ill be spared. But the Japanese were shoved back on their haunches, and we did get a respite of two months while our transport ships came through. Shortly afterward the Navy won the decisive Battle of Midway in the Central Pacific. Much of this happened before I ever set foot in Australia, but no one had to

tell me that our sea line was our life line. It was a slow trickle of supply, but it meant the difference between inertia and activity, airplanes and no airplanes. Fighter planes don't fly the Pacific; they come in crates.

By midsummer of 1942 the Japanese were again on the march. They had established at Rabaul on New Britain Island a large and powerful feeder base, and, under sea and air protection, their transports streamed south from there in two roughly parallel lines. To the east they moved down the Solomons, building airfields as they went. To the west convoys rendezvoused off the coast of Papua. Despite savage blows by Allied Air, they landed eleven thousand men in the Buna-Gona area on July 21.

The Papuan peninsula lies at the lower end of the great island of New Guinea and directly across the Coral Sea from Australia. Papua was considered a part of Australia, as distinct from the rest of British New Guinea, which Australia had governed since World War I under a League of Nations mandate. The capital of Papua is Port Moresby, garrisoned at the beginning of the war by a few militia troops. The Battle of the Coral Sea disposed of an initial Japanese attempt to capture Moresby from the sea. Now, from the beachheads at Buna and Gona, the enemy decided to try again—overland.

Moresby, on the south coast of Papua, and Buna, on the north coast, are only a hundred and twenty miles apart by airline, but between them lies the Owen Stanley mountain range, and some of the most difficult country in the world. The highest peak of the Owen Stanleys rises to more than thirteen thousand feet. Australians with a knowledge of the terrain believed an overland expedition impossible and the Owen Stanleys impassable. The Japanese, as they had proved in Malaya, were hard to convince. General Horii's experienced jungle fighters swept out of the coastal swamps and into the foothills, climbed the steep mountains, and started down the southern slopes. The Australian militia troops steadily fell back before them. On September 14 the Japanese were on the Imita Range, only twenty miles above Port Moresby.

The repercussions of this Japanese advance were many in Australia. In the scattered villages of the north there was understandable anxiety, and in the south, where horse racing continued as usual, there was considerable perturbation. To the Allied Air Forces the preservation of our advance airfields in the vicinity of Moresby was vital. Heavy bombers with their long cruising range could base in Australia, but George Kenney's fighters and light bombers, which steadily kept the Japanese off-balance, needed the forward outposts.

General MacArthur had already decided to take the offensive. The 7th Australian Division, which had fought in North Africa, was to be sent to New Guinea along with American troops. On September 14 I was in Brisbane and at about nine in the evening General MacArthur called me to his hotel apartment. I had a forty-five-minute interview with him and, immediately afterward, wrote down an informal report on our conversation, which is still in my files. General MacArthur told me I was to go to New Guinea about October 1 and that I would be, in effect, a task force commander. I was to have the 32nd Division, and I was to capture the Buna-Gona area.

I asked whether his chief of staff had been informed of this plan. He answered in the negative but added, "I'll tell Sutherland in the morning."

Nothing ever came of this. General Sutherland informed me the following day that General MacArthur's plan—it was detailed enough to include even the specific trails which my regiments were to follow—had been abandoned. But two regiments of the 32nd Division, the 126th and the 128th, did go to New Guinea.

In Washington I had read General MacArthur's estimates of his two infantry divisions, and these reports and our own inspections had convinced my staff and me that the American troops were in no sense ready for jungle warfare. It was true that we were newcomers, but I had expected to learn lessons in jungle training in Australia. And it seemed to me that our troops in training were just being given more of the same thing they had had back home.

My opinion was not popular. I am sure it would not have been popular with the troops themselves. I told Generals MacArthur and Sutherland that I thought the 32nd Division was not sufficiently trained to meet Japanese veterans on equal terms. After an inspection—and this must be in the War Department records somewhere—

I gave the 32nd Division a "barely satisfactory" rating in combat efficiency. This, I hasten to add, meant no criticism of the gallantry or the willingness of the GIs in that Middle-Western outfit.

I was to lead these troops later, and I recall one soldier who told me that in twenty months of service he had had only one night problem. He asked me how he could be expected to be proficient in night patrolling against the Japanese under those conditions. I had no answer. Training is a dreary job for soldiers, but it is amazing in war how much proper and intelligent training helps not only to win battles but to keep men alive.

Anyway, by September 25, the 128th Infantry and a detachment of the 126th had been flown into Port Moresby—without their artillery. This was the first major movement of American troops by air in World War II, and General Kenney deserves great credit. He not only used all his own transports; he drafted into service all the transport planes on Australian civilian airlines.

Three days later (when the rest of the 126th Infantry arrived by boat) the 128th was already opening a road in the Goldie River valley, and elements of the 126th were attempting to work their way up from Moresby over the almost impassable Kapa Kapa Trail.

The Japanese advance over the Owen Stanleys, from a military point of view, was a triumph of discipline and rugged determination. Allied air strafing undoubtedly made the maintenance of supply difficult, but I imagine that the inefficiencies of Japanese headquarters planning were equally guilty in the situation. Fortitude is admirable under any flag, and those Japanese foot soldiers had it. They pressed on—ill and empty bellied. They had no way to evacuate their sick and wounded. Sanitation was wretched, and they suffered from tropical fevers and exhaustion.

There is a limit to human faithfulness and fervor. Men must be rested and fed. The Japanese reached the Imita Range, and there a halt was called. Now, on orders from Tokyo, a rearguard was left behind, and the retreat began. Soon the Australians knew that the Japanese were attempting to retire over the same difficult mountain trails they had chosen for their offensive. General Blamey, the Allied

Ground Forces commander in New Guinea, sent the 7th Australian Division in pursuit.

This was not the first failure of the Japanese in New Guinea. In late August a small seaborne expeditionary force had landed at Milne Bay, which is located at the southeastern tip of Papua. Enemy intelligence officers did not know that the Australians had strongly garrisoned Milne Bay and constructed airfields there. The invading Japanese found themselves faced, to their surprise, with a numerically superior force, and after several days of fierce fighting the invaders were virtually annihilated.

There are two routes overland from Port Moresby to the Buna area. One is the Kokoda Trail, which the Japanese had followed. It is the longer, but permits the footsore traveler to get through the Owen Stanleys at the Kokoda Gap, where the altitude is sixty-five hundred feet. The other route is the Kapa Kapa Trail, which is more direct but climbs over the backbone of the Owen Stanleys at the height of nine thousand feet.

The 7th Australian Division pressed after the Japanese over the Kokoda Trail while a part of the American 126th Infantry Regiment challenged the steep wilderness of the Kapa Kapa Trail. Both expeditions could be supplied only by airdrop, and Kenney's fliers again did an excellent job in the misty, treacherous reaches of the Owen Stanleys. For the troops the going was slow and the going was difficult. General Blamey's plan called for a junction of the two Allied forces on the other side of the mountains and then the assault on Buna and Gona. The Americans did not make contact with the enemy—rugged nature was enemy enough. Old New Guinea hands told me later that no expedition of white men had been over the Kapa Kapa in half a century. The log of the 126th seems to bear this out: in many places the trail was so overgrown that the soldiers had to chop their way through. A tough assignment for youngsters whose knowledge of mountains and jungles came mostly out of the movies!

Under the curious Allied chain of command, the troops of I Corps passed over to Australian control when they touched New Guinea soil. I flew to New Guinea with three of my staff officers in late

September and made a brief inspection visit; at that time the Americans were not yet in combat. With a considerable section of the 32nd Division gone, I concentrated at Rockhampton on stepped-up jungle training for the 41st Division. During October I received my promotion to lieutenant general. This, I suppose, should have made a career officer happy, but, to tell the truth, I wasn't happy at all.

I knew the road to Tokyo would be long, and I felt that a responsible commander should be learning Japanese methods of warfare and getting firsthand information on problems which were certain to engage American attention throughout the foreseeable island-to-island campaign ahead. I was sure that I had plenty to learn—and the best way for a general to learn is to go up where the bullets are being fired. Then he doesn't have to take other men's opinions on what the problems are. He finds out for himself.

When the decision was made to send the 32nd to New Guinea I had suggested that I go with them, taking along an advance section of the I Corps staff. The main purpose was to enable I Corps to plan intelligently a training program to fit other troops for combat against the Japanese. General MacArthur told me he favored the idea but since Sutherland was opposed the answer was no, and that was that.

By the beginning of November the Australians and Americans were ready to strike against the Japanese strongholds on the north coast of Papua, and Generals MacArthur, Kenney, and Sutherland went forward to establish an advanced Allied headquarters at Port Moresby. The opinion in military circles apparently was that our first ground victory against the Japanese was immediately in the offing. A fortnight later, accompanied by Colonel Rex Chandler, my deputy chief of staff, I flew to Moresby to observe our troops in combat. This journey was made with the hearty approval of General MacArthur, and his chief of staff had been so informed.

My experience there was a baffling one. I saw General Ennis Whitehead, who commanded the Air Forces at Moresby and was in charge of the airlift. Whitehead was a good friend of mine, and when he remarked that he was going over the Owen Stanleys next day by plane, I said, "Going over the mountains? How about taking me along?"

"I'd like to," said the rough, gruff Whitehead, "but Sutherland says he's going to run you out of New Guinea tomorrow."

This was surprising news to me, and I was a little incredulous. I had talked to General MacArthur earlier in the day, and he had said nothing about a hasty departure. I immediately called on General Sutherland. Had General MacArthur, Sutherland inquired, told me that I was to return to Australia and pick out a campsite for the incoming 25th Division? (Incidentally, the 25th Division never did come to Australia.) Of course General MacArthur hadn't, but Sutherland was chief of staff and I understood.

"Okay," I said, "I'll pick up a ride in a bomber tomorrow."

"He wants you to go on the courier plane," said Sutherland, "and you should be at the airfield at four tomorrow morning."

I had no quarrel with the courier planes. They were well-worn, two-engine Lockheeds and looked like accommodation cars on a whistle-stop railroad; they carried everything from rope to cable wire, and passengers sat on benches. Even the toilets were loaded with freight. I had flown in worse planes before, and I was to fly in many less stalwart later on. However, I recalled with some amusement that Sutherland had once told me that he would never essay the stormy and treacherous air currents over the Coral Sea—it was called "the graveyard of planes"—in anything except a four-engine job.

It was storming when Chandler and I reached the airstrip in the early morning darkness. But orders are orders, and we took off. Actually, at the time, I think I was more entertained than angry. I was then, for whatever it meant, the second-ranking American Army officer in the Pacific, and I was being given a monumental brush-off. I was amazed by General Sutherland's thoroughness. Air Force friends had advised me that the courier plane passed directly over my headquarters and would drop me at Rockhampton. Once aloft, the pilot reported that he had *orders* not to land at Rockhampton. Chandler and I were to be carried on to Brisbane, three hundred miles to the south, still in our jungle clothes.

Fate took a hand. At Townsville in Australia we dipped down to pick up a number of sick American soldiers. Their stretchers were placed on the floor of the plane. One of them was a very ill medical officer who was being rushed to the hospital in the custody of another medical officer. Because of the storm, the pilot swooped up to a high altitude, and there was melodrama in our cabin. The able-bodied doctor suffered a heart attack, and the ill doctor rose from his stretcher to give his colleague the hypodermic which probably saved his life. The pilot of the plane wirelessed ahead to Rockhampton for an ambulance and made an emergency landing there. Both sick men, I am glad to report, survived that extraordinary tussle with death, and Chandler and I got off at Rockhampton too.

General Sutherland had been rather explicit with me at Port Moresby and had gone to considerable pains to clarify I Corps' function: my officers and I were not headed for combat; our job was to train troops; and the training role was to be ours from then on. Neither Sutherland nor I knew that, in two weeks' time, I would take over American command in the embattled swamps of Buna.

SUMMONS TO BUNA

Buna was the first Allied Ground Force victory in the Pacific (the Buna campaign was ended before the fall of Guadalcanal), and it was bought at a substantial price in death, wounds, disease, despair, and human suffering. No one who fought there, however hard he tries, will ever forget it. I am a reasonably unimaginative man, but Buna is still to me, in retrospect, a nightmare. This long after, I can still remember every day and most of the nights as clearly as though they were days and nights last week.

Buna Village and Buna Mission are godforsaken little places on the inhospitable northern coast of New Guinea. A few score native huts and the coconut plantations around them represented, before the war, Buna's sole claim on an indifferent world's attention. The climate there is insufferable; the man-made gardens on the edge of swamp and jungle are only judicious scratchings of the rich earth near the ocean: the Australian planters (before they were dispossessed by the Japanese) didn't want to get very far away from the sea breeze which alone made life tolerable. In times of peace a package of used razor blades might be—in terms of barter—a reasonable price for a native hut in Buna Village. But Buna cost dearly in war, because possession of the north coast of New Guinea was vital to future Allied operations.

"Were the Buna and Sanananda campaigns really justified?" an

17

acquaintance asked recently. "Why didn't you just by-pass the Japanese garrisons and leave them there to starve and rot?"

The question shows a profound ignorance of the situation as it existed in 1942. It is true that later in the war we successfully bypassed many Japanese garrisons, cut across their sea and land supply lines, and, in the words of the callous amateur strategist, left them "to starve and rot." But that was at a time when we had secure bases from which such operations could be maintained, when we had achieved air superiority and were on the way to supremacy at sea as well.

At this same time, it should be made clear, the Allies were also dealing with another Japanese offensive in the Pacific, the drive down the Solomons. This theater of action was under Navy command with headquarters in Nouméa. The area was called "South Pacific" to differentiate it from "Southwest Pacific," where General MacArthur was Allied chief.

In the Solomons, operating on a shoestring and with heavy losses in fighting ships and planes, Americans were seeking to maintain a precarious foothold on the advanced beachhead at Guadalcanal. I still recall the dismal August day when Admiral Leary told me the results of the Battle of Savo Island. We had five heavy cruisers and a group of destroyers there to protect our Guadalcanal transports. The engagement lasted eight minutes. The Japanese had no losses. We lost four of our cruisers—the *Quincy*, *Vincennes*, *Astoria*, and *Canberra* (Royal Australian Navy). The fifth cruiser, the *Chicago*, was damaged. It took considerable optimism in those days to believe we were on the winning side of the fight.

It was a poor man's war in the Pacific, from the Allied point of view, when the Battle of Buna was fought. The miracles of production managed by American factories and American labor were slow to manifest themselves Down Under. We were at the end of the supply line. There were no landing craft for amphibious operations; indeed, because the Japanese had air control in New Guinea waters, no naval fighting ship of any size was permitted to enter the area. The Japanese had gone into the war fully prepared; in 1942 it was they who had the specially designed landing craft for amphibious campaigns, the equipment, the ships, the planes, and the battle experience.

Supplies for the Buna campaign came either by air or by small coastal luggers (and many of these were sunk by enemy action), which traveled at night. Supplies often were transferred, once they arrived off Allied-held beaches, to native canoes manned by what our troops called "Fuzzy Wuzzies." These dark-skinned natives working under able Australian straw-bosses, or foremen, carried the supplies overland pack-a-back or on long two-man poles. In the beginning seven quarter-ton trucks and three one-ton trucks represented our total motor transportation. Why? There were no roads through the jungles and swamps.

It was a poor man's war in a good many other ways. Army censorship concealed from the American public, as it very properly attempted to conceal from the Japanese, how weak we were. When I arrived in Australia, as I have said, there were two American combat divisions present and undergoing what was called jungle training. It was not until May of 1943—nine months later—that another American combat division arrived. This may answer the question: "Why didn't you relieve those tired men in New Guinea and send in replacements?" There were no American infantry replacements in Australia.

I shall comment only briefly on the first days of the New Guinea campaign. As it happened (and as it often happens in war), the Allies were under a number of misapprehensions concerning the Buna terrain, the strength and temper of the Japanese soldiers and marines, and the vulnerability of Japanese positions. We had been encouraged by Japanese failure to take Milne Bay, and we knew that only a remnant of the force which had threatened Moresby had survived Australian bullets and the natural hazards of the return trip across the Kokoda Trail.

Because of these Japanese reverses, I was told, Allied headquarters originally expected that Buna would be taken almost without opposition. But fresh troops had been landed there, most of them veterans of the Jap campaigns in China, Malaya, and the Philippines. Actual fighting at Buna started on November 20. So ill informed was the Intelligence Section of our 32nd Division that enemy strength east of the Girua River was estimated at only three hundred when there were about three thousand men there. It is perhaps not surprising that aerial photography failed to disclose the location and strength of the Jap defenses; in a dense jungle where a bunker or entrenchment cannot be seen from thirty yards away, aerial photography must be swallowed with a full shaker of salt.

Back at Rockhampton, on a sleepy Sunday afternoon, we of the I Corps got our first hint that the campaign was not going well. An alerting message came through from General Steve Chamberlin in Brisbane. General Byers, my chief of staff, was swimming thirty miles away at Yeppoon Beach, and I was obliged to send for him by messenger. Byers decided on his motor trip back to Rockhampton that Buna had gone wrong and that General MacArthur was about to select me to take over combat command.

Perhaps Byers was clairvoyant. The date was November 29. Sure enough, at midnight, orders came through that I was to take off at dawn for Port Moresby. Two C-47 planes, one of them MacArthur's own, were sent for me and my staff. I was permitted to take along six officers, one civilian, and nine enlisted men.

We flew the Coral Sea and landed at Moresby late in the afternoon. I was met at the airstrip by a staff officer who told me Byers and I were to sleep at General MacArthur's headquarters. This was the big, comfortable structure which had been used by the civilian Australian governor, in happier times, as both home and office. There was fine tropical furniture, a library, and, still more important, a breeze. This was the chain of command at the time: General MacArthur, of course, was Allied commander; General Sir Thomas Blamey, Australian, was Allied Ground Force commander and commander of New Guinea Forces; Lieutenant General Ned Herring, Australian, was commander of Advanced New Guinea Forces, which meant all Allied troops in the forward areas; and Major General E. F. Harding, commander of the American 32nd Division, commanded American forces in the Buna area.

Byers and I were conducted to a sweeping veranda where General Sutherland sat at a desk, grave-faced. He had just flown back over

the Owen Stanley Mountains from Dobodura, and it was plain that
his report on conditions at Buna was responsible for my abrupt summons. General MacArthur was striding up and down the long veranda. General Kenney, whose planes were to do so much to make
the ultimate victory possible, was the only man who greeted me with
a smile. There were no preliminaries.

"Bob," said General MacArthur in a grim voice, "I'm putting you
in command at Buna. Relieve Harding. I am sending you in, Bob,
and I want you to remove all officers who won't fight. Relieve regimental and battalion commanders; if necessary, put sergeants in
charge of battalions and corporals in charge of companies—anyone
who will fight. Time is of the essence; the Japs may land reinforcements any night."

General MacArthur strode down the breezy veranda again. He
said he had reports that American soldiers were throwing away their
weapons and running from the enemy. Then he stopped short and
spoke with emphasis. He wanted no misunderstandings about my
assignment.

"Bob," he said, "I want you to take Buna, or not come back alive."
He paused a moment and then, without looking at Byers, pointed a
finger. "And that goes for your chief of staff too. Do you understand?"

"Yes, sir," I said.

Well, that was our send-off, and hardly a merry one. There were
conferences and briefings until late at night, but there really wasn't
much information to be had at Moresby about our forthcoming job.
Perhaps I should say here that our campaign maps turned out to be
inaccurate and obsolete; it is significant of the confusions of that
early war period that, several months after the Buna campaign was
ended, I found to my wrath that new, large-scale aerial maps had
been made by the Air Forces before the campaign was even well
started. I never saw them. Somehow they had been lost in the shuffle.

I told General MacArthur that I would take off after breakfast,
and I did. That breakfast of orange juice, bacon and eggs, fruit, was
the last good meal I was to have for a long time. General MacArthur
and I joked at the table about old days in Washington, when I had

served under him as Secretary, General Staff. After breakfast he put an arm around my shoulders and led me into his office.

"If you capture Buna," the Allied commander said, "I'll give you a Distinguished Service Cross and recommend you for a high British decoration. Also," he continued, referring to the complete anonymity under which all American commanders in that theater functioned, "I'll release your name for newspaper publication."

Ribbons and publicity are well enough, but I soon was to find myself fighting against invisible jungle veterans in places where, short of the mandatory summons of duty, neither my soldiers nor I would have stayed a day for all the pretty ribbons of all the nations of the world. It takes many days to tramp over the mountain trails to Buna, and it is several days by sea. It took only forty minutes for us to go by plane. My staff and I landed at eleven A.M. on December 1. Forty minutes from Moresby—but when the stink of the swamp hit our nostrils, we knew that we, like the troops of the 32nd Division, were prisoners of geography. And like them we knew we would never get out unless we fought our way out.

A great deal has been said and whispered about the 32nd Division, and much of it makes no sense. The 32nd which "failed" at Buna was the same 32nd that won the victory there. No one else did. Later, rejuvenated and retrained, the division went on to establish a superior combat record in the Philippines campaign. The 32nd originally was a Wisconsin-Michigan National Guard outfit. It went into New Guinea "high" on itself, full of confidence, but quite unprepared and untrained for the miseries and terrors of jungle warfare so alien to the experience of boys from the clipped green lawns and serene streets of the small-town Middle West. Almost all troops are afraid in battle because almost all men are afraid. That is where leadership comes in. There were men and officers who failed at Buna. But any historian will be hard put to discover in this war a division which earned, and deserved, so many citations and decorations for individual bravery. The record is there. And often beside the printed citation is the sad and significant little star which means "posthumous."

To understand the 32nd, one must remember what it had gone through. One detachment had made that grueling and exhausting march over the Owen Stanleys on the Kapa Kapa Trail. Other units of the American force had been flown from Moresby in October to points east of Buna and then had trudged on foot to their present positions in the swamps. Two battalions of the 128th Infantry had tried to go overland from Wanigela Mission (an old Australian landing field) to Pongani; the rains started, as they regularly do at that time of year, and those battalions got nowhere. They found themselves bogged down in the Musa River valley, which had become an impassable quagmire. Subsequently they were carried to Pongani by an improvised ferry service of small coastal boats.

Although the 32nd did not have its baptism of fire until mid-November, these troops even then were riddled with malaria, dengue fever, tropical dysentery, and were covered with jungle ulcers. I'll give you personal testimony. Shortly after I arrived in Buna I ordered the medicos to take the temperatures of an entire company of hollow-eyed men near the front. Every member—I repeat, every member—of that company was running a fever. Yet to evacuate all those with fever at Buna would have meant immediate victory for the enemy. I had to encourage most of those troops back into combat.

Sick troops *can* fight: Colonel (later Major General) Clarence A. Martin, a brilliant commander in the field, fought throughout the entire campaign with a malarial fever well above the human boiling point. No commander wants to make sick troops fight, but, hard as was my decision, there was no alternative. If the Japanese could not be driven from their comfortable coastal positions, and quickly, the whole Buna Force would meet defeat and death in the swamps. Retreat back over the mountains was impossible.

I was well aware of the importance of the Buna area to the Allied cause. We needed it to provide ourselves with sea-level bases from which to attack main Japanese strongholds by air. Rabaul—where there were about one hundred and fifty thousand of the Emperor's soldiers—was 400 air miles away, Faisi 500 miles, Lae 167 miles, Salamaua 147 miles. Subsequently there were ten airfields in that

hard-won region which helped to make possible Australian advances against Lae, Salamaua, and Finschhaffen—each invasion a seven-league stride on The Hard Way Back.

That was much later. My first day at Buna was spent in a series of conferences, learning what I could from the officers already there. It was a mélange of information that I got, much of it incorrect. Too many of the officers who reported to me had never been up front with the doughboys. The military positions at Buna, however, can be described in a few words. The Japanese occupied a coastal perimeter extending from Buna Village to the coconut plantation at Cape Endaiadere. This was in all not more than three miles in length, and sometimes as shallow as five hundred yards in depth, but it was all on dry land. A good military road extended the whole length of the beach so that Jap troops could be moved quickly by motor to points of concentration whenever an American attack took place.

The Jap utilization of terrain was admirable. At their back was the sea (no danger from that quarter in those days); their left flank also rested on the ocean while on their right were two unfordable streams—the Girua River and tidal Entrance Creek. Almost the entire Japanese position was in a coconut plantation in which they had built up a series of concealed bunkers and connecting trenches which took weeks, and artillery and tanks, to penetrate. In front of the enemy were the morasses where Michigan and Wisconsin boys hunched themselves above water on extruded tree roots to eat their rations. Since American advances from the morasses could only be made on a few known trails or tracks, it was simple enough for Japanese machine guns to cover them with fields of fire.

When I went to the front on December 2 I couldn't find a front. I had been told the day before that our men were within seventy-five yards of Buna Village and attacking. I knew that four hundred artillery rounds had been laid into the troubled sector. When I came back that evening to my headquarters tent on a creek bank at Hena-hamburi, I wrote to General Sutherland in Port Moresby:

"The rear areas are strong and the front line is weak. Inspired leadership is lacking. In a circuit of Buna Village I found men hungry and generally without cigarettes and vitamins. Yesterday afternoon the men immediately in contact with the Japanese had had no food since the day before. About four o'clock the rations arrived, two tins of C ration!"

Our troops were divided, because of swamps, into two units—the Urbana Force on the left and the Warren Force on the right. That same day I sent two of my staff officers, Colonel Martin and Colonel Gordon Rogers, to observe the attack on the Warren front. There was no more reality to the purported attack on the Warren front than there had been on the front I saw. The attack had been ordered, and it could be entered on the headquarters diary, but it didn't exist. Here is what Colonel Rogers, then I Corps intelligence officer, wrote me about his inspection trip:

"The troops were deplorable. They wore long dirty beards. Their clothing was in rags. Their shoes were uncared for, or worn out. They were receiving far less than adequate rations and there was little discipline or military courtesy. . . . When Martin and I visited a regimental combat team to observe what was supposed to be an attack, it was found that the regimental post was four and a half miles behind the front line. The regimental commander and his staff went forward from this location rarely, if ever.

"Troops were scattered along a trail toward the front line in small groups, engaged in eating, sleeping, during the time they were supposed to be in an attack. At the front there were portions of two companies, aggregating 150 men.

"Outside of the 150 men in the foxholes in the front lines, the remainder of the 2000 men in the combat area could not have been even considered a reserve—since three or four hours would have been required to organize and move them on any tactical mission."

This was Rogers' picture of the situation at the time. Eventually it turned out that his report was not entirely accurate. For instance, the regimental command post, although distant from one part of the front lines, was actually fairly close to the vital Japanese positions at Cape Endaiadere.

Two things were imperatively necessary: reorganization of the troops and immediate improvement of supply. The latter assignment I placed on the capable shoulders of Colonel George De Graaf, I

Corps supply officer, who throughout the rest of the campaign performed prodigious and sometimes ruthless feats of magic to bring in food and medicine and clothing by air and sea.

But of De Graaf, more later. Men in the front lines were half starved and what rations they had they were eating cold. They had been told that the cooking of rice to augment their tinned food would draw enemy fire. I changed all that. Hot food and warmed stomachs are elemental as morale builders and well worth the hazard of a sniper's bullet. Anyway, our troops were clearly visible to any Japanese who wanted to look at them; it was only the Japanese, high in the trees, low under tree roots, and secure in concealed bunkers, who were invisible to us.

Reorganization began at once. Brigadier General Albert W. Waldron, artillery officer of the 32nd, succeeded General Harding as division commander. I replaced some ranking officers. There is a legend that corps officers sleep between sheets in the rear areas while field officers sleep on the ground. It didn't happen that way at Buna. Several of my corps officers quickly assumed combat commands. Even one of my aides was soon leading troops. I am sure no lieutenant general ever had a smaller personal staff. Toward the end, because of illness and wounds, it seemed that my staff might be reduced to Sergeant Clyde Shuck, my secretary, and Sergeant Thaddeus Dombrowski, my orderly. There was no time at Buna for protocol.

The first thing I found out was that troops in the front-line positions had no trustworthy knowledge of Japanese positions. Our patrols were dazed by the hazards of swamp and jungle; they were unwilling to undertake the patrolling which alone could safeguard their own interests. To get accurate information was almost impossible—and yet men die if orders are based on incorrect information.

Actually, this long after, I'm inclined to believe that the men were more frightened by the jungle than by the Japanese. It was the terror of the new and the unknown. There is nothing pleasant about sinking into a foul-smelling bog up to your knees. There is nothing pleasant about lying in a slit trench, half submerged, while a tropical rain turns it into a river. Jungle night noises were strange to

Americans—and in the moist hot darkness the rustling of small animals in the bush was easily misinterpreted as the stealthy approach of the enemy. I can recall one night hearing a noise that sounded like a man brushing against my tent. It turned out that a leaf had fallen from a tree and struck the canvas side. The stem of the leaf was as thick as my thumb. It measured two and a half feet long by one and a half feet wide.

Then, too, there was the understandable but exaggerated fear of snakes and crocodiles. I never saw a crocodile in that whole region of creeks and bayous, and the only snake I saw was satisfactorily dead. The geographies report that snakes and crocodiles live there, but, if so, the war must have prompted them to emigrate to calmer and more peaceful places.

It was obvious that there was need of personal leadership. Two members of my staff, Colonel John E. Grose, I Corps inspector general, and Colonel Martin, my operations officer, had had combat experience as infantrymen in World War I. I placed Grose in command of Urbana Force on the left, which was committed to the capture of Buna Village and Buna Mission. Martin took command of Warren Force on the right, which had one flank on the sea.

Although the two forces were only two or three miles apart as the crow flies, liaison between them could only be managed by walking over roundabout native trails; and, as a result, distance became not a matter of miles but of hours. Trails were narrower than your two arms outstretched—I carried a big Japanese knife to cut my way through undergrowth—and jeep transportation was out of the question except for short distances on a few trails. It took six or seven hours to walk from one flank to the other and sometimes during the rains, as I can testify from personal experience, the traveler walked up to his hips in water.

One result of this lack of communication and the density of the jungle was that companies and platoons were as scrambled as pied type on the floor of a printing office. There were breaks in the chain of command, and any assay of the situation added up to confusion. I stopped all fighting, and it took two days to effect the unscrambling of the units and an orderly chain of command. While jungle fighting

is usually and necessarily carried on independently by small clusters of men, they must know where they are going, and, more important, why.

We attacked all along the line on December 5. Our artillery and mortar fire failed to neutralize enemy positions, and there was heavy resistance. On the Warren front, five Bren-gun carriers leading the attack on our right were knocked out thirty minutes after the jump-off. Throughout the day our troops there hammered determinedly away, but by nightfall our gains were negligible. Long after dark the litters of the wounded continued to stream down the difficult trails toward the field hospital.

I went to the Urbana front with a party consisting of, among others, General Waldron, Colonel De Graaf, Colonel Rogers, and Captain Daniel K. Edwards, my senior aide. Edwards, a North Carolina boy, had been with me for a considerable time and my regard for him was akin to that of father for son. Rogers and Edwards had already distinguished themselves a day or so before. Rogers, unable to recruit volunteers for patrol, had snaked his way through five-foot, knife-bladed kunai grass to discover that the Old Strip, the original Jap airfield, was comparatively undefended. Edwards had crawled forward to look into Buna Village, and he had brought back our first concrete information about enemy positions there.

I watched the advance from the forward regimental command post, which was about a hundred and twenty-five yards from Buna Village. The troops moved forward a few yards, heard the typewriter clatter of Jap machine guns, ducked down, and stayed down. My little group and I left the observation post and moved through one company that was bogged down.

I spoke to the troops as we walked along. "Lads, come along with us."

And they did. In the same fashion we were able to lead several units against the bunkers at Buna Village. There is an ancient military maxim that a commander must be seen by his troops in combat. When I arrived at Buna there was a rule against officers wearing insignia of rank at the front because this might draw enemy fire. I was glad on that particular day that there were three stars on my collar which glittered in the sun. How else would those sick and cast-down soldiers have known their commander was in there with them? They knew, being sensible men, that a bullet is no respecter of rank. As I wrote to General Sutherland that evening: "The number of our troops who tried to avoid combat today could be numbered on your fingers."

The snipers were there, all right. On one occasion all of us were pinned to the ground for fifteen minutes while tracer bullets cleared our backs with inches to spare. Fifteen minutes, with imminent death blowing coolly on your sweat-wet shirt, can seem like a long time! Later a sniper in a tree opened fire at a range of about fifteen yards. My companions returned the fire with tommy guns, although, in that green and steaming jungle, they couldn't see the sniper. Someone scored a direct hit.

The afternoon, all told, was eventful. I wanted to take Buna Village and I had thrown in my last reserves under the very best commanders I could find. The observation post was at a junction of two native trails, and as we attempted to advance from that junction point we encountered, in no man's land, other snipers in and under trees. Their expertness in concealment is well known; obviously they had been there for several days. During those days, for inexplicable reasons of their own, the Japs had held their fire, allowing litter bearers carrying the wounded to pass in broad daylight and ignoring any of our troops who made targets of themselves. Doc Waldron had gone some fifty yards ahead of me along the right-hand trail when a sniper drilled him through the shoulder. General Waldron's wound did not seem like a grave injury when he was carried to the rear, but it eventually ended that fine soldier's military career. After a long siege in hospitals and subsequent return to duty, he was retired for disability.

Edwards and I went forward along the left trail, seeking a favorable spot to observe enemy activities in the village. I had watched a Medical Corps sergeant cross this trail several times to go into the high grass to look for wounded. The corpsman had not been fired on, so Eddie and I headed for a big tree with luxuriant overhanging branches, which, we thought, might provide both concealment and

a view of the near-at-hand Japanese positions. Suddenly a bullet (the type technically called a disruptive cartridge) whizzed past my stomach and struck Edwards in the side. It was like a slow-motion picture; slowly his knees began to bend and then he fell forward, calling to me to keep cover. I dropped to the ground automatically when he was hit.

There was then no more firing. It was some time before our group could round up a stretcher. Finally Colonel De Graaf returned with four litter bearers. They put Eddie on their stretcher, and we all started toward the presumable safety of our rear—which, ironically enough, was all of seventy-five yards away. Just as we did a machine gun opened up from Buna Village, and the tracer ammunition passed directly between De Graaf and me. Then all hell broke loose. Three snipers, completely invisible to us, began firing, and Colonel Rogers rushed toward us from the observation post with a tommy gun and blazed over our heads into the trees from which this new assault seemed to come. Eddie's litter bearers dropped him three times during this battle of bullets, but finally there was silence: There were no more casualties.

Such enemy concealment may seem implausible to people who have never seen wet, luxuriant, close-branched jungle. I looked over the whole situation a few days later. The sniper who shot Edwards had been living in a "spider hole" under the roots of that big and luxuriant tree. He had used immense palm fronds to conceal the opening to his lair. I believe he was the same man who wounded General Waldron.

An abdominal wound is always serious; that sinister explosive Japanese bullet had carried through to make a gaping hole near Edwards' spine. But after I accompanied my young aide out of the combat area I had to turn back. We were still battling away at Buna Village. Edwards' litter was only one of the many which were going to the rear. By four-thirty that afternoon we had pressed up tight against the Buna defenses but we couldn't get through. On the way back to my headquarters, still full of grief about the shooting of Captain Edwards, I stopped at the trailside hospital. The physician there told me that Edwards would probably die. There were no facilities forward for taking care of a man so severely wounded, and Edwards, he said, was so ill he must not be moved.

Right then and there I decided to take Edwards back to the field hospital. If he were going to die, he might as well die on the hood of my jeep. We carted him out like a sack of meal, lashed him to the hood, and started down the trail. Much of it was a corduroy road; coconut logs had been imbedded in the mud to give our vehicles purchase. Edwards took a terrific and painful jolting, but he offered only one protest. Once he said, "Could you stop just a minute while I rest?"

We stopped. We got him to the field hospital where he was operated on next morning. The operation saved his life.

There had been one important success in that day's fighting. A platoon of G Company, 126th Infantry, had found a crevice in the Japanese defenses and had driven through to the sea on the narrow spit of land between Buna Village and Buna Mission. The commander of the platoon was Staff Sergeant Herman J. Bottcher, a fine combat soldier. The breakthrough was, possibly, lucky: the holding of the position was accomplished by intelligence and sheer guts.

Bottcher had only eighteen men with him, and he was sure that next morning his toehold on the sea would be attacked from both sides by infuriated Japs. He kept his men at work all night in the darkness. They dug themselves in. Before morning I managed to see to it that ammunition and a few additional men were sent in to the spot. Their one machine gun was emplaced in the sand. It seemed unlikely that this small force could hold off an attack from two sides. But Bottcher, in his calculations, accepted gambler's odds. It was a narrow beach, and he guessed that there would not be simultaneous attacks because of enemy lack of communications.

Bottcher was right. Japanese from Buna Village attacked about dawn, and the machine gun discouraged them. Japanese from Buna Mission attacked in force a while later, wading across the shallows from the other direction. With his hand on the hot machine gun, Bottcher was able to mow them down like wheat in a field. It was sharp and clear daylight when the last attack took place. For days after, the evidence of Sergeant Bottcher's victory rolled in and out

with the tide—the evidence was the sea-carried and drifting bodies of Japanese soldiers. Because American newspaper and magazine photographers appeared some days later to snap grim, realistic pictures of the Japanese dead, that stretch of sand between Buna Village and Giropa Point is now identified in history as Maggot Beach, and, if I may say so, with reason.

We never lost that beachhead. On my recommendation the Allied commander commissioned Bottcher as a captain of infantry for bravery on the field of battle. He was one of the best Americans I have ever known. He had been born in Germany and still talked with a faint Germanic accent. A profound anti-Nazi, he came to this country early in the 1930's, took out his first papers, spent a year at the University of California, and then went to Spain to fight against Franco. His combat experience was extremely useful at Buna, and his patriotism as a new American was vigorous and determined. Two years later, as a major of infantry, he was killed in combat in the Philippines campaign.

Bottcher's platoon at Buna had absorbed some of his devil-may-care attitude. Byers, whom I had appointed to succeed the wounded Waldron as commander of the forward elements of the 32nd Division, went forward on the morning of the 6th to confer with the troops who had achieved that heartening success. He chatted with the friendly, bear-like Bottcher, who said they could hold out. Then Byers talked with the thin group of doughboys. He was prepared to promise deliveries of—figuratively speaking—peacock tongues and garlic pickles and hot sausages and beef steaks and turkey, if they would just maintain their hard-won position on the sea.

"What do you need?" Byers demanded.

The American soldier is nonconformist and unpredictable. One member of Bottcher's platoon gave the answer. He turned a half-somersault on the sand and held the pose. Swamp water had rotted away the seat of his trousers and his naked buttocks were exposed.

"Pants," said the GI. "For God's sake, General, pants!"

Bare-buttocked or not, we had reached the ocean at Buna. That was only the beginning. For punishing weeks the ultimate outcome of the battle was to be agonizingly in doubt.

THE BITTER DAYS AT BUNA

When the going is tough, in a brawl or a battle, there is no better fighting partner than the man from Down Under. While the Americans, new to combat, slugged it out at Buna, the 7th Australian Division was driving against Japanese strongholds in the region of Sanananda, a few difficult miles to the west.

These Australians were not the untrained militia troops who earlier had fallen back along the Kokoda Trail before the Japanese advance. The 7th Division and the 18th Brigade, which came in later, were crack outfits with three years of war behind them. They were troops, tanned by a desert sun, who had served with the British in North Africa. They belonged, in fact, to the celebrated fraternity of the "Rats of Tobruk," who, encircled by the Germans, held out indomitably for many months. Churchill, reluctantly, had dispatched them home when invasion of Australia seemed threatened.

They were intrepid, hard-bitten soldiers, but they too were strangers to jungle fighting. All of us were to learn a lot before the New Guinea campaign was done. For jungle fighting against the Japanese was a good deal like the Indian fighting of America's pioneer past.

It was a sly and sneaky kind of combat which never resembled the massive and thunderous operations in Europe, where tank battalions were pitted against tank battalions and armies the size of

33

city populations ponderously moved and maneuvered. The Pacific was a different war. In New Guinea, when the rains came, wounded men might drown before the litter bearers found them. Many did. No war is a good war, and death ignores geography. But out there I was convinced, as were my soldiers, that death was pleasanter in the Temperate Zone.

The New Guinea campaign was an Allied operation. My immediate superior in the field was Lieutenant General Herring. He is now Sir Edmund Herring, Lord Chief Justice of Victoria, and the friendship we established in the wilderness will, I'm sure, last out our lifetimes. Allied operations are always difficult; there are jealousies, rivalries, suspicions, and it is only normal for commanders to favor their own. These things are to be expected. But I can honestly say that from Australian commanders in the field I received cooperation, sound advice, and the fraternal understanding which arises from what St. Paul describes as the "fellowship of suffering."

When disagreements occur among Allies, you may count on it that both sides have a case. Luckily for American troops, Colonel George De Graaf was prosecuting—I use the word advisedly—our case in the matter of supply. It is not too much to say that Colonel De Graaf's independence and indifference to good relations between Allies were responsible for the fact that, by the middle of December, hungry American infantrymen got enough to eat.

They were living, when my staff and I arrived, on about a third of a ration. It is a little late now to fix responsibility for this state of affairs. The Australians, to be sure, were in charge of supply, and De Graaf felt strongly that our forces were not receiving an equitable division of the transport available. Australian officers at Port Moresby determined the character and allotment of cargo. But the basic fact was: there just wasn't sufficient transport to go around. Almost everything—food, clothing, ammunition, field wire, engineer material, American reinforcements, Australian troop replacements —had to come in from Port Moresby by plane.

The transport planes were American planes piloted by American fliers. Both Australian and American Ground Forces would have perished without "George Kenney's Air." There were two airfields

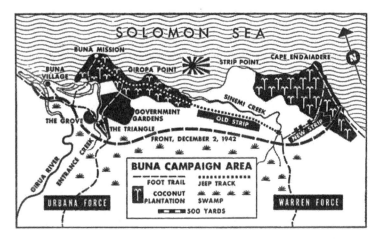

on our side of the mountains, and the mire was so soft and thick at both that I have seen clots of mud fly fifty feet high when planes took off. Dobodura Field was in our sector. Poppondetta Field was in the Aussie sector.

The Owen Stanley Mountains were capricious and closed in much of the day by tropical storms. Some days planes could not fly at all. However hard he and his subordinates might try, General Kenney could not supply adequately all the Allied troops in the field with all they needed. When De Graaf went to Moresby to seek to increase American shipments of food, he got no results at Allied headquarters. So he went to our own General Whitehead, commander of air transport. Whitehead studied De Graaf's inventories closely.

"Do you realize," he demanded, "that if there were bad luck at the Gap—if the Owen Stanleys were closed in for three or four days —your troops would starve to death?"

De Graaf understood it very well. At Moresby he pleaded, blustered, cajoled, threatened, and made a thorny nuisance of himself. He ignored military protocol and stepped completely outside of regular channels. Eventually Whitehead placed every available American transport plane at his disposal, and at the end of three days we had accumulated at Dobodura a reserve of three hundred thousand pounds of critically needed supplies. The Australians were wroth at De Graaf, but the storm blew over, and the whole incident had a happy ending.

Not long afterward, recognizing efficiency in the field, General Herring placed De Graaf in charge of both Australian and American supply depots. De Graaf was one of the few Americans at Buna to receive a decoration from Britain's king. He also won a Distinguished Service Cross for risking his life in Buna's front lines.

Another staff officer was Lieutenant Colonel S. S. Auchincloss, my signal officer. In civilian life "The Auk" had directed the communications system of the New York Stock Exchange. At Buna he performed miracles under outrageous conditions. There were three hundred miles of telephone wire to be kept open. In impassable terrain, signal parties sometimes laid wire along creek banks while floating downstream on rafts. At night Jap patrols cut our communication lines, which lay imbedded in the swamp mud, and each morning Auchincloss and his men sallied forth to make repairs. The Auk would take his linesmen as far forward as a jeep could go, put them out to continue on foot, and then load the jeep with battle wounded for a quick return trip. Often this shuttling back and forth between trouble spots lasted from dawn until nightfall.

One anecdote about Auchincloss is warm in my memory. On our first night at Buna a young captain who was signal officer for the 32nd Division came into headquarters with news that the vital telephone line to the Urbana front was dead. He reported also that his men were loath to go forward because of the steady infiltration of the Japanese. Auchincloss said, "That's my job. I'll handle it." He walked across to the signal tent, glanced at the men assembled there, and then, with considerable care, selected a sharp knife and a pair of pliers and put them in his leather linesman's kit. As he started out of the tent he looked over his shoulder at the silent signalmen.

"I'm going out to fix that line," he said. "Any of you people want to come along?"

Every man rose to follow him. It was only a relatively short time

before the telephone rang at headquarters. It was Auchincloss. His
report was terse. The line to the Urbana front was repaired.

I have told these stories to show the kind of staff officers I was
blessed with. I needed them. Our line to the sea was a noose around
Buna Village, and the enemy in subsequent attacks failed to break
through. The morale of our troops improved, and daily we inched
forward. Rations were better. Patrolling became extensive. We began to look like an army. It is significant that morale improved while
the weather grew worse and the incidence of malaria and dengue
fever and scrub typhus increased—for now we were visited with a
series of torrential nightly rains which turned all the jungle into
tanglefoot morass.

Sometimes I have wondered whether the High Command back at
Port Moresby ever really understood our battle with weather.
Moresby in winter months (summer there) is brown and burned
and ugly. Yearly rainfall is forty inches a year, about the same as
my native Ohio. Mountains intercept the rainclouds. North of the
mountains—and all this is dramatically evident from the air—the
whole landscape is a voluptuous, dripping, and sinister green. At
Buna that year it rained about a hundred and seventy inches.

I have found out since that we got more than our share in December and January of 1942–43, but it is small comfort now. My first
tent camp was located beside a small crystal-clear creek, which,
after an eight-inch rain in a single night, became a roaring torrent.
I was so tired that night that not even nature's explosions waked
me. Next morning I found the creek in my tent and within an inch
of the bottom of my cot. Various personal possessions floated around
like chips in a millstream. I waded knee-deep to get to my shaving
mirror, which hung on a bamboo tree outside. I could (and did)
move my headquarters, but that same morning, it should be remembered, the soldier up forward had to stay where he was.

Japanese Air added to our misery. American combat planes were
ordinarily in complete command of the sky during the early morning. Then big, black, tropical disturbances gathered over the Owen
Stanleys, sometimes to heights of thirty to forty thousand feet, and

our planes had to scurry home. From noon until next morning the Japs usually came over as they pleased.

Our field hospital, crowded with three times the number of patients it was designed to accommodate, was a favorite target. The hospital was plainly marked with many immense red crosses. I recall vividly a visit by twenty-one Japanese bombers on the afternoon of December 7, the first anniversary of Pearl Harbor. I was returning from the front when the bombing began.

American doctors distinguished themselves that day. There were desperately wounded men on the operating table when the trouble began. The Japs did both high level and dive bombing, ignoring our front lines and headquarters positions to concentrate on the hospital site. Surgeons continued to operate bravely and coolly. Anesthetists did not leave their posts. But the tent installation was a shambles. There were forty casualties from the bombing.

When I got there medical corpsmen were proceeding efficiently with first-aid measures, but shock and terror had created hysteria among the sick and the wounded: they were sure the Japs would be back next day. I immediately picked a new location for the hospital, and the transfer of patients and equipment went on all night in the darkness. I chose a spot which was near enough to Dobodura to make air evacuation easier, but which also offered jungle protection and concealment.

That afternoon as I picked my way through the scene of carnage and desolation I came upon the beaten-about but still lively Captain Edwards. Trussed up in bandages, supposedly within nodding distance of death, he had heard the first whistle of bombs and rolled himself off his cot and under it. Edwards, who had been an intercollegiate boxing champion while a student at Duke University, did not give up easily. Once again I laid him across the hood of my jeep. I carried him to an empty native shack near Dobodura and then went back for saline solution and blood plasma. Somehow the incredible Edwards lived through it all. He was evacuated by air next day.

We took Buna Village on December 14, and I received a congratulatory message from General MacArthur. The worst of the campaign still lay ahead of us. The prodigious rains continued. Because of the inundation it took miles of winding communications and many stumbling, heavy-laden men to get food and ammunition forward. At a place like Buna, figures on "available" riflemen are completely deceptive as to the real strength of the front line. We had virtually no motor transport, and no roads for truck travel anyway. Native bearers flatly refused to go near the front lines. This left us no alternative but to use many of our combat troops as carriers to sustain the rest.

No one could remember when he had been dry. The feet, arms, bellies, chests, armpits of my soldiers were hideous with jungle rot. The sun appeared when the skies wrung themselves out briefly, and steam rose like gray smoke in the dank undergrowth. Then the soldiers themselves steamed and sweated in their heavy jungle suits. These suits were supposedly porous. Back in Australia, before the New Guinea expedition, it was I who had ordered them dyed a mottled green to aid troop concealment. This was well meant but a serious error. The dye closed the "breathing spaces" in the cloth.

The Australian headquarters at Soputa was only nine miles away from my new camp at Sinemi, but so difficult were the trails that I usually went by air to attend military conferences. It saved time. I traveled in a Gypsy Moth, standing up and hanging on to a wooden crosspiece, or sitting in the rear seat of a Wirraway with a machine gun between my knees. The Gypsy Moth was a small, frail Australian plane which looked to our men (and to me) antiquated enough to be an exhibit in the Smithsonian Institution. It was a fabric-covered job with two tiny engines. There was no self-starter; the propeller had to be spun by hand. One of our Cubs (artillery liaison planes) would have been worth its weight in gold there. We received no Cubs until months later.

A squadron of Wirraways was stationed at Dobodura. The Wirraways were more substantial than the Moths, and we depended upon them exclusively for aerial reconnaissance. They were manned by fliers who knew the terrain and knew our ground force positions. In command was a grand soldier, Flight Officer O'Loan. Every one

of those planes, and their selfless pilots, crashed in the jungle or were shot down over enemy lines during my tour of duty at Buna. The Wirraway pilots have never received adequate credit, even in their homeland, for their deeds of exceptional gallantry during those rough early days.

In those days there was not adequate communication between Ground Forces and Combat Air. I am an old enough campaigner to admit that some of these failures in coordination were inevitable; to new and unvetted troops—who dread even their own artillery fire because an occasional shell falls short—such lamentable accidents are dispiriting. American bombers and strafers did not always drop their eggs or direct their machine-gun fire on Japanese coastal positions. I remember that the first day we put the new troops of the 127th Infantry into the line a stick of American bombs fell among them, causing more than a dozen casualties in one company.

I sent a number of messages to Port Moresby, suggesting methods by which such accidents might be avoided; I never received a reply. It was not until after the Buna campaign that I was able to make my point. Then General Blamey came over the mountains on an inspection trip. In my jeep we were weaving around bomb craters along the captured Jap motor road when an American A-20 came over, flying treetop high and firing with everything it had. Troops on the ground answered with everything *they* had.

"My God," said General Blamey. "What's that?"

Nobody had been hurt, and I could laugh. "Just another all-American battle," I said, "similar to those I have been reporting all along. Those planes think they are firing on the Japs at Sanananda three miles away. Our men get fed up and fire back."

Five or ten minutes later any possible humor vanished from the situation. Another friendly plane came over and strafed us. Three infantrymen were wounded.

Back home our Army Command and General Staff School was located at Leavenworth, Kansas. In a letter to the Allied commander (no matter how weary I was or how late the hour, I wrote two letters a night during this period, one to my wife and one to the MacArthur headquarters), I described the Buna tactical picture as a

"Leavenworth Nightmare." Everything favored the enemy. It may be enlightening to compare Buna to Guadalcanal.

At Guadalcanal the Americans were in the coconut groves and on the dry land at the coast. They had the sea breeze, and the Japanese were in the jungle. At Buna the situation was reversed. We were in the jungle, and the trails by which we could advance splayed down from the seacoast through otherwise impenetrable territory, like the fingers of a hand. It was easy for the Japs, secure in buried log bunkers, able to move reinforcements swiftly along a motor road, to command our approaches with heavy automatic weapons fire.

General Byers was wounded during December 16 operations and was evacuated several days later to Australia. Buna was not a happy climate for generals. Brigadier General Hanford MacNider had been wounded earlier, and now both Waldron and Byers were hospitalized along with him. I was the only general left in action, so I added direct command of the forward elements of the 32nd Division to the command of I Corps. I permitted myself a grim chuckle as I did so, because I suddenly remembered a fragment from a roaring ballad of World War I:

> The General won the Croix de Guerre
> But the so-and-so was never there,
> Hinkey dinkey parlez-vous.

Obviously Buna was a different kind of battle. Three generals had been shot, and the one farthest removed from the Japanese lines had been seventy-five yards away.

I can quickly record the casualties among my other staff officers. Colonel Gordon Rogers was shot through both legs on December 28 while directing the bridging of Entrance Creek. Major William Duncan, standing beside Rogers, also suffered two wounds. Duncan, who served as a courier between Buna and Moresby, had arrived at Dobodura only that morning. He asked to see something of the front and went forward with me for a visit that was brief indeed. Captain M. G. Gray came on from Australia to succeed Eddie Edwards as my aide and asked for combat duty. Gray was never

creased by a bullet, but after many days as a brilliant infantry leader
he was invalided out with a rich, ripe case of malaria.

There were many great combat commanders among the National
Guard officers of the 32nd Division. In crises, I would like to have
them again as comrades. I can mention only a few here: Colonels
Merle H. Howe and Herbert M. Smith of Wisconsin, Major H. E.
Hantlemann of Iowa, Major Edmund R. Schroeder of Wisconsin, the
inimitable Captain W. H. Dames, whose Company G, 127th Infantry, never made a wrong move in battle.

A tower of strength at this time, and later, was Colonel Frank S.
Bowen. Bowen served under me for eight years—from the summer
of 1939 to the summer of 1947. He was with me in the 30th Infantry,
went along to West Point as my aide, served as G-1 (personnel officer) of the 77th Division, and became assistant G-3 (operations
officer) of I Corps. When I found it necessary to put Colonel Clarence Martin in command of my right flank at Buna, Bill Bowen succeeded him as G-3. Bowen was about thirty-seven years old at that
time. He was an indefatigable worker, had an extraordinarily clear
mind, and was one of the bravest soldiers I have ever served with.

By mid-December the 126th and the 128th Infantry were badly
depleted by illness and wounds; companies with a strength of two
hundred and fifty at full muster were down to forty and fifty men,
and attrition among line officers was tragic. There were subordinates
of mine—understandably torn by the sufferings of their troops—who
suggested we abandon attempts to advance and settle down to
"starve out the Japanese."

But my orders were to advance; General MacArthur continued to
advise me that "time was of the essence." Here is one letter and
military order I received from him:

GENERAL HEADQUARTERS
Southwest Pacific Area
Office of the Commander in Chief

13 December 1942

Dear Bob:

Time is fleeting and our dangers increase with its passage. However
admirable individual acts of courage may be; however important adminis-

trative functions may seem; however splendid and electrical your presence has proven; remember that your mission is to take Buna. All other things are merely subsidiary to this. No alchemy is going to produce this for you; it can only be done in battle and sooner or later this battle must be engaged. Hasten your preparations, and when you are ready—strike, for as I have said, time is working desperately against us.

Cordially,

/s/ MacArthur
DOUGLAS MacARTHUR
Allied Commander

There was the constant danger of enemy reinforcements by sea. Indeed, on the night of December 13-14 Allied Air sighted a convoy moving toward Buna; despite bombing missions the enemy was able to land twelve hundred troops to the north of the immediate battlefront. There were a number of attempts to reinforce Buna by small boats under the cover of night. More important still was the fact that time was on the side of the Japanese. Disease was a surer and more deadly peril to us than enemy marksmanship. We had to whip the Japanese before the malarial mosquito whipped us.

It is useless, I suppose, to comment on how much easier our job would have been if we had had better tools. Later on in the war we would have been able to use Napalm, a bomb of jellied gasoline which would have burned out the log bunkers which resisted artillery and mortar fire. The American flame-thrower also proved invaluable later for similar jobs. But that was an improved flame-thrower. The flame-thrower we had at Buna was mechanically deficient. In that wet wilderness it accomplished only the death of our chemical warfare officer and made casualties of his personnel.

Our artillery consisted mainly of Australian 25-pounders and one prized .105 howitzer. This had been taken down in Australia and the parts flown to New Guinea in three airplanes. The howitzer, when again assembled, did excellent service until the ammunition supply we penuriously rationed ran out. We would have had more ammunition if the Japs had not sunk the boats which were bringing it up. I would have been delighted to have had many more howitzers, because they were effective against the Japanese bunkers, but since

we ran out of ammunition for *one*, what would we have done with others? The simple truth is that transport, by air or sea, was unequal to the job demanded. We made out as best we could.

Along about this time there was some cheering news. Fresh troops of the 32nd's own 127th Infantry began arriving in job lots via the overworked transport planes. And over at Hariko, our port on the sea, seven light tanks and a battalion of the 18th Australian Brigade came in by water.

Shortly after my arrival at Buna it had been agreed at a conference between General Herring's staff and mine that we would attempt to bring in secretly from Milne Bay a platoon of light tanks. Our hope was that a surprise tank attack against Cape Endaiadere might plow through to the sea. The stubbornly resistant Japanese positions at the Cape were nearly all in a coconut grove. There were firm approaches which tanks might use without bogging down. Combat-wise Brigadier George F. Wootten was to command the Australians, and because he was senior to Colonel Martin I suggested he assume command of the American right flank, which we called Warren Force.

The tanks were of American manufacture. Back in the States they were called M-3s; the Aussies called them Matildas. With great caution they were moved from Hariko and jockeyed up under the cover of night to the edge of a Japanese dummy airfield which we had named the New Strip. There was no discovery. Surprise was complete.

On December 18 tanks and troops jumped off. It was a spectacular and dramatic assault, and a brave one. From the New Strip to the sea was about half a mile. American troops wheeled to the west in support, and other Americans were assigned to mopping-up duties. But behind the tanks went the fresh and jaunty Aussie veterans, tall, mustached, erect, with their blazing tommy guns swinging before them. Concealed Japanese positions—which were even more formidable than our patrols had indicated—burst into flame. There was the greasy smell of tracer fire from the snipers' seats in the trees, and heavy machine-gun fire from barricades and entrenchments.

Steadily tanks and infantrymen advanced through the spare, high coconut trees, seemingly impervious to the heavy opposition. There were a hundred and fifty Japanese bunkers on Cape Endaiadere. Three tanks were destroyed by Japanese pompom fire, and infantry casualties were extraordinarily high. I have never seen Australian official figures, but I'm sure that Aussie battalion lost nearly half its fighting force in killed and wounded. Nevertheless, the job was done. The sea was reached, and mopping-up began.

The next day the attack changed direction, and the Americans and the Australians pushed the surviving enemy toward Buna Mission. Now Allied troops of the right flank were on dry ground at last.

Back in the swamp area, American troops were struggling still to cross Entrance Creek. Tanks would have been useless there. Even horse-drawn carts would have bogged down. I had orders from General Herring to break through to the sea between Buna Mission and Giropa Point. This made military sense. The Japanese were in a pocket. If our troops on the left flank could drive through to the coast there was an excellent chance that the enemy forces could be cut in half and Buna Mission isolated. To accomplish this, American troops on the left flank had to advance straight through the jungle and cross tidal streams.

We had already had our troubles. After the fall of Buna Village we pushed hard against two important Japanese positions. They were known to the men as The Grove and The Triangle, and even in retrospect those names ring no happy, chiming bell. The Grove was on our side of unfordable Entrance Creek. On December 16 we laid on mortar and artillery fire, and twenty minutes later our troops attacked. The attack was short-lived; our artillery preparations had failed to neutralize enemy positions. By sundown our troops managed to reach the edge of The Grove but were unable to enter it. Throughout the night they clung to their positions in rain reminiscent of Niagara. At dawn they charged and overran The Grove.

The next job was The Triangle. It had been believed at my headquarters that The Triangle was lightly held, but battle intelligence showed us, at considerable cost, our error. Actually it was a carefully prepared defensive area with seventeen mutually supporting bunkers. Our forces determinedly tried to advance. Despite their best efforts, they failed to gain.

Still, Entrance Creek had to be crossed, and I ordered the sore spot of The Triangle "contained" while the fresh troops of the 127th Infantry came forward. They were brisk and free of malaria; they were full of enthusiasm and full of fight. These troops took on the job of crossing Entrance Creek, and I still am proud of them. The job chosen for them in their first introduction to battle was the most difficult of all military maneuvers—a crossing of an unfordable stream under fire at night.

They made it. The first men crossed in small canvas boats and established a narrow bridgehead on the western border of Government Gardens. Then pontoons were laid down, and the anchored boats became steppingstones. Once upon a time the Gardens had been cultivated ground: now they were overgrown, high in kunai grass, and well fortified. Enemy resistance was stiff; every crossing of the deep stream drew heavy fire; every inch on the east bank was sorely contested. Yet by December 23 the bridgehead had been so enlarged that the Americans could take off from there in an all-out attack next morning.

Now five other companies were poised to make the projected breakthrough between Buna Mission and Giropa Point. For the first time in many days I felt a lightening of spirit and a surge of optimism. The tanks had been successful. The rains had let up. As a result of clearing weather Allied combat planes were in our sky again. On December 24 the rolling barrage started on the American left flank, and the troops jumped off.

The calendar being what it is, Christmas Eve and Christmas Day rolled around to New Guinea inevitably. They were hard to recognize. There were no lights and no tinsel on the palm trees, and a chubby-cheeked Santa would have found himself sweating in his furs. The Red Cross had valiantly delivered some Christmas packages and Christmas delicacies to Dobodura, but only the rear echelons could enjoy them. The soldiers up front already had their hands full. I am glad that none of them knew of the peculiar communiqué released to the press of the world by Allied headquarters. It read:

"On Christmas Day our activities were limited to routine safety precautions. Divine services were held."

I am convinced that this equable and pious sentiment was issued by rear echelons in Australia without General MacArthur's knowledge, because on Christmas Day at Buna—the only place in the theater where there *could* be American Ground Force activities—the fighting was desperate and the outcome of the whole miserable, tortured campaign was in doubt.

Indeed it was on the day before Christmas that two now famous Wisconsin infantrymen were killed. They were Sergeants Kenneth E. Gruennert and Elmer J. Burr, two men posthumously awarded the Congressional Medal of Honor. During an attack Sergeant Burr lost his life but saved his company commander by smothering the explosion of an enemy hand grenade with his own body. Sergeant Gruennert was second in command of a platoon pushing toward the sea which encountered two hostile pillboxes when within a hundred and fifty yards of the objective. He advanced alone on the first pillbox and put it out of action with grenades and rifle fire, killing three of the enemy. Shot through the shoulder, he bandaged his wound under cover of the pillbox and refused to go to the rear. Still alone, he attacked the second pillbox. He threw grenades which forced out the Japanese defenders, who then became easy targets for his men. Before his platoon could reach him, Gruennert was killed by snipers.

I was awakened on Christmas morning by heavy Japanese bombing from the air, and my Christmas dinner was a cup of soup given me by a thoughtful doctor at a trailside hospital. For the projected American advance had not proceeded as expected. Troops of Urbana Force bogged down in the kunai grass of Government Gardens and their commander lost contact with his forward units. One platoon of L Company, 127th Infantry, went on to the sea in a glorious manner. They waited for other Americans to reinforce them. One officer and eight men got through as reinforcements, but that was all The platoon of L Company took a wistful, farewell look at the ocean and retired.

Next morning I wrote General MacArthur: "I think the low point of my life occurred yesterday." I was wrong. I was to explore the

depths of depression more thoroughly on the night of December 27. My diary tells me that was the evening I received a dismal telephone call from Colonel Bowen, my operations officer. He told me there was grave news on the Urbana front; an American commander who had just toured the lines was on his way back to headquarters with a summation of the situation.

At two A.M. a conference took place in my tent. We heard the reports, and they were grave all right. Our troops, if the reports were to be credited, were suffering badly from battle shock and had become incapable of advance. A number of my senior officers were convinced the situation was desperate. I think I said, as I had said before, "Let us not take counsel of our fears." Nevertheless I was thoroughly alarmed. There was no way to evacuate our units. Could I get reinforcements? I decided to sleep an hour or so and then go forward to discover the truth for myself. Tossing on my cot, there in the tropical darkness, I remembered my conversation with General MacArthur three weeks before on the veranda at Port Moresby. At one point he had turned to me with the memory of Bataan in his eyes and a bitter query on his lips.

"Must I always," he demanded, "lead a forlorn hope?"

Was Buna, I asked myself, to be an American military disaster? Were the sacrifices represented by the rude crosses in Buna Cemetery to have been made in vain?

Daylight is good medicine for the fears of darkness. When I reached the Urbana command post Bill Bowen was already receiving telephone messages from such line commanders as Colonel Howe and Major Schroeder. The tenor of all messages was the same: the military situation was not desperate; it was encouraging. The field commanders were confident of attaining the beach—and a little more than twenty-four hours later they did. Buna Mission was isolated, and final victory became a certainty.

In battle the margin between victory and defeat is often narrow. Under the terrific pressures of combat, officers and men alike tend to forget that the enemy is hard pressed too. Sometimes just plain stubbornness wins the battle that awareness and wisdom might have lost. That's what happened at Buna. The Japanese morale cracked before ours did. Major Schroeder was one of the brave, stubborn men. He was killed in the very attack that won us the sea.

Several days of hard fighting followed. On January 2 a coordinated attack was made by both the Urbana and Warren Forces. More tanks had come in to spearhead the Warren Force attack, and the Urbana Force had succeeded in surrounding the Mission. Before nightfall we controlled the entire coastline east of the Girua River. I find that I wrote that evening: "At 4:30 P.M. I crossed the bridge (from the Island), after C Company had passed, and I saw American troops with their bellies out of the mud and their eyes in the sun. . . . It was one of the grandest sights I have ever seen."

Organized resistance ended on January 3, but for many days thereafter our soldiers were hunting out Japanese stragglers in the jungle and swamps. Almost all resisted capture and had to be killed.

It is difficult to convey to the reader the immense relief, the feeling of freedom, the outright joy, that came with victory. I was pleased, of course, by the warm congratulations of Generals Blamey and Herring. I was also pleased when General MacArthur wrote six days later to advise me that he was returning to Brisbane, and to congratulate me on the success which had been achieved. He ended his note:

> I am so glad that you were not injured in the fighting. I always feared your incessant exposure might result fatally. With a hearty slap on the back.
>
> Most cordially,
MacArthur.

There was something about winning at Buna which was above and beyond personal satisfactions and gratitude for survival. I had been luckier than most of my soldiers. I had not been wounded and I had not been ill. To be sure, I was having trouble with the waistband of my trousers; I had lost thirty pounds in thirty days. But I think I can honestly say that the real reason for my joy was to be found in the fact that brave men who had fought one of the weariest campaigns in history—albeit an important and decisive campaign—could see the sea again. They had proved themselves.

SANANANDA

No new principles of warfare were learned at Buna, but the nature of the terrain and the disposition of enemy positions necessitated some novel applications of well-known principles. In the beginning there was an unwise willingness to accept success of the Buna campaign as a foregone conclusion. Air reconnaissance reports, for instance, said flatly that there were only straggling Japanese in the area at a time when three thousand enemy troops were busily at work constructing fortifications. Many members of the General Staff were overconfident and, in the large sense, ignorant of conditions as they actually existed. Few of them came to the jungle front to learn at first hand.

There is one rather entertaining personal story which I have told many times. Back in the United States on Christmas morning the newspapers reported for the first time that three American generals —MacNider, Waldron, and Byers—had been wounded at Buna. Mrs. Eichelberger was living in Asheville, North Carolina, and a local paper, at about the same time, printed news of the wounding of Dan Edwards, my aide. Naturally my wife was tremendously worried. She was without news, but she drew the logical conclusion that if Byers and Edwards had been hit in New Guinea I must not be too far away.

She telephoned mutual friends in the War Department, but, lying like gentlemen, they assured her I was still in Australia. Miss Em was a little crisp in her comment: "If he's in New Guinea, the Japanese already know it, and you're only fooling me."

On December 27 or 28 an article written by Murlin Spencer of the Associated Press was published by many newspapers under a New Guinea dateline. Without being able, because of censorship, to mention my name, Spencer described a trip he made to the front with me on Christmas Day: by jeep as far as we could go, and then wearily, through the swamp, by foot. Spencer described the wounded and sick we saw in the litters along the trail, and how the "tall, gray-haired general" commanding Buna "frequently stopped to speak to them in this fashion: 'Good morning, lads. I only hope you will all be home next Christmas.'"

Miss Em read this story at her breakfast table. She immediately wrote Murlin Spencer, a superb correspondent and a good friend of mine still: "I recognize my husband from your description, because he is the only general I know in the Army who uses the term 'lads' to address soldiers. Thank God I know he was alive on Christmas morning."

At Buna it was siege warfare, and that, as history records, is the bitterest and most punishing kind of warfare. Considering the number of troops in the front lines, the fatalities closely approach, percentage-wise, the heaviest losses in our own Civil War battles. Few prisoners were taken on either side, and the record indicates the quality of opposition which our troops met. The battle had to be fought through until, as one Australian writer phrased it, there was "not one Japanese left who was capable of lifting a rifle."

The Japanese had had time enough to construct an excellent complex of bunkers and dugouts, and there were connecting trenches. Foot-wide coconut logs increased protection, so that small-arms fire made no impression, and, because the bunkers were so close to the ground, 25-pounders were often ineffective. Dense jungle and the camouflage of grasses and tree branches made these strongholds almost invisible in daylight.

Clever concealment and thick vegetation made reconnaissance very difficult for our soldiers, and, also, very important. Not only the hard-pressed GI but experienced commanders frequently erred in

estimating the strength of an enemy position. For one thing, the
Japanese hesitated to deliver fire which might disclose a bunker's
whereabouts and generally fired only when being actively attacked.
Frequently the enemy allowed our troops to expose themselves un-
knowingly for hours without a trigger being pressed. This led casual
observers to believe that few or no Japanese were present in areas
where, in fact, they might be concentrated in force.

An example comes to mind. It was reported that one spot along
the Sanananda Track west of the Girua River was defended only by
one machine gun and a few riflemen. This was attacked by the Australians and elements of the American 126th Infantry. Resistance
was stubborn. Reconnaissance parties were sent out and reported
themselves unable to determine the enemy's strength. When the
position was finally captured, between seventy-five and eighty machine guns were discovered and more than three hundred dead
Japanese were counted in the overrun bunkers.

The invisibility of the Japanese gave a haunting and fearsome
quality to any advance, and, indeed, even to a routine supply trip
forward with rations. Every GI knew there were snipers high in the
trees, but he could not see them. And there seemed to him no rhyme
or reason in their tactics. For three days a patrol might proceed forward and backward over a trail without molestation. On the fourth
day enemy bullets would turn the swamp mud red, and our survivors would shoot angrily but unseeingly into the impenetrable
green above. This was, of course, a calculated Japanese technique
intended to mystify the Western soldier and to heighten that sense
of insecurity which is inevitable in combat. I can say this: the technique worked.

Frequently the enemy would allow a large part of an attacking
force to pass by his concealed strongholds and then open up with
automatic weapons and grenades. I find in one of my own military
reports a calm sentence which now provides me with a certain grim
amusement. I wrote: "This procedure proved disconcerting to our
troops." Another masterpiece of understatement!

The Japanese troops were not improvising. Over a period of many
years expeditionary forces had been built up and trained for just

that kind of fighting. They had been conditioned for it too. They could exist on short rations, and they could travel light. They could climb trees stealthily, and they were willing to live and die underground with surprising patience and unflagging courage.

As a matter of fact, in strategy and tactics, the Japanese were rarely improvisers. They fought a battle just as they had been told to fight it; once the plan of a campaign had been drawn up, commanders in the field adhered adamantly to their book instructions— there was no flexibility of decision to meet unexpected situations. During the worst period at Buna, when the advantage lay with the enemy, it would have been greatly to their benefit to take the offensive. I have frequently said at military conferences that I would have been happy to exchange tactical positions with the Japanese; with the natural advantages which accrued to them I would have guaranteed to encircle and rout the prisoners of the swamps. But the Japs, whose interior position permitted them to concentrate great numbers at any one point, would not leave their strongholds.

It is always interesting to look at a battle through the enemy's eyes but rarely possible. After Buna we captured many diaries kept by individual Japanese soldiers. These diaries, when translated, were informative. From them we learned that the enemy feared our mortars most, our artillery next, and our aerial strafing and bombing least. During the early stages of the campaign the entries clearly reflect the official Japanese Army propaganda line that the American was not a formidable soldier.

As the siege proceeded the point of view of the besieged began to change. But the diaries tell their own story. Dates of the entries are omitted here, but the excerpts selected follow chronologically the progress of the battle:

The enemy has received almost no training. Even though we fire a shot they present a large portion of their body and look around. Their movements are very slow. At this rate they cannot make a night attack.

The enemy has been repulsed by our keen-eyed snipers. In the jungle it seems they fire at any sound, due to illusion. From sundown until about 10 P.M. they fire light machine guns and throw hand grenades recklessly.

They hit coconuts that are fifteen meters from us. There are some low shots but most of them are high. They do not look out and determine their targets from the jungle. They are in the jungle firing as long as their ammunition lasts. Maybe they get more money for firing so many rounds.

The enemy is using ammunition wildly. I wish the main force would hurry and come.

The enemy has become considerably more accurate in firing.

Enemy approached to about 50 meters. Difficult to distinguish their forms in the jungle. Can't see their figures.

The nature of the enemy is superior and they excel in firing techniques. Their tactics are to neutralize our positions with fire power, approach our positions under concentrated mortar fire. Furthermore, it seems that in firing they are using treetops. During daytime mess, if our smoke is discovered, we receive mortar fire.

This entry was a turning point in the diary serial-story. It seems to me probable that this was the enemy's unconscious acknowledgment that we Americans had learned our hard lessons and that the 32nd Division had found itself. From that time on the military observations are discouraged and very brief:

From today's mortar fire the third platoon received great damage.

Headquarters is a pitiful sight due to artillery fire.

Carried in one coconut tree and filled in all of the shelter. Now we are safe from mortar fire.

Artillery raking the area. We cannot hold out much longer.

Our nerves are strained; there is a lack of sleep due to the continuous shelling.

The enemy scouts which have been bothering us all night quit about two hours before dawn. The night strain has passed.

Enemy scouts appear everywhere and attack, shooting automatic rifles.

A second series of diary excerpts collected by my staff presents an even more interesting and unusual picture of the garrison troops.

These paragraphs are highly personal and represent the aspirations, fears, and frustrations of men. They demolish the idea that the Japanese soldier, however rigorously trained, is "unemotional," an automaton.

Morale of troops is good because we feel reinforcements will come.

Received word of praise from the Emperor today. We will hold out to the last. . . . Our troops do not come. Even though they do come, they are driven away by enemy planes. Every day my comrades die one by one and our provisions disappear.

We are now in a delaying holding action. The amount of provisions is small and there is no chance of replenishing ammunition. But we have bullets of flesh. No matter what comes we are not afraid. If they come, let them come, even though there be a thousand. We will not be surprised. We have the aid of Heaven. We are the warriors of Yamamoto.

How I wish we could change to the offensive! Human beings must die once. It is only natural instinct to want to live; but only those with military spirit can cast that away.

Now the tempo of retrogression heightens, and despair takes hold. Like young men everywhere, the Japanese soldiers are sad and unwilling and self-pitying in the coming presence of death. Sentences from the journals tell the story in a staccato fashion: "There are some who are completely deteriorating spiritually. . . . We can't eat today. Mess gear is gone because of the terrific mortar fire. . . . Everyone is depressed. Nothing we can do. . . . It is only fate that I am alive today. This may be the place where I shall find my death. I will fight to the last. . . ."

December becomes January and the final onrush of the Americans is at hand. These are the last entries:

With the dawn, the enemy started shooting all over. All I can do is shed tears of resentment. Now we are waiting only for death. The news that reinforcements had come turned out to be a rumor. All day we stay in the bunkers. We are filled with vexation. Comrades, are you going to stand by and watch us die? Even the invincible Imperial Army is at a loss. Can't anything be done? Please God.

Night falls. Thought we saw two enemy scouts. It turned out to be a bird and a rat.

It is certainly lamentable when everyone runs off and not a single person remains to take care of things. Can these be called soldiers of Japan?

I pray—with the symbol of the clan deity in my hand.

At the time of the fall of Buna the battle west of the Girua River was still in a condition of stalemate. The 7th Australian Division and the American elements of the 126th Infantry had been fighting there for weeks. Casualties had been high and luck had been low. The Australians were the hardy veterans who had crossed the Kokoda Trail, driving the Japanese before them, and the soldiers of the 126th (less the 1st and 3rd Battalions) were the courageous lads who had conquered the Kapa Kapa Trail. Both the Aussies and the Americans were tired, ill, and depleted by those epic-making marches. And, after arrival in the lowlands, they were committed to a battle of attrition and trench warfare which resembled, in miniature, the hateful Battle of the Somme in World War I.

In the beginning it had been decided that the Girua River would be the separating line between Australian and American commands. The 126th crossed the Girua River in November and joined up with the Australians at Soputa, and thus came under Australian command. This geographic inadvertence caused a considerable bitterness among officers of the 32nd Division, and their position was understandable.

Early in December the Allied Command decided to fly in a regiment of the American 41st Division to take the place of the exhausted American units before Sanananda. The 163rd Infantry was alerted about mid-month and appeared in the Buna-Gona sector just after the victory at Buna had been won. I had some knowledge of the condition of both Australian and American troops in the Sanananda operation, but I was soon to discover that it was infinitely worse than I had known.

When the 163rd went forward, the 126th was returned to American command with rather elaborate military ceremony. I received these troops with band music and with what might well be described as a martial welcome. Actually it was, whatever face could be put upon it, a melancholy homecoming. Sickness, death, and wounds had taken an appalling toll. Out of the eleven hundred able-bodied men who had been sent from Australia, only ninety-five were left to cross the Girua River and answer the muster. They were so ragged and so pitiful that when I greeted them my eyes were wet.

When Buna was taken, I had supposed my job was done. The first American Army victory over the Japanese had been announced to the world, and Generals MacArthur and Blamey had returned to Australia. General Herring took over the Port Moresby headquarters, and, abruptly, and with no joy, I found myself commander of the Allied forces on the north coast of Papua.

Public-relations officers on General MacArthur's staff chose to call this last phase of the Papuan campaign a "mopping-up operation." Instead, it was a completely savage and expensive battle. Australian commanders who had been engaged in the nutcracker job at Sanananda were pessimistic about the chances of early victory, and many of them foresaw, as a result of optimistic reports released to the press, the ruin of their own careers—and mine. Sanananda would not be easy.

I did not have an exact picture of the situation, but I had both admiration and friendship for the Aussie field commanders. Major General George Alan Vasey was a thin-faced, delicate-appearing veteran who had internal muscularity. He and I, from opposite sides of a river, had ridden a nightmare for many weeks and had been uneasy in the saddle. I listened while he and his staff officers told me what had happened in that theater. I shall summarize it as best I can.

After arriving, over the mountains, at Poppondetta, the Australians had struck immediately at Gona. They did well until storms closed the cleft in the Owen Stanleys for three days and no supply planes got through. Short of food and short of ammunition, the 25th Brigade and the attached 3rd Battalion were forced to retire some three miles south of Gona.

Actually, Gona was a rest home for sick and wounded Japanese soldiers. But defensive positions had been effectively prepared, and the sick and wounded, in pillboxes and timbered redoubts, defended themselves very well. After an air attack and an artillery assault, the

21st Brigade hit the beach stronghold and broke through to the sea. The Japanese fell back into a network of field fortifications around Gona Mission, and they were not finally routed until Brigadier Ivan Dougherty fought a second and bloody battle on the coastal dunes in mid-December.

Little progress was made in the Sanananda zone between the fall of Gona and the advent of the new year, although many men on both sides died. The Japanese held an area shaped like an isosceles triangle with the broad base on the ocean between Cape Killerton and Tarakena, and the apex of the triangle at a point three and a half miles inland from Sanananda. It was there that the trails from Killerton and Sanananda merged and continued on fairly solid ground to the Australian headquarters at Soputa. It was the trails which were fought for; the swamps between were almost impenetrable.

Immediately after the fall of Buna Mission the fresher troops took over the action. Brigadier Wootten's 18th Brigade moved from Buna to the Soputa area. Our own not-so-fresh 127th Infantry crossed the Girua River and started up a narrow coastal strip of sand and through an adjoining mangrove swamp toward Tarakena. It is simple to explain why this advance was hazardous. The strip of sand was so narrow that a man, at many places, could spit to his right in the ocean and spit to his left in a swamp. He had no concealment. This made Japanese marksmanship easy and communication lines difficult. Nevertheless, Tarakena was taken on January 8, and the advance continued toward Sanananda Point with some of the hardest fighting of the whole campaign ahead.

The strongest Japanese positions were at the inland apex of the triangle where in the past the Allied advance had been held up. In the rear of the Japanese, to the north, however, the Allies had established a roadblock which prevented the enemy from using the trail from Sanananda for supplies and forced them to rely on the roundabout and more arduous Killerton Track. The situation on the Sanananda Trail was truly extraordinary, with Jap positions and Allied positions lined up in leapfrog fashion. We were in their rear and they were in our rear.

The original Allied roadblock was about half a mile back of enemy advance positions. Just behind this was a second Japanese defensive position, and behind that another Allied roadblock. A quarter of a mile to the north there was another group of enemy defenses. The 163rd Infantry, under able Colonel Jens A. Doe, now took over these roadblocks. Our supply lines to them ran through dense jungle, and these dangerous routes were necessarily under constant patrol.

Censorship had been very strict during the Papuan campaign. Australian and American troops were always "Allied troops"; divisions and division commanders, brigades and brigadiers, were strictly anonymous. Yet over the radio on January 11 we heard from San Francisco an announcement that Brigadier Wootten would attack with his tanks next day. That was indeed the plan, and it was carried out. Wootten and the 18th Brigade struck north from Soputa. The Japanese were ready. Wootten's tanks were demolished by noontime and the 18th Brigade repulsed.

I took over formal command next day, and Major General F. H. Berryman, Australian, became my chief of staff. I was roughly familiar with General Vasey's plan for the envelopment of the Japanese, but I was not at all satisfied with our knowledge of enemy positions and supply lines. I wanted to know how the Japs were bringing in the food and ammunition which enabled them to fend us off.

I ordered vigorous and far-flung patrolling, which made life even more miserable for the American GI and the Australian "Digger." The rains had started again, with a ten-inch downpour in a single evening. Our patrols waded hip-deep and shoulder-deep in water. But the patrolling in the swamps paid off. Our troops discovered Japanese soldiers, with full packs on their backs, who were headed toward Cape Killerton. A general evacuation of the able-bodied (the sick and the wounded were left behind) was under way.

I gave orders at once for an attack with all the power we had. The Australians hit the enemy head-on, while the Americans cut in from behind. By the morning of January 15 Japanese strength at the apex of the triangle was wiped out; the 18th Brigade was pushing rapidly up the Killerton Track and meeting only slight resistance. When

Wootten reached the sea he turned down the coast and on January 18 made junction with the American 127th, which had fought its way up the coast from Tarakena to Girua under the leadership of colorful Merle Howe. Colonel Howe, a National Guard officer and a former schoolteacher, was the master *par excellence* of the indigo phrase, and a stalwart fighting man. He was to be killed in a plane crash in the Philippines three years later.

The encirclement of the Japanese was complete, but the battle was not done. I had shifted my Buna headquarters to General Herring's old command post at Samboga. I had been there many times before. The campsite was located on a dry grassy knoll, and to reach it one crossed over a small, calm creek on a rudimentary footbridge. When I came as commander in January I needed no measuring instruments to acquaint me with the amount of rainfall. The footbridge itself was under water, and I was paddled across what was now a wide river in a canvas boat. Even on dry land in New Guinea I often dug my own well with a shovel, struck water at two feet, and filled my canteen. Crystal-clear water gushed up through the black mud, but like every sensible GI I never failed to dump in germ-killer pellets.

It was at Samboga that I got news that General Herring in Port Moresby was not satisfied with the progress of Colonel Doe and the 163rd. Herring thought Doe was moving too slowly and was not in contact with the enemy. The truth was that the 163rd had its hands full. Up the Sanananda Trail it ran into the enemy's main resistance. Moreover, the 2nd Battalion of the 163rd, which attempted to cross over from the Killerton Track to the Sanananda Trail, found that its road vanished after half a mile. With only a compass as a guide, the troops had to chop their way through the jungle.

I had the utmost confidence in Colonel Doe, but to satisfy Herring I took General Vasey and our staff officers forward. The waters had retreated, and we were able to proceed by jeep beyond the apex of the triangle. We went up the Sanananda Trail. American soldiers were lying across the road and firing; there was also American and Japanese firing behind us. We were at the Fisk Perimeter—so called for Lieutenant Harold R. Fisk, the first officer of the 163rd to be hit in battle. Vasey and I got out of the jeep and crawled down into a trench.

This was Doe's command post. It had a roof of sorts and revetments to protect it. I said, "Where are the Japs?" Doe answered, "Right over there. See that bunker?" I saw it and Vasey saw it, and it was only fifty yards away. Doe was in the front line and so were we. He gave us some hot tea and then went on with the attack. Vasey was satisfied with Doe's determination, and so was I.

The 163rd had to do most of the nasty job of obliterating the enemy in a series of scattered skirmishes. The defeated Japanese would not give in. Because they were willing to accept death, because even hopeless odds did not hasten surrender, every single small outpost had to be taken at the sacrifice of Allied lives. But by January 22 all organized resistance of the Japanese in Papua was over, and the long, heartbreaking campaign was done.

General Herring, my Allied commander in Port Moresby, sent me this generous personal message: "Please accept on behalf yourself, your commanding officers and men, the heartiest congratulations and gratitude of General Blamey and myself for the carefully planned and magnificently executed operations which have resulted in capture of Sanananda and the virtual clearing of Japanese from Papua."

In those early days we consistently underestimated the enemy. Intelligence guessed there were three hundred Japanese at Buna, and there were three thousand. Intelligence guessed there were five hundred Japanese at Sanananda, and there were five thousand. However you look at it, the assignment was tough. Japanese casualties mounted up to about eight thousand dead. There were some high-ranking Japanese officers who did not become casualties at Buna and Sanananda. They dumped their wounded out of motor barges and saved their own skins by departure by sea.

What did it cost us? I have before me the casualties of the 32nd Division from September 26, 1942, to February 28, 1943. Killed in action and died of wounds: 690. Total deaths, including disease: 707. Wounded in action: 1680. Fever and disease cases (including shell shock and concussions): 8286. The Australian casualties should be added to the high purchase price for inhospitable jungle. Between September 25 and January 22, a period which covers their pursuit of the Japanese over the Kokoda Trail, 3359 Australians were wounded and 1602 were killed in action or died of wounds.

We had our victory, and we were started back.

AUSTRALIA AND THE AMPHIBS

My instructions from General MacArthur were to return to Australia as soon as the Sanananda operation was completed. The 32nd Division was to be rehabilitated in Australia, and a new division, the 24th, was scheduled to arrive there. Major General Horace Fuller of the 41st Division was on the ground to take over American troops in Advanced New Guinea for further operations under Australian command. Horace Fuller was a classmate and friend, and I was glad for the time being to bequeath the jungle to him and to Vasey. A young staff officer of mine, at the moment of departure, remarked alliteratively that he was "one of the lads not loath to leave." I was another.

I was very tired. But I knew, being a reasoning man, that I was not nearly so tired as many of the GIs who had already returned to Australia. In fact, with the removal of great responsibility, I felt reasonably good. Remembering the fallen, remembering the wounded and the maimed, I was convinced I had been lucky beyond my deserts. I had been shot at repeatedly and never hit. At the age of fifty-six, a man is not in the heyday of youth, but I had endured days of physical exertion calculated to kill an ox. Soldiers who served throughout the campaign and did not get malaria were few. Yet I never got it. I fed poorly and lost weight, but I must confess I did not even have indigestion.

63

Why I was never sick I did not know then and do not know now. The Anopheles mosquito is not choosy and, the doctors say, likes one blood stream just about as well as another. Yet the Anopheles mosquito avoided me. There are certain ancient superstitions which seem to be a part of soldiering; when I asked Brigadier Wootten to attack the commanding positions at Sanananda, where so many assaults had been beaten back before, he was silent for a little while and indecisive. Then he said: "If you want me to attack, I'll attack. I like a lucky man."

My corps officers and I—both General Byers and Colonel Rogers had come back from the hospital—took off by air on January 24 and spent that night in Port Moresby. Generous Ned Herring rolled out for us all the red carpets he had. There was a press conference with Australian newspapermen, and I took the occasion to tell them of the heroic job the Wirraway pilots had done beyond the mountains. Because of some curious caste system I failed to understand, the Wirraway pilots did not belong to the Royal Australian Air Forces; and I resented public indifference to their flying ability and heroism. My men saw one Wirraway shoot down a Zero. This was about like seeing Lindbergh's old *Spirit of St. Louis* shoot down a jet fighter.

It was comforting to go to General Herring's camp against a mountainside, and to feel dry, and to feel free, and to sleep. That night there was a Japanese air raid on Moresby, a great deal of excitement and an inordinate racket. The anti-aircraft guns were busy and noisy, and searchlights lighted the sky. I slept all night and never heard or saw a thing. I awoke clear minded, and ready to leave for Rockhampton.

Our Australian friends went to the airfields to see us off, and my own particular contingent traveled in three planes over the Coral Sea. There was a certain understandable exhilaration. Going back to Rockhampton seemed like going home. I have at hand a note to my wife, pencil written on the plane, which reveals some of our sense of release. Here is a paragraph:

"We are all as happy as kids. Eddie Grose, whom I have cussed so much, and decorated three times, is chewing gum. Gordon Rogers, with two holes through his legs, is reading a detective story. Also

Bill Bowen. Clovis is beside me, reading a magazine. There are fourteen of us in addition to the crew. Altitude has made the plane cool, but the aluminum seats were never intended for a boudoir. Sergeant Dombrowski, wrapped in a blanket, is asleep on the floor."

I find in the closing sentences of the note evidences of that loneliness which is the daily and unshakable companion of every soldier on foreign duty: "I hope you will sleep better now that the campaign for Papua is over. We fought them on the ground of their own choosing, under conditions which were indescribable. I believe I did my duty, and that is what you would have wanted me to do. I didn't have to ask anyone to do anything I was unwilling to do myself. I have received from the Australians and from my friends many compliments, but to do well in your eyes means a hundred times more than the things the others say."

Back at I Corps headquarters, our homecoming had been anticipated, and, to our surprise, there was a band on hand when our planes bounced to a halt on the grass landing field. Many of our Rockhampton Australian friends were also there, to make it an Allied welcome, and my officers and I proceeded with the greatest of pleasure to the comfortable living quarters we had deserted almost two months before. Because of censorship I was never able to describe my home—where five officers and three sergeants lived with me—to my wife, but some months later Mrs. Franklin D. Roosevelt came to Australia and did the job for me.

In her newspaper column, "My Day," she wrote of Rockhampton (without, of course, naming the town): "By five in the afternoon we reached our destination, a city of some thirty thousand inhabitants. My first impression is of the most beautiful and elaborate gardens I have ever seen. There are flowers everywhere, and opposite the General's home, a gorgeous hedge is in full bloom."

After the savagery and anarchy of the jungle it was agreeable indeed to be back in the beauty and order of Rockhampton. Most of us had forgotten what civilized living was like. Our Headquarters Company was established, through the good will of the citizens, in the City Park and Botanical Gardens. Flowering shrubs bloomed along camp streets, and there were flower beds among the tents.

The evening of our arrival back, General Byers, Colonel Bowen, and I sat out on Mr. Grant's lawn and savored the satisfaction of quiet and peace.

We remembered our first days in Australia. How long ago that now seemed! We remembered the fine group of American newspapermen who had been with us then and who now were scattered. In Brisbane they had asked for a press conference with me. I said that there would be a conference, but this time I wanted to ask the questions—because they knew much more about conditions in Australia than a new arrival like myself. Byron Darnton, a great reporter from the *New York Times,* was the unofficial but acknowledged dean of the American correspondents, and "Barney" arranged that unusual conference.

I went to dinner at the press house which the correspondents shared. After a little preliminary wassail and an excellent meal, coffee was brought in, and tunics were loosed at the neck. Barney acted as an informal chairman, wise, balanced, humorous, as I began the cross-examination of my hosts. Darnton had been a combat infantryman with the 32nd Division in World War I; he had known General Brett and General Barnes and other Americans who had been in Australia before me; he had watched the under-cover feuding between the American and the Australian military, and his perceptiveness had discovered some of the causes.

No military textbook with which I am familiar suggests the questioning of correspondents as a method by which a commander may inform himself. But around the dinner table that night—with everything off the record and no holds barred—I received from a group of intelligent newspapermen a first-rate orientation course. When they finished I had a pretty clear idea about the currents of the waters in which it was my unchosen destiny to swim.

Back in Rockhampton, and there on the pleasant lawn, everything seemed the same. But, remembering, Byers and Bowen and I knew it wasn't. It never is. Already, so early in the war, my friend Barney Darnton was gone. Many gallant newspapermen died subsequently in posts of danger, and many people forget—because the newspapermen were not soldiers—that all of them came to posts of danger voluntarily. Darnton was killed going forward with the 32nd Division in New Guinea.

I have described earlier the failure of our troops who tried to go overland from Wanigela to Pongani; they were mired down. As an improvisation it was decided to attempt a ferry service of small boats to the assembly point in the Buna area. Bruce Fahnestock, American explorer and yachtsman who was familiar with tropical waters, Barney Darnton, and a number of young American soldiers were passengers on one of those defenseless craft. Somewhere, there was a failure of communications. The Air Forces had been advised that all craft seen east of a certain coastal point must be considered enemy vessels. An American plane swooped down, dropped a bomb, and managed what is known technically as a "near-miss." The boat was not hit but shrapnel from the bomb killed both Fahnestock and Darnton.

They were brought sadly ashore by their comrades. Darnton was buried in the small weather-beaten cemetery at Port Moresby. There, among the scrub eucalyptus trees, Australians, British, American Negroes, American white men, and men of other nationalities lay side by side. "That would please Barney," said Robert Sherrod of *Time* magazine, in an interview; Sherrod had been Darnton's roommate in Australia. "Barney had a firm conviction that all men would one day be brothers, or they would be slaves."

In the Southwest Pacific, as in the Solomons, the first half of 1943 was a period of preparation, a lull in battle. An advance up the New Guinea coast had originally been contemplated, but heavy Australian and American casualties, and the attrition of illness, made such an advance impossible. Admiral Bill Halsey's furious sea battle off Guadalcanal (in which both Admirals Dan Callaghan and Norman Scott lost their lives) had made secure that American beachhead. The Japanese had been knocked back on their heels, and they too were concentrating on preparation and gathering strength for the next round of the battle.

Every enlisted man knows that weary Army phrase: "Hurry up and wait." In the Southwest Pacific the Americans hurried up and waited for many months. I had recommended that the 32nd Divi-

sion be given a thorough rest and a long one, but my recommendations were not followed out. Almost immediately, under efficient
Major General Bill Gill, who had come on from the States as their
new commander, they were returned to a routine of the most
arduous kind of training. Official releases minimized the casualties
they had taken. On one occasion, making an address to the GIs of
the 32nd, I made a solemn promise sometime to tell their story to
the American public. In this book I have tried my best to do so.

I have no intention of discussing here such an abstruse subject as
the "psychology of leadership." But it is just common sense that
cheerful leaders soothe the anxieties of men, that calm leaders allay
the hysterias which are both endemic and epidemic in battle, that
optimistic leaders imbue their subordinates with confidence. No
man in one section of a battle can have an accurate picture of the
battle as a whole. It may be that at the very moment of desperation,
comrades in another sector have broken through.

Though it seems incredible to the GI, the leader, in Shakespeare's
words, has "eyes, hands, organs, dimensions, senses, affections." He
has a breaking point too; but because of the responsibility upon him
he cannot admit it. Several months after my return to Australia I
went to visit a friend of mine, Brigadier General George Honnen,
who was a patient at the 42nd General Hospital near Brisbane.
George Honnen said that his young Army doctor had been with me
at Buna and had described me as a "cold, hard man." Honnen
challenged his judgment because Honnen had known me for a good
many years.

Just then the doctor came in. We were introduced. I did not
recognize him and I suspect he did not recognize me. Neither of us
wore jungle suits, neither had muddy pants legs and sweat-stained
shirts, neither of us had the greasy, tired faces which were a commonplace in the jungle. And the doctor, now so neat, had been
working all night with the wounded when I had last seen him, un-
shaven and splattered with blood. This is what we remembered in
common:

It was during December when the fate of Buna lay in the balance.
We were trying to drive through to the sea. I had been at the front

all day. I had seen the litters coming back. I had seen walking wounded being led from the front. I had seen men lying in ditches, weeping with battle shock. I had visited dressing stations. Yet there were advances to be made, and decisions which must not be governed by my own weaknesses or emotions.

It was then that the Army doctor asked me to enter his trailside hospital and to speak to the gravely wounded. I refused. He interpreted my refusal as callousness. Actually it was self-protection. I had seen pain and torture all that troubled day—and I did not know whether determination and a sense of duty would survive another scene of agony.

Eventually I mastered my weakness and went in to his wounded. Back in Brisbane, the doctor and I talked about that difficult time at the front. And I think he finally understood that war is such an unutterably cruel enterprise that generals, being human, must ration their own emotions in order to have reason about them when reason is imperative. They cannot afford to crack.

"You aren't the man I thought you were at all," said the doctor.

Perhaps not. I was the man who, after the last Japanese shot had been fired at Buna, stood at the edge of the Buna Cemetery with the tears running down my face. There is a time for all things. Even a time for tears.

In Australia we waited for reinforcements, we waited for supplies, we waited for ships and planes and landing craft. Some of us in positions of power waited with gnawing impatience, but in a war of two oceans and two hemispheres the nervous systems of commanding generals are expendable.

It was plain that a successful campaign in the Pacific must be based on amphibious landings. Water was the only way back. Americans were ill equipped for the job. The Navy and the Marines had practiced small movements in the Caribbean, there had been an amphibious landing in North Africa in the fall of 1942, but assault landings from the sea in the Pacific were brand-new stuff to a brand-new and hitherto land-bound Army.

The Japanese had already proved themselves masters of amphibious warfare. They had planned the conquest of Asia for a good

many years, and they had equipped themselves for it. They were far
ahead of us and far ahead of the British and—though few people
appear to realize it—far ahead of the Germans too. They invented
and accumulated in great quantity landing craft which vomited
troops directly on tropical shores. When their convoys crept down
the China Sea toward Malaya and the Philippines in the waning
autumn of 1941, they had the tools to do the job.

It is the fashion now, among some people who never fought
against them, to minimize the military abilities of the Japanese. No
veteran of the Pacific does. No fighter pilot who locked horns with
the early Zekes or Zeros does. Nor does anyone who knows about
equipment and supply. If the Germans had possessed the landing
craft the Japanese marshaled in the Pacific, Hitler would never have
abandoned the Channel crossing. Captured records of the German
High Command reveal that Hitler turned his troops away from the
beaches because he believed he did not have sufficient landing craft
to make the invasion of Britain feasible.

The first American landing boat I saw in Australia came off an
assembly line at Cairns in April of 1943—about a year and four
months after the war began. A few weeks earlier I had inspected
some of the just-arrived special troops who were to man these blunt
armor-plated craft. The troops belonged to an outfit new to the
American military roster: the Army Amphibian Engineers. To my
mind, their importance to the winning of the war in the Pacific
and their solid exploits under difficulties have been insufficiently
heralded.

The idea of the Amphibian Engineers was conceived in Washington but proved itself practicable on the brisk beaches of Cape Cod
—some ten thousand miles away from the coral and mangrove and
damp heat of New Guinea's shores. Major General Dan Noce (then
a colonel) was the pioneer who saw the need for Army amphibian
troops. The Navy had pushed hard for the development of landing
craft but, in view of the immense demands made upon it, felt it
could not train sufficient boatmen to meet the challenge of a Channel
crossing in Europe and simultaneous demands in the Pacific. The
Navy welcomed Army help.

Dan Noce was able to convince General McNair and Mark Clark of the need for these specialized troops. With their enthusiastic backing, Noce went to town. He and his staff did an admirable job in recruiting personnel. They tapped the records of two hundred thousand officers and three million enlisted men to search out maritime experience and aptitude. In ten weeks, by canvassing yacht clubs and boating organizations, they produced four hundred officers and commissioned them. Few had military or naval backgrounds, but they did have technical proficiency in the varied specialties which were part of the conception of an amphibian outfit.

Many of them were familiar with all types of propulsion: sail, steam, diesel, gasoline motor, or just plain oars. Some of them knew navigation, astronomy, and geography. Some had master's licenses, and some just wanted to go to sea. Some could lay steel-web on a beach, or man a radio, or handle the firing of 4.5-inch rockets when troops were going ashore. Their training was hardy, and it paid off. It paid off for Lieutenant General Walter Krueger when he came out in the spring of 1943 to command the Sixth Army (of which my I Corps became a part), and it paid off for me later when I became commander of the Eighth Army.

Eventually in the Pacific we had three brigades of these Amphibs. They were known as the 2nd, 3rd, and 4th Engineer Special Brigades. They were not only boatmen who put soldiers ashore, they were shore engineers who knew how to handle cargo on a beach. Their Engineer Base Shop Battalions and Boat Maintenance Battalions (I'm through with such technical subdivisions from now on) could assist in the construction and operations of shipyards, and they could supervise the assembly job of turning out the landing craft. Technical experts back in the States had worked out ways to send knocked-down landing craft overseas by transport ship. Certain of the Amphibs, who had been trained in the home plants, were experts in putting the parts back together. With transport ships landing at almost all the ports in Australia, and shipments subject to the hazards of war, mixups and confusion were inevitable. In consequence, many of these particular Amphibs had really a jigsaw job. Part A and Part B—each an integral part of the same vessel—were

not infrequently landed at harbors nine hundred miles apart. Often
it took weeks of effort to get the parts together for assembly.

The pioneer group of 2nd Brigade, the first Amphibs in Australia,
ran into a particularly tough situation. They expected to find an
assembly plant at Cairns. When they arrived there no plant had even
been started. Under considerable difficulties, by employing their mechanics as carpenters and electricians, they built one. Once the assembly line was ready, they began turning out seven completed
boats each day.

The original headquarters of the 2nd Brigade was ten miles from
Rockhampton, and in the company of the Brigade's commander,
Brigadier General W. F. Heavey, I had plenty of opportunity to
inspect the landing craft and the boatmen at the throttles. These
troops had also brought with them two important innovations in
amphibious warfare—the swimming truck known as the DUKW, and
the 4.5-inch barrage rocket. None of us had seen them before. Yet,
even at that time, American ingenuity was not so far ahead of the
Japanese. During the summer a detachment of Amphibs went to
Milne Bay, which, once a pestilential hole, was now being turned
into an important Army and Navy base. A number of Jap landing
craft, sunk in the original enemy invasion there, were raised, repaired, and put to use.

This gave the troops a chance to compare their craft with the
Japanese models of 1942. Officers of the 2nd Brigade told me there
were many good points about the enemy boats. Their design was
so much better than that of the American blunt-nose, flat-bottomed
boats, the experts said, that the Jap diesel engines needed only a
third as much horsepower as the American engines to make eight
knots. On the other hand, the ramps of the Jap craft were narrow
and unwieldy and restricted the types and sizes of vehicles which
could be carried aboard. But their general excellence was such as
to add one more injunction to the growing gospel that the Japanese
must not be taken lightly.

I had something to say along that line myself when I spoke in
June to four hundred graduates of an officers' candidate school near
Brisbane. These men from the ranks had had the advantages of

learning the principles of warfare from men, both Americans and Australians, who had had firsthand experience in the jungle. I was thrilled when I watched those four hundred "Yank" youngsters take the graduation oath en masse, and when I addressed them I was never more serious in my life. The successful campaign in North Africa had just ended.

"It will be a long time," I said, "before you hear of the surrender of a hundred thousand Japs as you have heard about the surrender of German and Italian troops. The enemy you are going to meet is one you can count on fighting to the last. You have read about soldiers in Allied armies accounting for hundreds of Japs, but I know one case where a lone Japanese routed out of a foxhole was discovered to have killed thirty-two Allied soldiers before he spent his own life. The Japanese is a wily, savage, courageous, and well-trained soldier who will make the job ahead of all of us a difficult one."

The 3rd Engineer Special Brigade, under Brigadier General D. A. D. Ogden, and the 4th Brigade, under Brigadier General Henry Hutchings, came to the Pacific some months later but they—like Bill Heavey's outfit—were tremendously valuable in the long climb up the ladder toward Tokyo. I remember many stories about the Jacks-of-all-trades who made up what was sometimes called the "Army's Navy." One of them concerned a lone LCM which was pushing along a tropical coastline with supplies for an outlying infantry patrol. One of the crew called attention to an unusual small island, a few hundred yards offshore, which was massed with underbrush and low coconut trees.

As a sort of automatic gesture of protection against snipers, the crewman gave the island a burst of machine-gun fire. He was surprised to receive machine-gun fire in return. Now the LCM maneuvered so that both .50-caliber machine guns could be brought to bear on the spot, then for several minutes the American gunners raked the island with fire. The enemy's shooting ceased, and the LCM closed cautiously in. To the astonishment of the Amphibs, the "island" turned out to be a landing craft heavily camouflaged. There were several dead Japanese aboard and a file of documents which our Intelligence Section found to be of considerable importance in the specific campaign then under way.

In June of 1943 the 2nd Brigade had three groups in New Guinea. One group was divided between Port Moresby and Milne Bay, another at Samarai was preparing a new base for the amphibians, and a third at Oro Bay was scheduled to support some of the troops of the American 41st Division in a drive from Buna to the northwest. Offshore at Cairns in Australia (in the waters where Zane Grey, the sportsman and novelist, once did his big-time fishing), a regiment of the 2nd Brigade was having combined training with the 9th Australian Division.

On June 29 a convoy of all available landing boats picked up troops of the 41st Division at Morobe and made a night landing back of the Japanese at Nassau Bay. In the convoy were twenty-nine LCVPs, an LCM, and three captured Jap barges—a very small sea force indeed—but the Amphibs were seeing first action. The thirty-odd-mile trip was made in wind, rain, and heavy seas. Only a few minutes behind schedule, the first wave hit the beach. No Japs were encountered, but a twelve-foot surf was too much for many of the thirty-six-foot boats. Only a few were able to retract before being swamped; twenty-one of the twenty-nine scattered LCVPs were pounded into distorted shapes by the heavy waves. But despite confusion and loss of equipment the troops landed without the loss of a man. The enemy did not attack that night; the roar of boats trying to extricate themselves from the shoals convinced them that tanks were being landed. At daylight the Japanese discovered there were no tanks and that the American force was small, and they counterattacked the following night. Sixty-eight boatmen fought in the line as infantry with the men of the 162nd Regiment. The Japs retired leaving their dead behind them.

One hero of the Nassau Bay engagement was 2nd Lieutenant Charles C. Keele. After the initial landing, medical supplies were urgently needed. Despite the probability of air attack, Keele took off in the small boat he commanded to make the delivery of supplies in broad daylight. Before the trip was half completed, enemy planes appeared and dived with guns blazing. Keele was wounded five times but refused to permit his crew to turn back from their mission. The supplies were delivered. More than ten hours elapsed before the lieutenant could reach a hospital, and he died of his wounds five days later. Keele was posthumously awarded the Distinguished Service Cross.

The Amphibs who had trained with the 9th Australian Division showed their mettle in the later Lae and Finschhafen campaigns. Lae involved, for those days, a large convoy: forty-four LCVPs, ten LCMs, three LCSs, and nine LCTs. The Amphibs took off from Morobe and made an after-dawn landing at a beach seventy-five miles away. During the twelve-day Lae campaign, which was fought in torrents of rain, Heavey's small boat force carried over twelve thousand passengers and ten thousand tons of cargo. Not even a jeep could negotiate the soaked coastal terrain during this period, and practically all supply had to be delivered by the Brigade craft.

One incident is memorable. A few days after the landing a severe storm caught the Aussies in the midst of an attempt to cross the flooded Buso River. One infantry battalion, using rubber boats and swimming, managed to cross to the enemy side and establish a foothold. Many of the soldiers had lost their rifles and no machine guns had been carried across. The Japanese, who held the coast just west of the river's mouth, soon realized that only a small and poorly armed force faced them; the Aussie battalion was cut off and virtually helpless.

Now the Amphibs turned to valiantly. Because of the continuing rain and the lack of visibility, their boats were able to go around the mouth of the river and get in the rear of the enemy. They worked for sixty continuous hours. They transported fifteen hundred Aussie soldiers and a great quantity of arms and supplies. They had absorbed bombing and strafing earlier; now they absorbed machine-gun bullets and fire from mortars. A typical story is that of 1st Lieutenant H. E. McPherson. He made forty trips to the beleaguered Allied troops and, declining relief, spent forty-eight hours on the job. When his steering gear was damaged by enemy fire, he rigged up an emergency tiller and steered his boat from an exposed position in the stern.

My old friend Wootten, by then deservedly a major general, was the field commander at Lae. He said of the American Amphibs: "Not for one hour has my advance on Lae been held up by the failure of the 2nd Engineer Special Brigade to deliver troops, supplies, or ammunition at the time and place needed." Perhaps more important at a period when relations between Americans and Australians were somewhat strained was this paragraph which appeared in an Australian newspaper:

The Lae and Finschhafen campaigns have provided a fine example of the effectiveness of Australian-American cooperation. In addition, the A.I.F. (Australian Imperial Force) has been supplied by its "Navy," a fleet of barges manned by the 2nd Engineer Special Brigade. Cooperation in the air is an impersonal detached matter. In an entirely different category is the active and man-to-man cooperation of the U.S. boys who man the supply barges. These Yanks have fought and some have died alongside Australians, and have done both so gamely as to win the respect and affection of the Diggers.

There is one final epic of the Amphibs. It is concerned with Private Junior N. Van Noy, a nineteen-year-old high-school boy from Brooklyn, who received, posthumously, the Congressional Medal of Honor. At Finschhafen Jap air reaction was more severe than at Lae. The men in the foxholes saw a good many aerial battles overhead as American fighters intercepted Japanese bombers. And occasionally the enemy broke through to blast boat and shore installations—particularly at dawn and twilight. During the day Kenney's planes kept the Japs at a reasonable distance. At night our boatmen frequently cut their motors to hide the sea wake from the sharp eyes of Japanese pilots aloft in the darkness.

Early one morning the Japanese attempted a surprise landing on an Allied supply terminal north of Finschhafen known as Scarlet Beach. They had taken advantage of a black night and a calm sea. They let their ramps down a half-mile off the coast and quietly paddled their boats toward shore. Two Americans manning a .50-caliber machine gun—Junior Van Noy and Stephen Popa—waited silently in the darkness until they were sure that the bullet-deflecting ramps were down. Then they opened up at a range of twenty-five yards.

It was slaughter. Japanese were killed on the beach, in the boats, in the water. Others jumped overboard and closed on the gun with grenades. Van Noy handled the machine gun. His companion, who later was decorated with the Silver Star, served as loader. There were shouted orders for the two men to retire to a bluff a hundred yards back of the beach, where the Aussies and other shore engineers were organizing to repel the attack. If Van Noy heard the orders he disregarded them.

So it was two men against more than a hundred men. When the machine-gun belt ran out, and with the grenades landing around them, Van Noy and Popa managed to load a second belt. Both were wounded by this time. More and more of the enemy fell before their fire, some only six or seven feet away. Prostrate on the ground, Popa managed to grab a rifle and shoot a Japanese who was about to bayonet him. He lost consciousness then, and when he woke up he found his dead adversary still across his chest. A grenade blew off one of Van Noy's legs, and later, when help came, he was found dead, with the machine-gun belt empty and his finger still on the trigger. The two-man crew, almost alone, defeated the enemy landing.

MY WARD MRS. ROOSEVELT

In August of 1943 I was given one of the most hazardous assignments of my career. It is one thing to have fortitude on a battlefield, but quite another to face the booby traps and land mines of international diplomacy. Any military man knows that. Summoned by General MacArthur, I flew from Rockhampton to Brisbane. There the General told me that Mrs. Franklin D. Roosevelt (traveling under the impressive code name "Flight 231, Pacific") would soon visit Australia and that I was to be in command of her.

This meant that I would conduct the negotiations with the Australian government, arrange her itinerary, provide her transportation, and be responsible for her safety. General MacArthur said at once that operations in New Guinea would require his presence at Port Moresby during the period of her visit, and I envied him his plausible escape. I had entertained Mrs. Roosevelt when I was Superintendent at West Point and I liked her. General Pa Watson, the President's military aide, was a lifelong friend of mine. But I viewed my assignment with apprehension. Commanding a corps seemed easier.

My apprehensions were justified. After forming a staff to make the arrangements I spent most of the next week in airplanes. Nelson Johnson, American Minister to Australia, advised me he was having difficulty with the Australian government. It was the viewpoint of

Dr. Herbert V. Evatt, the Foreign Minister, and of Colonel W. R. Hodgson, his personal representative, that Mrs. Roosevelt had been invited to visit Australia officially, that she would be the official guest of the Commonwealth, and that *they* would arrange her itinerary. It all seems like a tempest in a teapot now, but General MacArthur had direct orders from the War Department to assume responsibility for all phases of her visit. This job he passed on to me. I flew three times to Canberra, the capital, attempting to quiet the diplomatic fracas. It was Australian winter, and two of those times my plane iced up; we were blown out to sea, and made emergency landings at Sydney. On the third visit to Canberra I suggested, in order to resolve the disagreement, that Colonel Hodgson and I fly to New Caledonia to meet Mrs. Roosevelt on her arrival there and to let her give the Solomon's decision on the ownership of the baby.

Hodgson agreed, and we set off next day by Navy bomber. Nouméa in New Caledonia was the headquarters of Admiral Halsey. General "Miff" Harmon, Army commander in the South Pacific under Halsey, met us, and a trip I had dreaded became a pleasant one. To my surprise, Robert P. Patterson, then Undersecretary of War, and Lieutenant General William S. Knudsen, the Dauntless Dane who had abandoned General Motors for public service, were both Harmon's guests. I talked late with Judge Patterson and then shared a bedroom with Knudsen.

That same afternoon I met Halsey for the first time (Patterson and Knudsen were to leave in the morning before Mrs. Roosevelt's arrival), and it was the beginning of a firm friendship. Two years later I was able to repay Halsey's New Caledonia hospitality in occupied Japan. Knowing his distaste for the militarists of Nippon, I provided the Admiral with a pleasant day by taking him on a tour of the Yokohama prison where various Japanese war criminals and Filipino collaborators were incarcerated.

But that day in Nouméa there seemed to be some doubt of my welcome. Halsey, I was told, had no idea why Hodgson and I had come there and was considerably irked by our presence. I learned subsequently that the explanatory message I had tried to send from Brisbane had been edited and garbled by Navy communications. Such things happen.

However, when I wryly explained my diplomatic difficulties with a friendly Australian government over Mrs. Roosevelt's Australian tour, Halsey felt his own responsibilities lighten and he laughed until the tears ran down his face. I did not feel so funny, and the next day he seemed bothered too. We were ferried by plane to the airfield where our guest was to land. All of us worried when her converted B-24 circled endlessly, or so it seemed, in the overcast before the pilot—and he was expert—nosed down for a landing.

Mrs. Roosevelt came off the plane in her Red Cross uniform, looking as fresh as a daisy, and Colonel Hodgson and I had an immediate interview. I explained that General MacArthur had received orders from the War Department that her visit to Australia was to be in his charge. Colonel Hodgson explained that the Australian government insisted that, as the President's wife, the American "Queen," she was to be the government's guest. Mrs. Roosevelt listened patiently—and solved the problem.

She recalled an earlier visit to England where she had been the official guest of the King and Queen at Buckingham Palace for several days and then had toured installations under American Army auspices. She said she would like to follow a similar procedure in Australia: to visit the Governor-General and his wife in Canberra and then to place herself under my direction for the rest of her stay. She wanted to see hospitals, troops, Red Cross installations, and the simpler her reception the better she would like it.

We were guests of Admiral Halsey that night at dinner, and next day Colonel Hodgson and I returned to Brisbane. Mrs. Roosevelt was to spend a week in New Zealand before her arrival in Australia, and this gave my staff time to set up her itinerary and to send representatives by air to make arrangements at every place where she would stop. In short, the staff work for the visit of the President's wife was handled like a small military operation.

Because Colonel Hodgson was a fighting man (he had an honorable limp from a battle wound in World War I), I suspected at Nouméa that he had not yet abandoned his case, and in consequence

I asked Mrs. Roosevelt to send me a wire confirming her statement that she placed herself under my direction. This was wise insurance. When the Australian government did renew its persuasions, I was able to forward to Nelson Johnson a copy of Mrs. Roosevelt's telegram, which made her wishes a matter of record. From that time on, I am happy to report, the Australians were as cooperative and hospitable as only my friends the Australians can be.

We met Mrs. Roosevelt at Mascot Field near Sydney on Friday, September 3, and I have never seen such an unrehearsed reception. When Mrs. Roosevelt and her aide, Major George E. Durno (in peacetime a well-known Washington correspondent), stepped off the plane, thousands of people were waiting on the field. They had come just to get a glimpse of her; they knew she was to leave in half an hour for Canberra. Flowers were thrown, and there was an electric welcome that any veteran of crowds could recognize at once as real and spontaneous. A few days later, in Melbourne, General Rupertus of the Marines had to rope off the entrance to a hotel to prevent Mrs. Roosevelt from being mobbed by a friendly multitude.

The first day's program called for a quiet dinner in Canberra with Lord and Lady Gowrie, and then a two-day visit with the Commonwealth's officialdom. Lord Gowrie was the Governor-General, the representative of the British Crown. Early in the summer he had inspected my installations near Rockhampton and been my guest overnight. I found his reminiscences fascinating. A retired four-star general, he had been Lord Kitchener's aide at Khartoum in 1898. This was of particular interest to me; I had studied the Sudanese campaign, but he was the only man I'd ever met who had taken part in it.

Canberra is a small city and new; only since 1927 has it been the Commonwealth's capital. A stone's throw from handsome buildings of state, sheep graze on green and brown hillsides. At Government House the American party was quartered pleasantly and well. I had appointed Admiral Carey Jones as my naval aide and General Byers as my military aide. Admiral Jones and I shared a suite. We were rough customers and a little rusty on the traditional punctilio of the English country house.

When we went to our rooms in the late afternoon we found that our luggage had been unpacked and our clean clothing laid out. Submissively I put on fresh clothing. Jones, a character of a sturdier type, rebelled. He went down to dinner without changing. An English butler is a hard man to lick. The next evening Jones again found his clothes laid out—but, in polite recognition of his eccentricity, they were the soiled garments he had worn the day before.

On Saturday Mrs. Roosevelt and I (her guardian Army angel) set off on the repetitive cycle of formal events. There was a state luncheon, with all of the cabinet ministers present, and speeches by Prime Minister Curtin, Mr. Hughes, and Mrs. Roosevelt. A reception was given by Nelson Johnson at the Canberra Hotel, and then a state dinner at Government House. There I sat next to Mr. Hughes. William Morris Hughes, Prime Minister of Australia during World War I, was a salty and delightful character. He reminded me of my father's friends in a pioneer America. Hughes was a Welshman who had come to Australia at the age of twenty. He had worked on farms, he had driven sheep across New South Wales and Queensland, he had cooked for harvesting gangs, he had been a sailor on coastal vessels, he had taught school, and he had prospected for gold. He had been a power in Australian politics since 1904, and he was an excellent storyteller. I enjoyed every story he told.

Mr. Hughes was seventy-seven years old at the time of the dinner at Government House, and definitely hard of hearing. I was told later, by disapproving aides, that between Mr. Hughes roaring at me and my roaring at Mr. Hughes we deafened most of the guests and kept a formal dinner lively.

Consulting my diary this long after, I find a mollifying quotation: "Had a hell of a good time. To bed late."

Consulting the same diary, I find we took off for Melbourne at nine-fifteen the next morning. Our original instructions were that Mrs. Roosevelt's visit was to be a quiet one; she wanted to see American soldiers and Red Cross workers, and there was to be no fuss about it. My single adventure in diplomacy has made me sympathetic with diplomats. Events supersede instructions. The Australians demanded a chance to see her, and the Lord Mayors of Melbourne, Sydney, and Brisbane were insistent that she appear in their cities for official receptions.

Eventually a compromise was arrived at. Mrs. Roosevelt said she had no official standing and could not attend official receptions. But if a Lord Mayor wanted to assemble his city's ladies in the Town Hall to listen to her, she would be glad to talk to them. This worked out satisfactorily. Tens of thousands of Australians had an opportunity to see her in the big towns and many thousands heard her talk. At each stop a smaller group had a chance to chat informally with the President's wife over a cup of tea.

I shared an airplane with her on three thousand miles of travel, and my legs ached as I walked with her through hospitals and Army camps. In hospitals she stopped at beds to talk with soldiers and wrote down messages to send to families. She sent them too. As she went down a corridor she neglected no one. She called on them all, listened to their complaints, made notes, spoke cheering words. She was indifferent to personal hardship, and always gracious. She could not be kept out of wards where wounds smelled evilly and agony was a commonplace. These were the men, she said, who needed comfort the most.

She asked permission to go to Port Moresby, but, to my surprise, General MacArthur refused. However, one night, traveling by jeep, we came upon a group of soldiers who were on *their* way to embarkation for New Guinea. They were traveling by truck and they seemed crowded in like cattle. Mrs. Roosevelt got out of the jeep and went along to each truck and talked to the disconsolate soldiers. She introduced herself and asked what communications she could send home to their families.

I suppose in these days of peace it will be hard for people to understand how warming it was for a sick or wounded or well soldier in a foreign land to see the wife of the President of the United States at his elbow. It made him, ten thousand miles away from his childhood, confronted with unknown and incalculable future dan-

gers, somehow feel remembered and secure. And perhaps, in some mystic way—and I do not want to sound sentimental—Mrs. Roosevelt served as his own mother's deputy.

I am fully aware that some people back in the States criticized Mrs. Roosevelt for her wartime travels. In Australia we had become inured, if not agreeable, to the visits of Very Important Personages. Some of us referred privately to these high-priority official vagabonds as "feather merchants" and accepted them philosophically as necessary nuisances. But not Mrs. Roosevelt. I had dreaded her coming, but I knew when she departed that she had been the most valuable VIP who had ever come to Australia. Her simplicity and lack of side endeared her to the troops; her graciousness endeared her to the Australians; and her visit stored up a reserve of good will that was like a family bank account. Even by the end of hostilities we had not checked it all out.

A good many million Americans who went overseas probably share my reminiscent wonderment at how quickly the soldier feels himself estranged from his native land. New sights, new scenes, new situations have something to do with it, of course, but there is something more. Letters home are a connecting link, but the letters become more attenuated as time passes. There is so much censorship will not allow you to tell that after a while you no longer try to tell it. Letters between husband and wife, in normal times, usually take on a kind of shorthand; they share so many friends and so many common interests that a letter is written conversation. But not in war. The letters may begin that way, but soon the soldier finds out that he is daily faced with problems that, within the censorship, he cannot explain. He is hungry for news about what is happening back home, but as he himself turns by necessity to the minutiae of his own life overseas he finds his own bulletins from home less informative. Censorship is catching, and distance is catching too. I was more fortunate than most in this because my wife had married a professional soldier and knew the pidgin of military talk.

Nevertheless, after only a year's absence, I found myself writing to her as though America were in another world. In Australia we had read reports of the establishment of rationing in the States. The "rationing" in New Guinea, because of lack of supply, had been such that a soldier often couldn't get a square meal. But in Australia the steak served for a single person (Australia is a cattle and sheep country) was the size of a platter—and, sometimes, almost as difficult to chew. I wrote this to Miss Em:

"Out here there are other things which interest me which you do not tell me. When you go to the Chevy Chase Club, it would be interesting to know what you can get to eat. What does dinner cost? Can you get ordinary cuts of meat? Is there any cream for the coffee? Is there any coffee? Any butter? Are there people who still play golf at the club? If so, how do they get there? Are private cars in general use any more?"

But I wrote her about other things too: the kindness to me of the Rockhampton people, the beautiful bougainvillea border that faced my veranda, the friendship of Bishop and Mrs. Ash of the Church of England and Bishop Hayes of the Catholic Church. Rockhampton was a conservative community and most of the town folk were consistent churchgoers. It was always a pleasure to me to see the large number of American soldiers who attended service, and old friends would have been surprised by the number of times I went to church myself. As a matter of fact, I can personally attest the fact that American soldiers conducted themselves in exemplary fashion in Rockhampton. I have too much regard for the truth to certify that this was always the case in such great leave centers as Brisbane, Sydney, and Melbourne.

I wrote to my wife about the oddities of daily life: the kangaroo that hopped across a flying field and wrecked a plane on its take-off, the giant bats (called flying foxes) which frequently electrocuted themselves because their wing spread was wide enough to touch two electric wires, the incessant clamor of the kookabura bird which is known out there as the laughing jackass. I described the USO troupes now coming our way. Gary Cooper, not previously or subsequently celebrated as a singer, achieved a footnote in history by introducing "Pistol Packin' Mama" to the Pacific. In his party were Andy Arcari, the accordion player, Una Merkel, and Phyllis Brooks. Nice people, all. Then there were Lansing Hatfield, singer, and Edwin McArthur,

pianist and conductor, then with the Metropolitan Opera Company. And Joe E. Brown who stayed with us in the Pacific for a long time; there was no obscure island too far forward for Joe E. Brown, and no trip by plane, jeep, or truck that he would not take. He loved the GIs and the GIs loved him. Behind his wide-mouthed merriment was a deep sadness; one of his sons had already been killed in the war. In public—and the GI public was a tough one—I only saw him non-plused once. That was when the city fathers of Rockhampton, ordinarily solemn men, presented him with his own kangaroo.

I also sent home frequent reports on our housekeeping in Australia, and snapshot sketches of various members of my staff. Miss Em, of course, knew Byers, Grose, Bowen, Dick McCreight, George De Graaf, and a good many others. But I introduced her by mail to the sergeants on my staff. Clovis Byers had chosen some of them at the time the 77th Division was organized back in the States. One of them was Clyde Shuck. Shuck, a graduate of Temple University, had been a private secretary to the president of the Campbell Soup Company. Byers calculated that if he were expert enough to be secretary to the president of a large corporation he might be useful to me. And he was. After Buna, Shuck was commissioned at my request and became one of my aides.

I have never been very expert at housekeeping and, during the first strenuous days at Buna, was quite unconscious of the fact that I was not being well looked after. It was Byers who brought forward taciturn Sergeant Dombrowski. Dombrowski, late of Fitchburg, Massachusetts, fed me my breakfast every morning, washed my clothes every night in the creek, and, when I took my daily swim, laid out newspapers at water's edge for me to step on. This ceremony had its bizarre aspects, but actually it was a sensible precaution. Wet soil in the tropics is luxuriant with Ancylostoma. Hookworm, prevalent among all New Guinea natives, enters their bodies through their bare feet. From that time on, Dombrowski was with me through every campaign and always a faithful friend. He continued to be my orderly until I retired from the Army.

Then there was Sergeant Matéo Ventura, a Filipino from Luzon. Before the war Ventura had worked as a chauffeur for Brock Pem-

berton, the eminent theatrical producer, and he had a lively sense of
drama himself. This sometimes proved embarrassing to me. Here is a
quotation from a letter to Miss Em:

"Last night when I came out of the movies Ventura (as usual) had
all the interior lights of the car turned on. This was so that the people on the sidewalks—he had managed to collect quite a crowd—
could all see the show. How he loves his job! If the streets aren't
crowded, he finds a crowded street to drive down instead of keeping
straight ahead for home. This is true at all times. He would like to
have a siren on the car or, better still, to tow a calliope behind us."

Ventura was a man of many talents to which he would not own up.
He pretended to be only a chauffeur. He was one of the finest of
cooks, and as we went along toward Tokyo I gradually found him
out. He could take ordinary canned rations and, with certain imag-
inative touches of his own, create delightful meals. Other Army
cooks, trained at the Quartermaster Corps citadel at Fort Lee, could
have done the same thing. Too many of them didn't.

Later, in the Philippines, I gave Ventura a leave of absence so he
could visit his mother on Luzon. Ventura's return to the old home
village was a production that Pemberton himself might have envied;
the party went on for several days. Ventura, whatever his vagaries,
was a sound and brave soldier. Some months ago I went to New
York to make a speech. As I came out of the auditorium on that cold
evening, I was accosted by a short man in a smart beaver-collared
chauffeur's uniform.

"Where can I drive you, sir?"

It was Ventura.

One of the most dangerous flights of the hundreds of flights I made
in the Pacific occurred during the Rockhampton period. And on a
completely ridiculous mission. One day, in the midst of training activities, all the generals in the Rockhampton area were abruptly ordered to Brisbane. A rather tired Australian Airways plane came for
us, and we adjusted ourselves as comfortably as possible on the
wooden benches. The pilot made no mention of the fact that we
would hit bad weather on the way to Brisbane.

Holding on to our hats and our diaphragms, we passed through nine successive storms, and rose on occasion to tremendous altitudes to fly over other storms. I have never seen so much scrambled weather in a three-hundred-mile journey. At last we reached our destination. All of us decided it must be a grave emergency which would demand such a hazardous trip.

Then we found out why we had been ordered to Brisbane. A famous (at least *he* said he was famous) photographer had arrived in Australia with instructions from the War Department to immortalize on film the visages of senior American officers. In other words, we were there to have our pictures taken! And that procedure occupied five days of the time of a lot of generals. At the end I asked the painstaking artist if I could have a copy of my picture to send to my wife.

"No," he said. "Your photograph will be put in a lead-impregnated envelope, and that in turn will be put in another lead-impregnated envelope and placed in the Roosevelt Library at Hyde Park, and in a thousand years it will be opened so the people of that time will know what our officers looked like."

I said I didn't really care what I would look like in a thousand years and doubted that it was worth five days of my time. Later I learned that the little genius of the lens flew directly over Rockhampton on his way to New Guinea and could have landed and taken his pictures then.

FIGHT FOR THE HUON PENINSULA

During this period of build-up in Australia, Allied Air continued active in bombing enemy strongholds and harassing shipping. American submarines, based near Perth, were busy on heroic exploits of their own. Attrition in the air was rapidly decreasing the number of our own planes available for duty, and no replacements were arriving. At a time when strength was already dangerously low in our particular theater, General Kenney's pilots and bombardiers distinguished themselves in what is now called the Battle of the Bismarck Sea.

A convoy of enemy transports, cruisers, and destroyers, presumably headed for Lae with reinforcements, was sighted off the north coast of New Guinea by reconnaissance pilots. A heavy storm made an immediate bomber attack impossible, but Allied planes kept the convoy under surveillance for several days. As the vessels turned south in the Vitiaz Strait the weather began to lift and the first attack was made. For three days Allied bombers and strafers punished the convoy. It was completely destroyed and defending Japanese air cover destroyed or dispersed. Sixteen war vessels and merchant ships were sunk, and many Jap planes were shot down. We lost six planes; thirteen men were killed and twelve wounded. It is impossible to say how many Japanese soldiers aboard the transports were lost, but the numbers probably ran to thousands.

89

Allied Air was to remember one incident of that battle for a long time. A B-17 formation was intercepted by thirty fighters. One B-17 lost a wing and plunged into the ocean, but seven of the nine-man crew managed to bail out. As the seven men hung in the air in their parachutes, ten Jap fighters dived down and machine-gunned them to death.

At some risk to the tempo of a personal narrative, I must pause here to discuss briefly the problem that faced the Allies in the South and Southwest Pacific at midsummer. Modest shipments of planes were at last coming in, and, invigorated, Allied Air was doing a stalwart job in both Admiral Halsey's and General MacArthur's areas. The Joint Chiefs of Staff had set up a plan known as "Elkton," which called for collaboration of the two commanders in a campaign to isolate or neutralize the great base at Rabaul.

Rabaul, located at the northeast end of the large island of New Britain, was the beating heart of the whole body of Japanese positions in that part of the Pacific. From it, in all directions, ran the arteries of supply and reinforcement to the other islands. The Japanese crushed the small Australian garrison at Rabaul only seven weeks after Pearl Harbor, and poured in troops and matériel. The magnificent harbor is surrounded by mountains. These were fortified. Five airfields were built. In a year's time Rabaul had become a bastion second in strength only to Truk, seven hundred miles northward.

Our fighter planes were unable to provide adequate cover for bombers headed for Rabaul. The distance from the Russell Islands, where Halsey's nearest airfields were located, and from Port Moresby and Oro Bay in New Guinea, prohibited round trips for fighters because of their limited gasoline capacity. One of the objectives of the Elkton plan was to obtain airfields closer to Rabaul. Halsey's ships and planes, and the Army troops and Marines under his leadership, were scheduled to fight their way up the Solomons to Bougainville, while New Guinea forces under MacArthur pushed north toward the Vitiaz Strait, which commands the southwestern end of New Britain.

The first assignments of the newly organized American Sixth Army were full-scale landings on Woodlark and Kiriwina Islands, which lay in the Solomon Sea about halfway between New Guinea and the

Solomons. They are three hundred miles from Rabaul and two hundred miles from Bougainville. Fighters based there could hit Rabaul and return with ease. My own I Corps lent Colonel C. C. W. Allen, who had been with us at Buna, to the Sixth Army staff for this expedition; Allen was my assistant supply officer. The 158th RCT (Regimental Combat Team) landed at Kiriwina, and the 112th Cavalry . RCT landed at Woodlark. There were no Japanese on these islands, but our troops were designedly kept in ignorance of this fact. The landings were made under full combat conditions, and, as a result, the troops gained experience that later proved valuable. The building of airfields immediately began.

Halsey's initial move was against New Georgia. After a series of preliminary landings the main thrust was made at Munda with the 43rd Division; American troops went more than a mile inland the first day and then ran up against the enemy's main defense line. Now Halsey and Miff Harmon had their troubles ashore. Advance toward the objective, the Munda Airfield, began to be measured in yards rather than in miles; another American outfit was having its first experience in jungle fighting, and day after day passed in deadlock. There were shifts in shore commands. After a fortnight Major General Oscar W. Griswold, commander of XIV Corps, became boss of the Ground Forces, and the advance soon gathered momentum. "Griz" Griswold, an old friend and a calm and able leader, will appear again in these pages.

The fighting on New Georgia lasted just short of a month. Halsey learned, as I had learned, that when the Japanese chose to stand and fight in the jungle, costs and casualties could be high. He has written: "Our original plan allotted fifteen thousand men to wipe out the nine thousand Japs on New Georgia; by the time the island was secured, we had sent in more than fifty thousand. When I look back on 'Elkton,' the smoke of charred reputations still makes me cough." Elements of the 43rd, 37th, and 25th American Divisions eventually were thrown into the struggle.

In New Guinea the fighting into the autumn was largely an Aussie show. Our Air made it possible, our Amphibs did much of the fetch-and-carry, elements of our 162nd Infantry Regiment handled them-

selves gallantly, but the main responsibility was borne by the 7th
and 9th Australian Divisions. Because of the term "Allied Forces,"
which the censors then employed, many Americans still believe
erroneously that our own troops carried the burden of that back-
busting advance against the Salamaua-Lae-Finschhafen sector. The
Aussie advance took off from the inland village of Wau, which is
about one hundred and fifty miles northwest of Port Moresby.
Around Wau, which is thirty-five hundred feet high, lies one of the
richest alluvial gold regions in the world. More important militarily
to the Australians was the small, steeply sloping Wau airfield. An
interesting and little known chapter of history was written there.

Sometimes the enemy makes our plans for us. After the fall of
Buna, Japanese assault troops landed at Lae and struck down toward
Wau. This action on the part of the Japanese is still a little hard to
fathom. Perhaps they were seeking an intermediate base for a new
approach to Port Moresby. If so, they were surprisingly indifferent
to geography; Wau nestles in a mountain cup, and a march from the
coast necessitated a climb of the Kuper Range, a very strenuous assignment indeed.

Nevertheless, the march over the mountains was made. A strong
force of Japanese took off from sea level and, without meeting resistance, reached Mubo, not too far away, as the crow flies, from Wau.
There were some Allied commanders who wanted to evacuate by
air the two or three companies which then garrisoned the village.
This course was not followed. The troops remained. The Australians
believed the Japanese would approach from Mubo only along well-
defined trails. There were two—the Black Cat (for the name of a
gold mine) and the Crystal Creek. Both ran through the gloom of
rain-forest and twisted across razor-back ridges.

The Japanese moved token forces along both the Black Cat and
the Crystal Creek Trails with the aim of deceiving the Australians.
Then they chose for their main force—an infantry regiment with artillery and engineers—a trail surveyed by a German explorer before
World War I and forgotten by New Guinea planters and prospectors.
The Australians, who had reconnoitered the area with considerable
thoroughness, had overlooked this trail. The Japs hoped for a com-

plete surprise. The task of hacking a way through an old and over-grown track, as the Americans who went over the Kapa Kapa Trail had discovered, is long and difficult. The strain on Japanese food sup-ply lines was almost at a breaking point when they reached the Wau valley.

At this point the Japanese advance was discovered. One mile north of Wandumi, a village very near Wau, the enemy came upon a com-pany commanded by Captain W. Sherlock. An immediate fight began. Outnumbered ten to one, the Australians were forced down a long, naturally terraced mountain spur. In a wilderness of kunai grass Sherlock's company found a defensible position on one of the ter-races. Reduced to forty men, the company held out for two days at a key point on the Wandumi track. Captain Sherlock was killed, but the company's resistance bought time.

It was time that was needed. Inclement weather had almost given the enemy the winning trick. Back at Port Moresby the Australian re-inforcements were stranded. Half of the 17th Australian Brigade waited at the Moresby airfields for several days, hoping that the clouds would lift and that the tropical rain would cease. Here was the rescue squad—and unable to travel because planes could not get over the Owen Stanleys. The impossibly slender forces at Wau were disposed as best they could be when the Japanese began a general attack. At that moment great cloud banks rolled back from the steep mountain ranges, a hot sun raised steam on the Wau Airstrip. One by one, the transport planes from Moresby began rolling in under fire. As fast as the planes landed the green-clad airborne Australians scampered to defensive positions. They got into action fast. Some of them went back on the same transports as casualties. In four days at Wau, Allied Air made two hundred and forty-four separate landings with reinforcements, ammunition, and supplies. And this on a field that was only eleven hundred yards long. The enemy was repulsed.

The slow pursuit of the Japanese back toward the strong points from which they had come now commenced. Not until summer, how-ever, could the Allies mount and support an offensive. This was the plan. The 17th Brigade based on Wau and reinforced by the 15th Brigade was committed to effect a junction with the 162nd Infantry

of the American 41st Division coming from Nassau Bay. The 9th Australian Division was to be landed near Lae by Admiral Dan Barbey's fleet, and the 7th Australian Division was to be brought in by air. The plan was to surround and demolish the formidable Japanese positions at Lae and Salamaua; they had been built up steadily after our victory at Buna, and undoubtedly the enemy's idea was to make the Vitiaz Strait secure.

The miserable and inconclusive overland fighting proceeded during July and August, and it was about one part fighting to three parts sheer misery of physical environment. It was climbing up one hill and down another, and then, when breath was short, fording streams with weapons held aloft or wading through swamps. It was sweat and then chill; it was a weariness of body and spirit; and once again tropical illness was a greater foe than enemy bullets. Troops in the jungle could not know that the steady, day-by-day missions of General Ennis Whitehead's airmen in New Guinea had achieved parity in the skies over the jungle. Or that later, after a culminating two-day heavy raid on Wewak in mid-August (two hundred Jap planes were destroyed), the Allies at last were the stronger in the air.

The 9th Division and the 7th Division were re-equipped and brought to full strength. The climax of the campaign for the section of New Guinea known as the Huon peninsula was at hand. General Whitehead and the Australians and the American 871st Airborne Engineers came up with a brilliant coup. Without discovery they constructed two airfields—at Marilinan and Tsili Tsili—in the heart of enemy territory. The fields were about forty miles from Wau. Tsili Tsili became headquarters for an important fighter group, which was slated to protect the airborne expedition. Back at Moresby the American 503rd Parachute Regiment had been assembled, and Barbey's amphibious group was already at sea.

On September 4 Wootten's 9th Division was put ashore in the Lae area. On September 5 the 503rd Parachute made a classic landing twenty miles behind the enemy lines in the beautiful grassy valley of the Markham River. I was to command these fine troops during the Philippines campaign and to plan and stage their drop on Corregidor. The 503rd had been stationed at Gordonvale, Australia, for many months, and General Byers had inspected them there. Byers went aloft and watched a jump. He reported back to me that the parachutists were the best-conditioned troops he had ever seen.

Although the 509th Parachute made three small drops in Africa in November 1942, and the 82nd Airborne Division dropped in Sicily, some military historians have described the drop of the 503rd Parachute as the first effective use of paratroopers in their proper strategic role. It was far and away the greatest show of air power we had seen in the Pacific. From ninety-odd transports flying twelve abreast the paratroopers jumped. The moment they touched ground they set about the task of making secure the airfield they had seized. One footnote may illustrate the ingenuity and courage of some of these men. A small detachment of Australian artillerymen had needled and annoyed the expeditionary command until they were allowed to accompany the 503rd. The artillerymen desired to set down in the Needham valley two 25-pounders, heavy weapons which are certainly no part of regular parachutist issue. The artillerymen-jumpers, volunteers, few of whom had ever hit the silk before, broke down the guns, and each man carried one section in his pack. Once on the ground, the group assembled and put the 25-pounders back together with skill and speed. I hardly need say that the 25-pounders were a welcome addition to the military furnishings of the Needham valley airfield.

The job of the paratroopers was to guard and hold the field for the airborne arrival of General Vasey's 7th Division. They set up roadblocks on all trails and made a protected perimeter around the airfield itself. There was no reaction from the Japanese, but no one felt secure. Darkness came. And daylight.

And then, when the sun was high, the transports roared over and landed. The troops came out of the DC-3s like chickens out of a hatchery and went immediately to their assigned positions. Within thirty minutes columns of the 7th Division were already on their way to join the Allies moving in to encircle Lae.

On September 11 Salamaua was captured. These troops were involved: the 15th and 17th Australian Brigades, and the American 162nd Infantry Regiment. On September 16 Lae was captured by the 25th Australian Brigade, 7th Division. On September 22 the

landing at Finschhafen was made by the 9th Division under Woot-ten. On October 2 Finschhafen was taken. A month later the Huon peninsula belonged to the Allies.

A few of the Japanese units fought it out to the death, but a good many of them retreated and tried to escape over the Finisterre Mountains to other enemy strongholds up the New Guinea coast. A few, gaunt and weak, reached Madang. But many died of starvation along the jungle trails.

Meantime, progress had been made in Halsey's theater. Vella La-vella was taken. Americans began the job; New Zealanders (the 3rd Division), under Major General H. E. Barrowclough, finished it. The next objective was violin-shaped Bougainville, largest island of the Solomons. The Japanese had built a seaplane base and five airfields there; a sixth was under construction. Bougainville was the last major obstacle—on the Solomons side—before Rabaul. Two small prelimi-nary landings were made. The 8th New Zealand Brigade went ashore in the lightly held Treasury Islands, and the 2nd Marine Parachute Battalion landed on Choiseul Island. Further to confuse the enemy, there were naval barrages and aerial assaults at several other places.

The main landing was made at Empress Augusta Bay in western Bougainville by the 3rd Marine Division, under Lieutenant Gen-eral A. A. Vandegrift, and the Army's 37th Division. The latter was an Ohio National Guard outfit commanded by an old friend of mine, Major General Robert S. Beightler. Later the Americal Division came into Bougainville from Guadalcanal, and control of the beach-head went over to General Griswold's XIV Corps.

It was a long ladder from Australia to Japan, but we had begun slowly to climb the rungs in 1943. By autumn there were five American combat divisions in Australia and a number of others in the Halsey theater. In Australia the 32nd Division, under I Corps command, and the 1st Cavalry Division were stationed outside Brisbane. The 1st Marine Division was at Melbourne. The 24th Division and the 41st were at Rockhampton with me. Elements of the 41st which had been in at the kill at Salamaua returned for rest, recuperation, and re-organization and joined their comrades at the old camp.

From the outset, it should be understood, Allied strategy had one

aim: to advance farther and farther our airfields for fighter planes
and to put those planes to work. Once the ground troops got a toehold, the bulldozers arrived and started scooping up the landscape
behind them. Often our fighter planes were landing and taking off
from brand-new strips while the doughboys were still wrestling it
out with the Japs in the jungle just a mile or two away. This was all
dirty fighting. As the year waned, however, we felt our muscles flex-
ing. We were not strong but we were stronger. We had more planes,
we had more ships, we had more troops. We were preparing to break
our lease in Poorhouse Row.

But to go forward we must control the Vitiaz Strait, the narrow
and dangerous stretch of water between New Guinea and the island
of New Britain. Two amphibious landings on New Britain just before
year's end made this possible. Brigadier General Julian Cunningham
and his 112th Cavalry RCT captured Arawe, and later were reinforced by the 158th Infantry. Eleven days later General Rupertus
and his fine 1st Marine Division went ashore at Cape Gloucester.
After rugged fighting they captured the vital airstrip which commanded the channel passage.

And just after the first of the year a regimental combat team of the
32nd Division, commanded by General Clarence Martin, occupied
Saidor, about halfway up the New Guinea coast between Finschhafen and the great Japanese base at Madang. A close personal friend
of mine died heroically at Saidor. Young Gordon Clarkson, then just
out of West Point, had served under me as a lieutenant in the 30th
Infantry. Bright, handsome, diligent, he later became a member of
I Corps staff. At Buna, by Clarence Martin's request, I sent him forward to command a battalion, and he performed brilliantly.

At Saidor, Lieutenant Colonel Clarkson was at the head of a chain
formation of American soldiers crossing a chest-deep tropical river.
A Japanese bullet killed him instantly. War is a heartbreaking pro-
fession. So often the brave go first.

One of the men I saw frequently on visits to General MacArthur's
headquarters at Brisbane during the summer and autumn was Brigadier General MacNider of the 32nd. Jack MacNider had been

wounded in the Buna fighting (before my arrival there) and was on temporary duty with the General Staff while undergoing medical treatment. A Jap grenade had blown up in MacNider's face, and there was a question, for some time, as to whether or not he would lose his sight. MacNider was a banker from Mason City, Iowa, a veteran of World War I, a former Assistant Secretary of War, and a onetime national commander of the American Legion. He was an engaging companion and a brave soldier. The doctors saved his eyes, and he took part in further combat operations in subsequent campaigns.

It is only human for soldiers and their commanders to become a little restive during a long period of troop training. We were perfecting our amphibious techniques, we were making experiments with atabrine, which was to reduce importantly the toll of malaria among our GIs, we were turning raw youngsters into tough and tenacious jungle warriors. But on the other side of the world the long bitter struggle for Italy was under way, and in England the Allies were already preparing for the great Normandy thrust.

I got back to the United States briefly in the fall, flying the ocean both ways. Mrs. Eichelberger met me in San Francisco and we spent two weeks together in California. But it was not vacations which interested me. I wanted to be useful. I knew that three times in particular that year the War Department had requested the Southwest Pacific headquarters to release me from my corps command in order that I might be given the greater responsibility of leadership of an army in the European theater of war. General MacArthur disapproved all three requests.

The late autumn passed quickly. There were many conferences with the Allied commander and with General Krueger concerning the disposition to be made of I Corps troops during the campaign we all realized was almost at hand. I flew to Sixth Army's new advanced headquarters at Milne Bay and marveled at the changes made in Papua by the engineer troops and their bulldozers. They had carved roads out of the jungle; they had dried up the swamps which had made Milne Bay a malarial pesthole. The Navy had carved its own new roads through the shallows of the harbor at Milne

Bay so that it could shelter many ships. Then I flew in a C-47 to Goodenough Island at the top of the Coral Sea, to which I Corps headquarters and the 24th Division would be moved in the fairly immediate future.

After a three-hour stay on Goodenough we took off again for the return trip to Milne Bay. Just at the take-off the clouds lifted and I could look back on the eight-thousand-foot green mountain range on the island. At the moment—and I'm not quite sure I would change my judgment now—Goodenough seemed to me the most beautiful place I had ever seen.

By the first of the year there was movement of troops everywhere in the Southwest Pacific theater. Trains were full of American troops going north in Australia, planes and vessels left American bases each day for unknown destinations. The Australian civilian population did not know *what* was up, but they certainly knew great events were in the air. The 1st Marine Division was long gone from its post-Guadalcanal home in Melbourne, the 32nd Division was on its way, the 1st Cavalry Division had pulled stakes, and—military censorship or not—it was evident that what one Australian newspaperman amiably called the "American occupation" was almost at an end. An appreciable number of our lads had been there long enough to achieve romantic or marital attachments, and there were many tears as the exodus began.

General MacArthur's birthday fell on January 26, and he spent the day with me at Rockhampton. He flew in from Brisbane with two of his aides, Colonel Sidney C. Huff and Colonel Larry Lehrbas, a former newspaperman. Rockhampton, as I am sure I have said before, was a perfect training area. It had beaches, hills—and jungle. I was amused to see in the American newspapers later a photograph of General MacArthur and me in a jeep at Rockhampton and to read the caption below the photograph: "General MacArthur and General Eichelberger at the New Guinea Front."

The dead giveaway was the unmistakable nose of a Packard motorcar in one corner of the picture. There weren't any Packards in the New Guinea jungle in early 1944.

UP THE LADDER TO HOLLANDIA

It was January of 1944 when I learned I was to be the task force commander of the biggest Pacific Army operation up until that time. (It was the first one of corps proportions since Sanananda.) Looking over my diaries, reading the letters I wrote to my wife, I find that I was a rather glum fellow during I Corps' period of recuperation and training. I had always thought I was a man with a green thumb for comfortable living. My house at Rockhampton was pleasant, the mangoes in the yard were tasty, my Australian friends were hospitable, and, with both the Catholic and Anglican bishops in my corner for a polite reception in the Great Beyond, even my future seemed secure.

I guess I just ask too much. At Buna I would have traded my best medal for a day of this kindly living. When I had it, I wanted something else. But after I moved my headquarters to mountainous Goodenough Island (my letters bear witness), I was brisk and optimistic and whole again. Things were about to happen.

There were several strategic choices in the Pacific at this juncture. The Japanese were located in force at three places: Rabaul on New Britain, and—up the New Guinea coast—at Wewak and Hansa Bay. The capture of Rabaul had been our original objective. But now were drawn. I have always been glad that my task force job was not to take Rabaul. Many months later, at the end of the war, and then only by the Emperor's command, some hundred and twenty-five thousand veteran Jap troops surrendered there. Imagine putting in two or three divisions to capture Rabaul!

It was decided that my next job would be an attack on Hansa Bay, and preparations went forward on this basis until early March. The Japanese saw this as a logical move and they were working feverishly to meet us. Hansa Bay is a concave harbor with high headlands, where, no doubt, the enemy would have given us a hearty reception.

Still another and much more ambitious project was buzzing in the minds of American strategists. Major General Steve Chamberlin at GHQ was one of them. It had taken us a year to advance 240 miles north from Buna—and some 2240 miles stretched ahead to Manila. The chief hope for increasing the tempo of the advance was to lengthen our jumps rather than to increase their number. Hitherto the short effective range of land-based fighter planes had been a limiting factor. But if Navy carriers and their fighter planes could be made available to support and cover landings that limitation would cease to exist.

Thus it was that General MacArthur proposed to the Joint Chiefs of Staff that the next jump be made to Hollandia, hundreds of miles up the coast into Dutch New Guinea. He estimated he could advance his time schedule at least six months by this one operation alone.

There were other cogent arguments for this leap into the unknown. It would by-pass and isolate the reinforced Jap strongholds at Madang, Hansa Bay, and Wewak. It would cut across their supply lines, since Hollandia was a depot from which a great enemy army lower down the coast was fed and munitioned. It would place all northeastern New Guinea under Allied domination and provide us with excellent naval and air bases for future operations.

The Hollandia operation was approved. A considerable section of the Pacific Fleet was lent to us for a limited period. March and April were intensely busy months; the magnitude of the plan (compared to our earlier activities) called for the most detailed logistical work and for complete cooperation between Ground, Air, and Naval Forces. This meant many practice sessions.

It was obvious that surprise would be our strongest ally. We knew from a study of maps that the Hollandia terrain was difficult; if the enemy suspected our intentions and reinforced there, assault landings would be bloody indeed. Consequently, determined efforts were made to preserve secrecy. The rumor that we were to attack Hansa Bay was encouraged, by calculated leaks, to perpetuate itself. Only the higher-echelon planners knew the strike would be at Hollandia.

My task force (code name, "Reckless") was built around I Corps. It consisted of the 24th Infantry Division and the 41st Infantry Division less one regimental combat team, reinforced by tanks, artillery, and many other units. Total strength of the original Hollandia force was thirty-seven thousand five hundred combat troops and eighteen thousand service troops. This involved specialists of all sorts, from experts in tropical medicine to hydrographic engineers. As it turned out, specialists in operating a bulldozer were the most valuable of all.

Our first objective was the capture of the three important airstrips just above Lake Sentani. To accomplish this, my task force must manage a pincer movement. Elements of the 41st would land on Humboldt Bay near Hollandia town and press inland. The 24th Division was to land at Tanahmerah Bay some thirty miles up the coast and seek a trail back through the seven-thousand-feet-high Cyclops Mountains in order that Americans might converge on the airdromes from two sides.

The staging of the Hollandia invasion was an immensely complicated job which proved that both the American Army and Navy had come of age. When the sailing date came, Reckless Task Force was the largest armada ever assembled up to that time in the Pacific, and it seemed to us veterans of the lean days that we were traveling in oriental splendor. Witness this contrast: there had been thirty landing craft for the assault on Nassau Bay ten months earlier. The naval escort then had consisted of two tiny PT boats. The skippers were fearless, but, armament-wise, the PT boats were beebee guns in a shotgun war.

Now we had transports, freighters, and many LSTs, LCIs, and other amphibious vessels. Also we had two hundred and eighty small

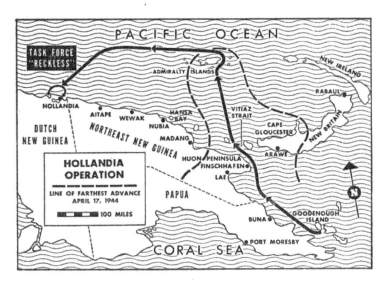

PACIFIC OCEAN

TASK FORCE "RECKLESS"

ADMIRALTY ISLANDS

NEW IRELAND

RABAUL

HOLLANDIA

AITAPE WEWAK

HANSA BAY

NUBIA

VITIAZ STRAIT

CAPE GLOUCESTER

NEW BRITAIN

DUTCH NEW GUINEA

NORTHEAST NEW GUINEA

MADANG

HUON PENINSULA

ARAWE

HOLLANDIA OPERATION

LINE OF FARTHEST ADVANCE
APRIL 17, 1944

100 MILES

FINSCHHAFEN

LAE

PAPUA

GOODENOUGH ISLAND

BUNA

PORT MORESBY

CORAL SEA

N

landing craft, including rocket and flak boats, and fifty magic-making "buffaloes" and "alligators" for negotiating coral beaches. These odd craft swam at sea like boats, and in shallow water walked ashore on tank treads. Our escort consisted of battleships, cruisers, destroyers, sub-chasers, and tugs. Most important of all, there were Navy heavy escort carriers with their deck-based fighters and bombers ready to protect the convoy as it moved beyond the range of our own land-based planes.

In March the 41st Division had moved north by sea from Gladstone harbor, near Rockhampton, to the raw new base at Finschhafen, where Sixth Army headquarters was now located. The 41st staged from Finschhafen. Our service troops for the expedition staged from such widely separated places as Milne Bay, Cape Gloucester, Lae, and Australia itself.

I sailed from Goodenough Island—Hollandia was about eight hundred and fifty miles away—on the destroyer *Swanson*. This was the command ship of Admiral Barbey, who was known to some of my

antic subordinates as "Uncle Dan, the Amphibious Man." General
Frederick A. Irving, commander of the 24th Division, and General
Byers shared passage with me. We embarked on April 17, and we
knew our cooped-in troops were to have five days at sea before the
assault. I wrote about the Navy to my wife: "Our sister service does
a fine job and a friendly one—no inefficiency here."

Despite the unchartable problems ahead, it was difficult for me to
choke down an exultant feeling when I went on deck and looked
across calm waters; grim and gray, the convoy extended in both
directions as far as my eyes could see. A fresh wet breeze swept
through my short brush of gray hair (I had had it scythed down so
it was only a half-inch high), and a shiver ran down my spine. This
was what I had waited for. At last we were going places!

Unchallenged, our great convoy moved through Vitiaz Strait. Hollandia lay to the west, but our course carried us straight to the north.
This was part of the plan of deception. Enemy observation planes
could not know where we were going. Hansa Bay, Wewak, the Admiralty Islands, Rabaul itself—all these were possible objectives.
Admiral Barbey led us a devious course. A deliberate three-hundred-
mile detour took us to the Admiralties. And then—on D-day minus
two—we headed west toward Hollandia.

I had plenty of time to examine my position as commander. I had
the utmost confidence in the combat divisions assigned to me. The
41st was battle-experienced. The 24th had been on duty at Pearl
Harbor at the time of the Japanese attack of December 7, 1941, and,
after two years of waiting and training, still cherished vigorous ideas
about paying back violence with violence.

General Horace Fuller (commander of the 41st) and I were, as I
have mentioned before, West Point classmates and had been friends
for years. General Irving, a younger man, had been commandant of
cadets when I was Superintendent at West Point. He was unassum-
ing, efficient, quiet, almost austere. Fuller, Irving, and I had worked
closely together at Rockhampton.

But, frankly, I was concerned by the ambitious scope of my orders
and the brief amount of time allowed me to carry them out. For
leisurely months we had planned and practiced. Yet now my orders

demanded that an entire primitive area be won and re-created into a base which would accommodate a hundred and forty thousand troops —and "at the double." By May 15 Hollandia must be able to stage the next advance toward the Philippines, and by May 27 another. In short, my forces were expected to establish beachheads, defeat the enemy, advance inland twenty miles on trails that were poor or non-existent, capture and construct airfields—all in about three weeks.

Our information about Hollandia, gathered principally by intercepts of Japanese communications, indicated that we would meet two regiments of infantry there and one regiment of marines. Estimates of enemy strength turned out to be exaggerated. But I didn't know that then. There was a great deal I didn't know. A fortnight earlier the Allied Intelligence Service had landed secretly a party of eleven scouts. They went ashore from submarines in rubber boats, and they were equipped with a short-wave radio. Nothing was heard from them. A day or so after the landings I found out why. I shall report in more detail on this small but hair-raising episode of war in a later chapter.

On D-day, April 22, I was awakened at three A.M. I dressed, according to my diary, "slowly and reluctantly." All I could do had been done. Other men were to lead the troops ashore; my job was to wait. Did the Japanese know we were coming? Had we fooled ourselves in thinking our convoy's roundabout route had fooled the enemy? Were Jap land-based planes poised to hit us and hit us hard? Were we walking into a trap? I was holding in reserve, at sea, troops to reinforce either the Humboldt Bay or the Tanahmerah landings if trouble developed. But I must wait for reports.

I went on deck in the darkness. It was yet a quiet darkness. I wandered down to the *Swanson's* messroom. The coffee ran hot from the urn, but breakfast had been prepared the night before. Along the table were pyramids of paper-wrapped sandwiches. You could eat them or put them in your pocket for future emergencies. Some sensible men did both.

It was not quite sunrise when I went on deck again, and it was a noisy half-darkness. The naval bombardment had begun. This was deep water, and cruisers and destroyers close inshore were letting go

deafeningly with all they had. The sun still had not appeared, and, in the dusk of almost-dawn, the flashes of the big guns were all around me. Soon, somewhere, I knew (like the battleships, they were at least a hundred miles at sea), the Navy carriers would launch their planes toward the objectives ashore.

Dawn broke over a calm and innocent sea, and the Navy planes swept down over the Hollandia airdromes and the landing beaches. They had bombed the airfields the day before and the day before that. So had Kenney's Fifth Air Force. Between them they had demolished two hundred and forty-five planes on the ground. The Japanese, however, did not know that these air attacks presaged an invasion.

The naval bombardment announced that. A total surprise had been achieved. There was no reply ashore. Now rocket craft closed in to their firing range of eleven hundred yards and gave the beaches a lethal fireworks display, while behind them wave after wave of landing craft lined up for the assault. Our long training in amphibious assault was rewarded. The landings were classical in their precision. Down to the most minute detail of planning, everything went off as scheduled.

At Humboldt Bay the surprise of the Japanese was so great that most of them fled at once from the beach area. Breakfast bowls of rice were only half consumed, and teapots were found still boiling when our first wave landed. Only scattered fire met the troops as they hit the shore. At Tanahmerah the enemy had already fled into the forested hills to escape the bombardment. There was automatic weapons fire from one island in the bay, and I watched the guns of the *Swanson* silence that.

General MacArthur, after flying from Brisbane, had joined the convoy the day before on the cruiser *Nashville*. About noon the *Nashville* appeared in the outer harbor, and Admiral Barbey and I were ordered to report aboard. A similar message was sent to General Krueger, our Sixth Army commander, who was aboard a destroyer on submarine patrol out at sea.

There is one passion of the Ohio small-town boy which I have

never outgrown—an unquenchable appetite for ice cream. So, to celebrate our fortunate landings, General MacArthur produced not a magnum of vintage-year champagne but chocolate ice-cream sodas! There at the Equator they certainly hit the spot. When I finished mine with celerity, the Allied commander grinned and gave me his own untouched, frosted glass. I polished off that soda too.

At three o'clock General MacArthur, General Krueger, and I went ashore in Tanahmerah Bay. With us was a considerable delegation of newspaper correspondents and newsreel men. We walked for an hour along a narrow stretch of mud and sand behind which rose a dense rain-forest. The sun poured down mercilessly, and my uniform was soggy and dark with wetness. I remember my astonishment that General MacArthur, despite the sweltering heat and the vigorous exercise, did not perspire at all. He was then three months beyond his sixty-fourth birthday.

As we returned to the *Nashville*, General MacArthur told me that he was trying to get another army in the Southwest Pacific. And, he added, if the Hollandia operation were brought off successfully, I would be its commander. I thanked him and shook hands. That was my first information about the Eighth Army, which I was to command in the Philippines and Japan.

Before the *Nashville* left that evening to return General Mac-Arthur to Australia, a conference was held at which he suggested that I move within three days to the Wakde area, a hundred miles up the coast. I shared his satisfaction over the success of our landings, but the uncertainties of the enemy situation both at Hollandia and to the northwest led me to argue against this precipitate movement. Three weeks later the heavy Japanese resistance at Wakde confirmed my apprehensions.

The second day of the invasion I was again wakened before daylight and was twice ashore before noon. General Krueger accompanied me on one of these inspection trips, and then departed for Finschhafen, four hundred miles away. He did not move his headquarters forward for more than a month.

Fred Irving is one of the ablest division commanders, and his per-

formance under trying conditions at Tanahmerah is firsthand testimony. There are two beaches in the bay. Our tactical plan called for
a main landing on Red Beach 2, and a smaller landing at Depapre
(Red Beach 1). Depapre was a tiny cove where the Japanese had
constructed a makeshift jetty; the mountainside lifted steeply above
it. The Navy planners objected to the Depapre landing; they pointed
out (correctly) that the sea bottom there was coral and that larger
landing craft could not get ashore at low tide.

Irving fought hard for the Depapre landing, and I backed him up.
If vessels could not get over the coral, buffaloes could. It seemed
to me important to get troops immediately inland—even a few troops
—to seize the steep primitive trail that led toward the dromes. The
Navy ultimately agreed. No single decision was more important.

The two landings were made simultaneously on D-day. From
Depapre three reinforced rifle teams under Lieutenant Colonel Jock
Clifford (they became known as "Clifford's Cowboys") climbed and
crawled their way up the hairpin turns of a sixty-degree slope. At
every one of the turns of the path they expected to meet point-blank
fire. But nothing happened. The enemy had really been surprised.
They had fled into the jungle. There were fire lanes, prepared fire
positions, and half-completed pillboxes. But no troops. In that terrain
a squad, literally, could have held up a division. The Japanese were
not yet ready. By evening of D-day the Cowboys were six miles
inland.

Back at Red Beach 2, scene of the major landing, there was the
devil to pay. There, and at Humboldt Bay, the beaches were less
useful than Army Intelligence and aerial photographs indicated. Rich
jungle growth concealed, on the films, the fact that some beaches
were really islands, with no exits whatever for troops and vehicles.

Remember the old saw: "The camera never lies"? The camera
lied at Red Beach 2. Thirty yards behind the sand there was an
almost impenetrable swamp. This was the area we had expected to
use for bivouacs and the dispersal of supplies. Our troops did not
hold back. One man sank out of sight before his comrades could
reach him. Another was down to his armpits when a sergeant
grabbed his rifle barrel with both hands. In the struggle between

man and morass the rifle was discharged. The sergeant was killed, but the man was rescued. Many other soldiers, bogged down in sink holes, were pulled to safety by their mire-smeared compatriots.

While troops and supplies continued to come automatically ashore, frenzied explorations were made in search of exits toward solid ground. It was believed the Japanese had constructed a road between Red Beach 2 and Depapre. A company of the 19th Infantry was sent to look for it. They arrived at Depapre next day, bedraggled and exhausted. It had taken them twenty-four hours to travel a distance of two miles through forest and mud. The road did not exist.

General Irving could now bless his stars (and his own foresight) that the Depapre landing had been approved. Small as was the cove —there was a channel through the coral but it was wide enough to accommodate no more than two landing craft and those only at high tide—it was our one open door to the airfields from the Tanahmerah side.

There was opposition from the Japanese on the Humboldt side, but Fuller's casualties were light and the Japanese were kept on the run. I had held the 34th Infantry of the 24th Division at sea as a reserve; now I sent it ashore on the Humboldt beaches. Once again the alligators and buffaloes were called upon to do a spectacular job. Crawling up out of the sea at Jautefa, a shallow bay within a bay at Humboldt, they moved slowly overland five miles to Lake Sentani. There, afloat again, they served as transports to carry troops fifteen miles down the lake for a landing which developed into a vital enflankment.

Our tanks stayed on the beaches. There was no way to use them. Not even a jeep could negotiate most of the precipitous, winding trails. As a result, throughout the operation all food, ammunition, and medical supplies from Depapre had to be carried from below by walking men. The forward surge of the supply-carrying troops was such that it took forty-eight hours for walking stretcher parties, coming down, to carry the wounded back to base. For the soldiers making the pincer movement on the dromes, there was nothing for it except slog, slog, slog. Fuller's troops had twenty-one miles to go; Irving's troops had only fourteen miles to go, but their going was

harder. They had fourteen streams to cross; they traveled, often in single file, through the peculiar twilight of rain-forests, and frequently they were tumbled head over heels by landslides.

Jock Clifford, center on the West Point football team of 1937—he met a gallant death later in Mindanao—was one of the best combat leaders I have known. On the fourth day of the advance he had got so far ahead that not even the elaborate train of human packhorses could catch and feed his troops. This had been anticipated, and from Lake Sentani I watched the B-17s which zoomed in to make food drops. The conjunction of the combat teams, and the capture of the dromes, came a day later. We owned the airfields on April 27.

Although we gained the dromes without heavy casualties, not everything went our way. On the second evening of the invasion—April 23—a single enemy bomber slipped in through the mountains and our anti-aircraft defenses and suddenly appeared over White Beach 1 at Humboldt Bay and released a stick of four bombs. Three bombs produced only geysers of sand and water, but the fourth scored a direct hit on a captured Jap ammunition dump near what we called Pancake Hill.

This was the curtain-lifting of a holocaust. Explosions from the ammunition set afire a nearby gasoline dump, and roaring flames spread in all directions. Intense heat drove back the most courageous efforts to salvage supplies. When I arrived there next morning Humboldt Bay seemed to be the scene of a devil's Fourth of July. Food, ammunition, bombs, were all going up in smoke. The fire burned for two days, and a large part of the supplies brought ashore on D-day and D-day plus 1 were a total loss. Twenty-four American soldiers were killed, and more than eleven were wounded. That stretch of ravaged and pitted beach was one of the saddest sights I have ever seen. And one Japanese bomber did it!

The capture of the airfields, unhappily, did not retire our combat troops to lives of leisure and feathery ease. We had not met the regiment of Jap marines and the two regiments of battle-tested infantry which G-2 predicted. Our adversaries were poorly trained service troops, but there were many of them, and on frequent occasions Japanese service troops fought courageously and well. On this occasion, we discovered, the commander of the Hollandia airfields did not lay out a plan of defense until two hours after we had landed. It is a military axiom that no plan for defense means no defense.

But the Japanese, slogging the trails inland and to the mountains, were still there. And it was the job of the doughboys to hunt them out and kill them. Our troops made ambushes and roadblocks along jungle trails. The 24th Division alone claims to have killed or captured five thousand Japanese during a period of weeks. There is no way to check these figures, but I believe they are substantially correct. Captives were few; only Koreans and Formosans and the Japanese sick surrendered.

Simultaneously with our attack upon Hollandia a smaller task force, which had been part of the same great convoy but was not under my command, hit the beach at Aitape, about a hundred miles down the coast. The object of the expedition was the seizure of Jap airfields in the Aitape-Tadji area and the quick preparation of those dromes to accommodate an Allied fighter group. We thought initially that close air support of troops in the Hollandia gamble might be of great importance in a battle of problematical odds.

Jens Doe, now a brigadier general, commanded this sortie. The 163rd Infantry of the 41st Division made the landing, and by one o'clock that afternoon the engineers were at work on the airstrips. Soon after, the 127th Infantry of the 32nd Division arrived and cleaned up Jap stragglers on two commanding islands which lay offshore. Japanese forces at Aitape retired into the jungle. Three days after the original landing the 78th Fighter Wing (Royal Australian Air Forces) flew there from Cape Gloucester and went into action.

The GIs at Aitape also had reserved seats for a one-plane bombing attack. This Jap adventurer came in over the Torricelli Mountains, dropped three 500-pound bombs, and scored a hit on the *Etamin*, which settled at the stern but did not sink. The *Etamin* had been carrying bombs and gasoline but was unloaded. One man was killed, five were reported missing, and thirteen were wounded. The rest of the crew went ashore in small boats, witnesses all to the im-

portance of the quick unloading of dangerous cargoes. If the bomber had hit them the day before—well!

The Aitape operation at that time seemed an easy one. In the first days field artillery, well ensconced, was not even called upon for a fire mission. Doe's 163rd had other commitments, and on May 3 the 32nd Division arrived and took charge. I am sure that throughout its history primitive Aitape had never seen such a parade of sea-going vessels. There were vessels to take the 163rd out, and there were vessels to bring in the 32nd Division. And above them always there was the drone of planes.

Aitape seemed an airfield cheaply won. But later there was to be bloody fighting there as Sixth Army Command sent troops farther into the jungle. General Bill Gill and the 32nd were to be occupied for two months by an engagement they describe in the Division's official history as "Death on the Driniumur." I shall come back to it later because the story is little known and should be told. The engagement at Aitape which began with a regimental combat command ended up with two infantry divisions involved.

WE BUILD THE AIRFIELDS

On April 28 began what one of my staff officers called the Big Engineering Phase at Hollandia. It was a race against time. The airfields must be ready to receive the Army fighter planes and bombers
which would launch the Wakde invasion on May 15 and the Biak
operation on May 27.

My day began at dawn and often ended at the airfields at midnight. Other men were the combat commanders in this campaign;
my job was to direct traffic and construction, and to demand speed,
speed, speed. Our engineers had full opportunity to prove themselves. Japanese airfields were not adequate for our war planes. A
Jap Zero weighed about six thousand pounds. An American bomber
weighed about sixty thousand pounds, and needed good ground and
good underpinnings, and a long stretch of hard-surface runway for
a take-off. I think I seemed like a factory foreman to a good many of
my subordinates while the landscape was being tamed. To me the
stench of hot asphalt became a fragrance in a region of many worse
smells. A week after D-day the first C-47 landed safely and taxied in
with its freight.

Road construction had proceeded simultaneously, and this was a
gigantic task. Sides of mountains were carved away, bridges and
culverts were thrown across rivers and creeks, gravel and stone "fill"
was poured into sago swamps to make highways as tall as Mississippi

113

levees. At Humboldt Bay the Japanese in two years had not been able to build a road from White Beach to Pim Jetty Hill. My engineers built a road in two weeks.

The record shows that the Wakde and Biak invasions were staged exactly on schedule. Much of the credit for this logistical triumph belongs to those who served immediately under me—officers like our chief engineer, Colonel Robbie Robinson, Colonel Mike Shea, our transportation officer, Colonel Dick McCreight, our G-4. A good deal more credit belongs to the enlisted men with the big muscles and wet feet. They made the four-lane road from Humboldt to the airfields. They made the famous scenic highway from Depapre. It was handy that they had been trained to carry their weapons to work: on the Depapre road alone, American engineers—while going ahead with their backbreaking jobs—killed one hundred and eight Japanese and captured twenty-eight.

Hollandia became one of the great bases of the war. In the deep waters of Humboldt Bay a complete fleet could lie at anchor. Tremendous docks were constructed, and one hundred and thirty-five miles of pipeline were led over the hills to feed gasoline to the airfields. Where once I had seen only a few native villages and an expanse of primeval forest, a city of one hundred and forty thousand men took occupancy.

Hollandia had also been important to the Japanese. This is witnessed by the thousands of tons of supplies we captured. There were more than six hundred supply dumps. There were clothing dumps as high as houses. There were ammunition dumps everywhere. There were pyramids of canned goods and tarpaulin-covered hills of rice which looked like Ohio haystacks. There were saki and beer. There were tons and tons of quinine and other medical supplies, which, as a result of our landing, never reached the Japanese troops at the front. I believe Hollandia was the richest prize—supply-wise—taken during the Pacific War.

But why, with so much booty, was there so little enemy opposition? Obviously because the Japanese thought—in view of past performance—we could not get there. I ran across one ironic story. The enemy had been so sure we would attack Wewak or Hansa Bay that

a high-ranking naval officer, Vice Admiral Endo, commander of the 8th and 9th Fleets, was brought back by submarine to Hollandia for safety's sake just five days before our assault. The story came from the Admiral's orderly whom we captured, emaciated and ill, in the Cyclops Mountains. This is a literal translation of the orderly's account:

When the American bombardment and attack came, the Admiral sat in his chair all morning without saying a word and just looked at the sea. About noon he ordered me to dress him in his dress uniform. Then, with other members of his staff, we went up in the mountains. When the Admiral felt his physical strength would carry him no farther, he halted and ordered the rest of us to go on. He still stood there when we had our last backward look.

The orderly had been a fugitive for thirty days when we captured him. Admiral Endo's body was never found, but the ceremony of the donning of the dress uniform convinces me that he killed himself in the Emperor's honor somewhere in those alien hills.

There are unimportant incidents in any campaign which are as permanently memorable as scar tissue. I established my corps headquarters ashore on the Humboldt Bay side at a place called Brinkman's Plantation. A tent had been put up for me and I had a bed and an office there. The 41st Division had already passed through the area, and there seemed to me no likelihood of attack. Liaison officers from other Allied governments were quartered there, and a perimeter defense had been established by a platoon from the 24th Division.

Sergeant Dombrowski, my orderly, and Sergeant Ventura, my chauffeur, slept immediately outside my tent in hammocks. All of us had witnessed that afternoon Ventura's swearing in as an American citizen. Naturally Ventura was proud and happy. We all were. I was anything but proud of the behavior of other American citizens, native born, that night.

I believe I went to bed about ten P.M. From just about that time until daylight the platoon guarding me carried on a terrific war. Tracer bullets from all directions made fireworks in the camp. Automatic rifles were fired and grenades were thrown. Troops on the in-

side and on the outside thought they were being attacked by Japanese, and the perimeter defense was standing like a rock.

From the beginning I was sure all the firing came from trigger-happy Americans. But, of course, I did not know. It *might* be Japanese. We had agreed that, in case of enemy attack, we would stay down and not run around in the dark. There in the night my aide, Captain Shuck, kept calling, "General, are you all right? General, are you all right?" About the fifteenth time Shuck called I became annoyed. "Shuck," I said, "for God's sake, abandon my rank until morning."

And he did. But I used my rank in the morning. The Battle of Brinkman's Plantation was, indeed, a battle among Americans. A master sergeant was killed and a number of troops were wounded. It was a disgraceful exhibition. It had not been Japanese but night and nerves which had caused the shooting. At daybreak I had the platoon lined up. I told them I never wanted to see them again; that I would feel safer (and I meant it) if I were guarded by Japanese. I had them marched away.

It was sheer coincidence that this same platoon was assigned to guard my camp on the island of Biak many weeks later. Then there were really Japs on a ridge above the camp. The guards never fired a shot all night. In the long dark hours they remained calm, watched the phantasmagoria of shadows and heard the snap of twigs without pressing a trigger. The combat lesson had been learned.

There was one humanitarian aspect of our surprise at Hollandia which has never ceased to give me satisfaction. When the Japanese garrison fled to the mountains and remote hinterland, where we were still hunting out and killing them many weeks later, they abandoned large numbers of East Indian military prisoners whom they had used as slave labor. These prisoners had been taken at Singapore. We also rescued, after a spirited chase of the Japanese units which had them in charge, about one hundred and twenty-five nuns and missionaries of many nations who were otherwise doomed to early death. They were Australian, Dutch, German, and American. They were starved and wraithlike; many were so weak from their prison life they could not walk.

I recall in particular an American couple named Braun. They had been in New Guinea for sixteen years. Dr. Braun was a medical missionary; although he was not a combatant he had been of considerable assistance to Allied Intelligence workers who had circulated secretly in his vicinity. When we arrived Mrs. Braun was at the point of death from malnutrition, and she, like many of the others, was immediately hospitalized by Army doctors. I visited her at the hospital and took along hard-to-get fruit juice and the highest protein foods I could find. Later—I should have thought of it sooner—I asked Colonel Les Skerry to take her several bars of perfumed soap, talcum powder, and a toothbrush. It was then Mrs. Braun, so disciplined before in spite of her illness, burst into tears. She had forgotten what toilet soap and talcum powder were like.

Almost all the missionaries, men and women alike, were barefooted, and all of us dug up shoes out of our lockers for them. Some of the nuns looked odd in ill-fitting combat boots, but shoes keep your feet off the ground. Our mess sergeants labored to fill them with food. The German missionaries were as happy to see us as the people from the States. Earlier some of the Germans had attempted to persuade the Japanese that they and their particular native flocks were neutrals. This turned out to be a serious mistake. The Germans told us the Japs treated them worse than they did the British and American missionaries.

These people remained with us for only a few days. Consequently I had no chance to talk to them all. But I remember a small Catholic priest who had been impressed into cooking for a Japanese troop camp. The camp was on Humboldt Bay, and his oppressors vanished when the warships began their bombardment. The good Father stayed with his pots. He decided if God so willed the Americans would save him, and that anyway he would save his breakfast.

When the missionaries were evacuated the weakest were carried on shipboard by stretcher. The finest of medical attention was available on the boat, since it was equipped in expectation of heavy casualties which, at Hollandia, did not occur. I have no doubt that more than half of this group owe their lives to our doctors.

Eventually I established my headquarters in an abandoned house

which—interestingly enough—had been built a number of years before by members of a National Geographic Society expedition. The
first two nights of the invasion I spent aboard the *Swanson* at sea.
The Navy expected Japanese retaliation by air. Cruising, without
lights, hugging the forested coastline, we moved as slowly as possible so that no phosphorescent wake would betray us to enemies
aloft. The throbbing of our engines could be heard ashore, and
fugitive Japanese had not yet given up hope of reinforcement. I saw
many surreptitious signals from the shore—flashlights and bolder
lights which winked in code. Up on deck, in the darkness, I realized
that scattered parties of Jap troops, unwilling to believe they had
been abandoned, were hopefully asking the *Swanson* to identify
itself as a friendly craft.

I shall never know why enemy air reaction was so weak. Up at
Manokwari Airfield, at the tip of New Guinea, there were ninety
Japanese planes; the Navy's flying lads saw them and told me.
Naturally I was apprehensive; if one plane could wreak havoc at
Humboldt, what could ninety planes do? I knew the Manokwari
strip lay beyond territorial limits set by the agreement between General MacArthur and Admiral Nimitz for the joint Hollandia operation, but I wanted those planes taken out. At a conference aboard a
destroyer on the third day I pleaded: "The same flag flies over my
troops that flies above the carriers." Admiral William M. Fechteler
and the flying boys from the Pacific Fleet backed me up; they were
ready and anxious to make the strike.

But Admiral Barbey refused to join me in an appeal to higher authority for permission to make the Manokwari raid. I do not report
this as a criticism of my good friend Dan Barbey, who was always
cooperative. I report it as one small argument for effective unification of our Armed Services. With the airplane in the picture, strict
area agreements between generals and admirals are not sacrosanct—
but dangerously academic. Those planes from Manokwari, as it
happens, made little trouble at Hollandia, but they certainly raised
hell with us later at Biak.

Captured Japanese records shed some light on the situation we
found at Hollandia. First, the enemy expected us to attack Hansa

Bay or Wewak. Second, whatever happened at Hansa Bay or Wewak, they did not expect us to be in a position to threaten their great supply depot until June at the earliest.

If we had obliged the enemy by a two months' delay, there is evidence they would have been ready. Japanese orders unearthed by the researchers of Allied Intelligence indicate that at one period the High Command intended to pull the entire Eighteenth Army out of eastern New Guinea for the purpose of holding Hollandia. This included three infantry divisions and seventy thousand men. The least ambitious of the alternate defense plans called for one crack division there.

Of interest, also, is the fact that our attack came very shortly after a grave shake-up in the enemy command at Hollandia. Allied Air can be credited with bringing about this internal combustion. The headquarters of the Fourth Japanese Air Army and the headquarters of a subordinate organization, the 6th Air Division, were both located at Hollandia. When our Fifth Air Force carried out devastating raids in late March and early April, the bombs blasted not only Japanese installations but Japanese reputations and Japanese military careers.

Most of the enemy planes on the Hollandia dromes never got off the ground to resist the Allied raiders. They were destroyed on the runways. As a result, the entire staff of Fourth Air Army was transferred, and the commanding general of 6th Air Division and his chief of staff were summoned back to Japan in disgrace. This left already demoralized garrison troops without leadership. Major General Inada, new commanding general of 6th Air, did not arrive until April 15. Major General Kitazona, who apparently was sent to be the senior officer in charge of all services, did not arrive until several days after that. There is considerable evidence that Inada and Kitazona did not see eye to eye on their duties, and that each believed himself to be charged with the over-all job of defense. It is possible that this situation explains why no coordinated plan for defense of the whole area was ever worked out.

The captured documents establish that General Kitazona was there, but no orders issued in his name were found. Nor did we ever

discover what became of him. Probably he died in the jungle with hundreds of other miserable stragglers who tried to find their way northwest to Toem-Sarmi. This was over a hundred miles farther along the coast and there were strong Jap garrisons there. As a matter of fact we had thought it just possible that Japanese from Toem-Sarmi would be dispatched overland to reinforce the Hollandia defenders. We know now that they were sent. But Japanese air and Japanese sea transport had vanished, and jungle trails were slow. The enemy reinforcements turned back.

On Ferguson Island, not too far from Goodenough, Sixth Army had trained a group of soldiers known as the "Alamo Scouts." A good many of them were former football players, and all of them were put through exercises and disciplines which are supposed to harden muscles and mercy. They all learned jujitsu. Thousands of troops learned jujitsu in the United States under the tutelage of Colonel Anthony Drexel Biddle and others, but I know of few cases where jujitsu was used in battle. Battles usually are not fought at such short distances. Marksmanship is more important than muscles, and a small, thin man with an accurate eye may kill more Japanese than a big-muscled fullback from the University of Minnesota. You don't wrestle with the enemy; either you kill him or he kills you. Nobody bothers with the rabbit punch; your adversaries are armed with guns, bayonets, and hand grenades.

The Alamo Scouts, however, needed all the toughening exercises and the teachings of rough-and-ready scuffling. The Scouts were trained to be expendible, and they knew it. Just after the Hollandia invasion a group of them were put ashore fifteen or twenty miles up the Dutch New Guinea coast. They took with them a radio, and their assignment was to plow inland and to find out whether the Japanese were sending reinforcements from Toem-Sarmi. The Scouts did their job. A submarine called at the appointed beach to take off the Scouts. Their rubber boats foundered, and the submarine abandoned them. By the hard terms of their hazardous job, the Scouts were then on their own. They started back toward Hollandia along the same trails the Japs from Hollandia were using for flight.

The Scouts had lost all their weapons in the sea. They had lost their supplies. They were hungry. They ate taro roots from native gardens, and they equipped themselves with wooden clubs. Taking turns, one or two men were always sent ahead to pioneer the trail and to give warning when they sighted approaching Japanese evacuees. Then the Scouts scattered in the jungle. Sometimes they laid traps for the Japanese and smashed Japanese heads with their rude clubs. Their main duty, of course, was to get back to Hollandia. They got back, but very thin.

Clovis Byers brought into my headquarters the sergeant who had commanded this extraordinary unarmed sortie through unknown terrain. I told the sergeant I was going to award him the Silver Star for gallantry and to give every member of his expedition the Bronze Star. The sergeant frowned. He was not ungrateful, but he was troubled—as all men of principle are—by judicial evaluations. After he pondered the matter a while he told me that his men had really done the job; he wouldn't like to receive a higher award than they received. The sergeant and all the rest got the Bronze Star.

Any chronicle of the Hollandia expedition must, because of space limitations, be unsatisfactory to those who participated in it. But I cannot sign off without an account of the misadventure of General Lumsden of the British Army. War is a grim business, but it does have its lighter moments. Lumsden I recall with admiring affection. He had been assigned by Mr. Churchill to be Britain's liaison officer with General MacArthur. A year later (along with Bill Chickering of *Time* magazine) he was killed aboard the USS *New Mexico* at Lingayen Gulf during a kamikaze attack.

Lumsden saw Hollandia before our engineers made it into a civilized suburb. I early took him ashore at Pim Jetty. The footing was slippery, and the engineering was mostly ditching. At Pim Jetty there was a brand-new latrine which had not yet been covered over. Lumsden, inspired by an admirable desire for personal exploration, managed to get far enough from the official party to fall into the latrine. He was a tall, slender cavalryman, and we fished him out with considerable difficulty. Lumsden was bedraggled, but his dignity was undismayed. Obviously he was familiar with the Chic Sale type of American architecture. As he shook himself like a dog after a swim, he remarked to me without even a smile, "At least it may be said, in England's interest, that I was the first thing through the hole."

The decision to jump eight hundred and fifty miles to Hollandia was one of the great strategic decisions of the Pacific War. It did indeed advance our progress by many months. The base became invaluable to future operations. Our casualties in its capture were unforeseeably small, and there can be no happier news for a task force commander—or for anyone else—than that. In view of its importance, I think (in the matter of blood and tears), Hollandia was the American victory most economically purchased.

But during the planning phase, of course, I could not know that G-2's estimate of garrison strength was vastly in error. We were lucky enough to meet not the predicted regiments of combat infantry and the fanatical Japanese marines, but harassed and uncertain and poorly commanded service troops. A task force commander, in all good sense, must prepare for the worst of luck and hope for the best.

At this late date I can look back on the operation with calmness and a certain satisfaction. But I cannot forget my apprehensions during the Finschhafen conferences. At the first one Generals Chamberlin and Krueger urged a single-minded drive on the Hollandia strips: "Sacrifice tanks, sacrifice artillery! Get those dromes!" Consequently I laid down narrow attack lines. At the next conference General Krueger's orders were: "Capture all of Humboldt Bay. Get a great supply base started there." At a third conference it developed that I was also to capture a Japanese airfield ten miles below the beaches where we would land. And all of this in difficult terrain and against an enemy of unknown strength.

Orders are orders, and Clovis Byers, my chief of staff, was my only confidant.

"I intend to do my damnedest," I told Byers, "but it looks like we've got to attack north, south, east, and west."

Well, that is what we did.

General George C. Marshall, then Chief of Staff, described the Hollandia campaign as "a model of strategic and tactical maneuver."

OPERATION FERDINAND

One of the most interesting and unconventional military outfits I ran into during the Pacific War is almost unknown to the American public. Members of the outfit—many of them middle-aged civilians and nearly all volunteers—were called "The Coastwatchers." This small group of venturesome men, at top strength numbering only a few hundred, risked their lives—and frequently lost them—in order to supply the Allies with accurate and firsthand information from the widely scattered tropical islands the Emperor's troops had occupied.

The code name of the organization was "Ferdinand," and the title was peculiarly apt. Ferdinand, as you may recall from the American nursery book, was a completely unaggressive bull; he liked to sit under a tree and smell flowers. The Coastwatchers avoided combat, except in dire extremity. It was their duty, figuratively, to sit inconspicuously under a tree, gather information, and send it out.

Equipped with bulky teleradios, difficult both to conceal and to transport, the Coastwatchers sat in some extremely uncomfortable spots. Throughout the period of the war they lived among the Japanese, hiding in the jungles of Papua, New Guinea, the Solomons, moving from place to place with their cumbersome and risky equipment. White men can't pass themselves off as natives, nor can they exist in the jungle without help. The Coastwatchers on their hazardous assignments were obliged to trust the natives who served them. Too often the trust was misplaced and they were betrayed to torture and death.

Needless to say, the operation was top secret. Until the armistice, the Allies did not even admit the existence of such an organization. Operated originally under the auspices of Australian Naval Intelligence, Ferdinand later became a part of the Allied Intelligence Service which was headed up by Major General Charles A. Willoughby, General MacArthur's able G-2. A group of Coastwatchers went into Hollandia to collect information five weeks before I led our invasion there. From an emaciated survivor, who rowed out to see me while I was still aboard the *Swanson,* I learned of the disaster that befell the party.

Before telling the story, I would like to describe a little of the background of this highly unorthodox organization whose members performed a useful service in modern war while remaining as individualistic and, on occasion, as undisciplined as our own old-time Indian fighters. After World War I the Australian Navy became uneasily conscious of its interminable, undefended coastline. Australia is an immense subcontinent, about the size of the United States; most of its eight million population is crowded into the southeastern corner of the country. Elsewhere lie immeasurable plains, plateaus, deserts, wastes, and wooded lands. In these empty areas, in the vast ring of islands and atolls which surround Australia, it seemed obvious that an enemy might operate without opposition and, indeed, without discovery. As a precautionary measure the Navy selected certain civilians, living in remote and isolated places, whose duty in time of war would be to report suspicious activities and events and subversive behavior. Generally they were postmasters, harbormasters, schoolteachers, police or railway officials—people who had access to telegraph instruments. The watchers received no pay in the beginning.

Before the 1930's the few scattered missionaries and managers of cattle stations settled on the north and northwest coasts had no means of swift communication. The invention of the pedal radio (charged by foot power) gave these frontiersmen a link with the outside world and they were enrolled. Later, government administrative officials, prospectors, miners, and planters in Papua, New Guinea, and the Solomon Islands joined the Coastwatcher network.

It was in this screen of islands which Americans call the Southwest Pacific and Australians call the Northeast Area that the main job of Ferdinand was to be done. When the war began the Australian Navy directed the secret organization to start functioning. Eric A. Feldt, a former naval officer, was placed in charge of the Coastwatchers located in Papua, New Guinea, and the Solomons. Commander Feldt has written the definitive history of the Ferdinand operation.*

With the Japanese invasion, inevitably, immediate cracks appeared in the volunteer communications system. On Nissan Island there was a superannuated Australian Navy telegrapher who had retired on pension and become a planter. He watched an enemy ship approach his undefended atoll, calmly coded his report, and was never heard of again. From Gasmata, just off the south coast of New Britain, an Australian government official warned Port Moresby of its first Jap air raid—which allowed the town ample opportunity to prepare. Unfortunately this friend in need was betrayed by journalistic enterprise: news that the Moresby-bound enemy planes had been sighted over Gasmata was broadcast on the Australian radio. This gave direct information to the Japanese that there was a reporting station on Gasmata. J. Daymond, the Coastwatcher in question, escaped the raid. But two weeks after the fall of Rabaul the Japanese landed troops on Gasmata. Daymond and his assistant were taken immediately, and a third member of the staff radioed news of their capture. He never sent another message, and undoubtedly died with the others.

In the early days the Coastwatchers were of considerable assistance to the Americans. For example, when the Japanese made their first air attack on our landing forces at Guadalcanal, twenty-three out of the twenty-four enemy bombers in the raid were brought down, and our expedition suffered little damage. The defeat of this particular sortie was partially the result of a Coastwatcher's warning.

* *The Coastwatchers* (New York: Oxford University Press, 1946)

Hidden in a jungle three hundred miles away, with a bulky receiving and sending set as an incriminating companion, he had sighted the Japanese flight and passed on the information in time for our fighters to rise at Guadalcanal and for our anti-aircraft to be alerted. This was only one of many Jap air raids which were intercepted because of mysterious information from the islands. Detailed reports on the movements of Japanese transports, the daytime hiding places of destroyers and barges, the speed and progress of Japanese naval movements, also figured in the radio bulletins.

In the Solomons campaign a handful of Coastwatchers worked with picked American Marine signalmen in the jungles of Bougainville. Their knowledge of uncharted trails and of secret channels where small boats could land proved to be very valuable. General MacArthur was later to decorate several of the leaders with the Distinguished Service Cross, an event necessarily unheralded at the time. When General Vandegrift left Guadalcanal, in his final Order of the Day he spoke cryptically of "our small band of devoted Allies, who have contributed so vastly in proportion to their numbers." This, of course, referred to the Coastwatchers.

One of my favorite stories concerns Cornelius Page, a planter living at the extreme outer perimeter of the Coastwatcher network on a dot of land called Tabar Island. Page was a twenty-mile canoe journey from New Ireland, but his own inconsequential island was a landfall by which Japanese bombers flying from Truk fixed their navigational positions. Night and day Page radioed news of the oncoming flights. These reports did not go unnoticed by the Japanese. After the fall of Rabaul and Kavieng, they decided to hunt Page out. A warship bombarded his plantation. Page had moved his awkward teleradio—the power system was so heavy that fourteen native carriers were required to transport it—to a hut in the jungle, and he was not discovered. He reported the departure of the Japanese vessel to his superiors back in Townsville. He was congratulated on his work, ordered to bury his teleradio, and escape.

Page ignored the command. Ordered to maintain radio silence, he continued to code and send in his daily reports. He told about the enemy guns and positions at Kavieng, the names of the Europeans

captured; he was able to pass on information gathered from runaway natives that the Namatani Airfield on New Ireland was mined. On one occasion he wanted to send a particularly urgent message. Two missionaries in Papua were conversing over the air channel and both were depressed. Page waited with impatience while one missionary said, "I will pray for you, Brother." The other replied, "And I will pray for you, Brother."

At this point Page's patience vanished. He broke in and roared, "Get off the ruddy air, and I will pray for you both."

Soon Page was a lone voice in enemy-held territory. The natives on Tabar, cognizant of Japanese victories, deserted him. Page hid in caves. He had no weapons, and his plantation supplies were virtually exhausted. When the Japanese began enrolling native police, Page at long last agreed to be evacuated. It was arranged that a submarine would take him off Tabar. For three nights in a row Page went out in a small boat and flashed recognition signals but without result. The rescuing submarine had developed engine trouble and was hard put to get back to port. Eventually Page signaled that a party of Japs and natives with hunting dogs was on its way to seek out his hiding place. The hunting party found him. When Page was next called on the radio no answer came.

Not all Ferdinand stories had the same dismal end. The saga of K. D. Hay, with its humorous anticlimax, was told and retold by Americans after the victory at Guadalcanal. Hay was an extremely obese planter, a veteran of World War I, who maintained a watch station with two other Australians in an abandoned mining camp at Gold Ridge, high in the hills south of Lunga. Hay did not come out of the bush until January of 1943. A good part of this time he had been sheltering an ill and aged nun, sole survivor of a Japanese massacre.

The great fat man had difficulty getting down the rough and roundabout mountain trails. When he finally reached a roadhead he collapsed and sent on a note by a native, saying he was "knocked up." In Australian slang this means to be exhausted; to Americans, it means to be pregnant. A bewildered American lieutenant set off in a jeep to meet the planter. When the lieutenant encountered Hay,

he took one look at that monumental belly and said in awe: "My God! It's true!"

Young Leigh G. Vial was an assistant district officer at Rabaul. He was evacuated by the Australian Air Force and set down in Salamaua before the Japanese moved in. He was provided with a teleradio, codes, instructions, and food. Hidden in the hills above Salamaua Airfield, he reported for six months the arrivals and departures of Jap aircraft. Because of his technical knowledge—at a premium then —he was able to report types of Jap planes in the skies and their numbers, the heights at which they were flying, and their courses. Vial, living in the rudest of circumstances, did not know that he was the voice most listened to at Port Moresby; indeed, one romantic correspondent referred to him as "The Golden Voice." Vial was one of the watchers awarded our Distinguished Service Cross. Later he was killed in an air crash over central New Guinea while attempting to succor another hard-pressed Ferdinand group.

Another Coastwatcher, less technically proficient than Vial, was perched for weeks near the important Japanese anchorage between Bougainville and the Shortland Islands. Pages torn from a copy of *Jane's Fighting Ships* were dropped to him by air. After studying the illustrations, the watcher became usefully expert at identifying and reporting the types and classes of Japanese vessels circulating in those waters.

One of the boldest and ablest of Ferdinand's operatives was G. C. Harris, an Australian naval lieutenant. His lifeline almost—but not quite—crossed mine at Hollandia. It was Harris who headed the secret expedition which went ashore at Hollandia a month before the carriers and battlewagons led us there. His mission was to get exact information on landing beaches (information that would have been very handy for us at Tanahmerah Bay), on Japanese strength in the area, and on Japanese defenses.

Harris was not new to dangerous enterprises. After the Japanese landed at Rabaul, he assembled from various points along the New Guinea coast a flying-on-one-wing flotilla of launches; some of them could manage as much as six knots. With these sea-going flivvers he crossed the Vitiaz Strait and managed a partial evacuation of troops and European refugees stranded on the island of New Britain. The launches, which were always breaking down, were known sardonically as the "Harris Navy." They traveled by night, and when daylight came were quickly beached on some island shore and covered with tree limbs to conceal them from Japanese air reconnaissance. Regular companions of the obstreperous and somewhat irreligious Harris on these chancy expeditions were four missionaries.

Dr. Braun, the medical missionary rescued by my task force at Hollandia, was one of Harris's close friends. In the unquiet interval after the Japanese landed at Lae and Finschhafen, Dr. Braun directed the American Lutheran Mission Hospital near Madang. At various times Harris and about fifteen other Coastwatchers showed up in his vicinity. Nearly all suffered from malaria and other tropical diseases, and the doctor treated them. On one occasion an Australian who had licked a violent bout of fever and was convalescent broke his upper dental plate and could not chew the food necessary to his recovery. A radio message went to Ferdinand headquarters, and a day or so later a plane dropped by parachute the materials necessary for repair. Dr. Braun fixed the plate.

Talking to Dr. Braun and his wife, I got a fair picture of "Blue" Harris. He was a plump young man in his twenties, with a courteous manner and a truculent disposition. He had the hard, weathered face of a frontiersman, and a soft, gentle voice. He lisped. A strip of blazing red hair wrapped itself around the edge of a shining bald pate; "Blue" is the usual Aussie nickname for a redhead.

In 1943 Ferdinand, at the request of Allied Intelligence, sent several expeditions overland in New Guinea in an effort to get concrete information about such Jap positions as Wewak, Hansa Bay, Aitape, and Hollandia. Despite the fact that they were led by men of jungle experience, the expeditions were failures. Every member of one group was wiped out. After these disheartening failures Blue Harris was given the Hollandia job. Since the assignment meant landing on an enemy-held coast, among natives who were an unknown quantity, his party was carefully chosen. Lieutenant R. L. Webber, a companion on previous ventures, was second in com-

mand. The others in the landing team included three Australian Army privates, one able seaman, and four native New Guinea policemen. None knew the dialects of Dutch New Guinea tribes. Consequently the Dutch government detailed Sergeant Launcelot, an Indonesian trooper, to accompany them as interpreter. If possible, however, the party intended to avoid any contact with natives.

Harris expected to land from a submarine thirty miles west of Hollandia, then push inland to the mountains. To make sure of proper communications, another Ferdinand group, under Captain C. J. Miller, was landed by plane at the Idenberg River, about one hundred miles south of Hollandia. If base stations found Harris's radio signals too weak, Miller would pick them up with his power set and relay them on.

Harris and his men embarked on the U.S. submarine *Dace* on March 13. Four days later the submarine was off Cape Tanahmerah. After dark the *Dace* surfaced and approached the coast; just then a powerful searchlight bloomed out on shore. The submarine hastily withdrew and submerged. Next day, after further cruising, it was decided to land the party on a small beach on the open coast, even though a periscope inspection showed there were several native huts nearby. According to plan, the team was to remain ashore fourteen days, and then to be picked up at the same spot by the *Dace*.

Because of those native huts Harris decided not to commit his entire party. He would go ashore with a reconnaissance group, sound out the situation, and then communicate with the *Dace* by flashlight. If everything looked all right, the signal would be "Groggo." But if the signal "Washout" was sent, the other members of the party were not to be landed and the whole plan would be revised.

That night the submarine surfaced about a mile offshore. The sea was calm, and Harris set off in a rubber boat. With him went Webber, Launcelot, and two others. They carried a walkie-talkie radio, guns, flashlights, and other equipment. The rubber boat came in smoothly on a low ground swell until it was suddenly caught up in heavy breakers caused by an invisible reef. The boat swamped. The radio equipment was ruined. As the drenched men reached dry sand a fire flared up near a native hut.

Harris knew that any further attempt at concealment was futile. He and Launcelot walked up to the hut. The natives seemed friendly, and they reported through Launcelot that the nearest Japanese were two or three miles to the west. Years of working with New Guinea tribes had equipped Harris with delicate and highly sensitized intuitions. He was not satisfied.

Purely on the basis of the smell of danger, Harris ordered the signal "Washout" to be flashed. Webber gave the message and then sent a further signal asking the *Dace* to return at once for them. There was no acknowledgment, and Webber climbed a small hill to repeat. From the hill Webber was appalled to see two rubber boats just beyond the reef. The rest of the party mistakenly had been sent ashore. The signal had been misinterpreted.

Blue Harris quickly assembled his water-logged men. A turn of bad luck, and the loss of radio equipment, had already robbed the group of most of its importance as an Intelligence unit. The problem now was survival. A dawn assessment of strength disclosed that the eleven men had among them four submachine guns, two carbines, six pistols; also a box of hand grenades and some medical kits and maps; about a week's supply of rations had been saved from the surf. They would strike inland, Harris said, and try to reach Miller's headquarters on the Idenberg River. He knew, of course, that if the natives were unfriendly the news of the landing was no longer a secret. Again he went to the native hut.

There had been only four people in the hut the night before. But that morning the natives had been joined by another man who seemed to be a chief. He agreed that one of the boys in the hut would guide the Ferdinand party around the Japanese areas. The rubber boats were hidden, and the expedition moved inland—finally making camp in a dry creek bed. The guide then abruptly departed, telling Launcelot that he would search for a better campsite. He never returned. Harris's intuitions had been correct: the Japanese had been tipped off as soon as the little group left the beach.

The following morning, ignoring the absence of a guide, Blue Harris moved his men quickly along a path through the jungle. This led them to a wide patch of kunai grass. There they paused to recon-

noiter before venturing into the open. At that point voices were heard behind them. Lieutenant Webber, second in command, dropped his pack and went to the rear to investigate. He saw a line of Japanese moving forward through the jungle. It was an entrapment. Webber ran to warn Blue Harris, but Harris was already hurrying his group across the open area to the protection of the jungle on the other side. Four of the men reached shelter before the Japanese firing began. Webber and two others were able to hide themselves in the high grass.

Machine guns and mortars soon joined in the firing. Caught in the open space were Blue Harris and two of the Australian privates, J. I. Bunning and G. Shortis. The position was surrounded and the Japanese were moving in. At the last moment Sergeant Launcelot, the Indonesian interpreter, reached the jungle uninjured. Still in the open, Harris, Bunning, and Shortis kept up an accurate fire and drew the enemy on themselves in order that the others might escape.

The Japanese attack centered on those three. Launcelot, concealed only a few yards away, witnessed much of this action. The three men sold their lives expensively. For four hours they held off the enemy. Then, at last, Bunning and Shortis were dead, and Blue Harris faced the Japanese alone with an empty pistol. Harris was already wounded in three places. He was propped up against a tree and savagely cross-examined. He was asked about the ship which landed him, about future Allied plans and military movements. He said nothing. In the end, the Japanese bayoneted him to death—a welcome release for Blue Harris.

Sergeant Launcelot lay hidden for four days in one spot while the Japanese conducted an over-all search of the area. For drinking water he licked raindrops off the leaves. A few days later he met a friendly native who concealed him and fed him until our task force hit the beach. At that time Launcelot believed himself to be the only survivor of the Blue Harris party. When he saw the warships move in, he paddled out to the *Swanson* and came aboard to tell me, in part, the story I have just told you.

Since then I have learned more details. Two members of the Harris party simply disappeared; they were undoubtedly executed by the

Japanese. Astonishingly, five men out of the original eleven managed to live through their experiences. Lieutenant Webber and Private P. C. Jeune were among the survivors. Until sundown they remained hidden in the kunai grass, and then they crawled into the jungle. They had an Owen gun, a pistol, two knives, one can of rations, five bouillon cubes, and a compass. They decided they would try to reach Idenberg, but after five days of wandering that project was abandoned. They realized their only chance of survival was to conceal themselves until the Americans arrived. Seven starvation days later they dragged themselves into two small caves where they hid for a fortnight. They had only raw hearts of palm buds to eat. On April 21 came the bombardment which heralded the attack.

The following day they set out for the Hollandia beach, but by now Jeune was so weak he could hardly walk. They approached a native hut, where he intended to stay while Webber sought out an American patrol. Just as they reached the hut a Japanese charged out at them, armed with a sword. Jeune fended off the saber blow and, holding on to the sharp blade, was cut on his hands, forearms, neck, and ears. Webber was afraid that firing his pistol might bring enemy reinforcements. He tried to knock out the Jap with punches to the face. But in the end—so desperate was the struggle by two weak men—he buried his pistol in the adversary's belly and pulled the trigger. Then, to prevent outcry, Jeune grabbed the saber and drove it through the soldier's heart. The Japanese was alone; no reinforcements came.

After that Webber and Jeune went on. Webber scouted ahead and supported himself on the saber while Jeune staggered along behind, using a long stick as a cane. There were many pauses for rest, but finally they met up with American soldiers who carried them to a battalion hospital.

For thirty-two days Julius McNicol, the seaman of the party, existed by foraging in the jungle. He too reached the beach after our arrival. Probably the most incredible journey of all was made by one of the New Guinea native policemen. Four hundred miles away at Saidor, he knew, the American 32nd Division had landed. He walked there. A companion, who started with him, died on the way.

One note from the official report of the trip reads: "As we had no food or matches and could not cook any of the food stolen from native gardens, we grew weaker."

All five of the survivors of the expedition gave the credit to the redheaded leader who deliberately drew the Japanese fire on himself when they were ambushed. I never met Blue Harris, but I think I have the measure of the man.

BIAK: BATTLE OF THE CAVES

Americans who fought at Biak, just off the coast of upper New Guinea, remember that sun-baked island as something as unreal and frightening as Conan Doyle's "Lost World." The geography was scarred and pitted by the accidents of nature's past, and some of the cliffs and limestone terraces along its southern shore seemed as barren as the mountains of the moon.

Biak is an island of innumerable caves—caves with the dimensions of a narrow dark hallway, caves as deep and large as five-story tenement buildings and with as many levels of connecting galleries, caves with weird stalactite and stalagmite formations reminiscent of the Carlsbad Caverns of New Mexico. It is also an island of subterranean streams, and scarce (and evil-tasting) surface water. Soldiers fought for the precious water holes, and more than one American died as he crawled forward in the night to replenish his canteen.

The mystery of Biak's caves is probably explained by volcanic upthrusts. Long ago busy coral built beneath the sea, and rainbow fish swam through the tunnels and mazes which later housed hundreds of men. Repeated volcanic convulsions in forgotten eras lifted the coral formations and water-made faults until some of them were two hundred feet or more above the sea where they originated. Then we came.

An American task force built around the 41st Division landed at

135

Biak on May 27, 1944, and discovered the Japanese had established themselves both on the cliffs overlooking the beaches and in invincible underground fortresses. The Japanese had been on the island only a few months but their explorations had been thorough. They had located and staked claim to an intricate subterranean network with many secret places of ingress and egress. These widely scattered caverns were altogether absent from our maps. A full month before our arrival (captured records indicate our invasion was anticipated) the Japanese proceeded to exploit their knowledge. They took every advantage of nature's fantasies, and with foresight and able engineering constructed themselves an island stronghold with a considerable claim to impregnability.

General Fuller, who led the Biak task force, called at my Lake Sentani headquarters shortly before his departure. In a general discussion of the situation facing him, Fuller expressed some apprehension. It is not an easy matter to lead a division on one full-dress amphibious expedition, and then, in five or six weeks' time, to prepare that division for another. Fuller was also concerned about the size of his force. Only two combat regiments had been assigned to the landing.

Just a short time earlier, as we both knew, an expedition launched against Toem-Sarmi had run into unexpected trouble. As I have previously said, my first task after the capture of Hollandia was to rush the construction of airfields so that the invasions of both Biak and Toem-Sarmi could be supported by the Fifth Air Force. Twelve days before the strike against Biak—on May 17 to be exact—the landing at Toem-Sarmi took place.

On Wakde Island, two miles off the New Guinea coast and directly opposite the wild jungle region called Toem-Sarmi, were located a number of commanding Japanese airstrips. These airstrips were our principal objective there. First landings were made at Arare Village on the mainland. The troops then moved three miles overland to Toem Village, where preparations were laid for a shore-to-shore movement to Wakde Island the next morning. Reconnaissance planes had seen no Japanese on Wakde; strafers had not encountered return fire. One officer on a scouting expedition to a nearby tiny island reported back jovially that if "my orderly didn't have sore feet" the two of them could have waded over and captured Wakde.

There were others who were deceived. One of them was General Byers, my chief of staff. Brigadier General Donald R. Hutchinson commanded the fighter planes from Hollandia which provided the air cover for Toem-Sarmi. Byers rode "piggy back" with Hutchinson in a P-39 to witness the D-day landings. They flew over Wakde at treetop level and found no enemy reaction. Indeed, they saw no one. At one end of a seemingly deserted Jap runway they spotted a fresh crater made by our bombers. "Fighter Hutch" cut his motors in the air and said to Byers, "Shall we land?" Just then American bombers dug another deep crater on the strip. Hutchinson and Byers decided to return to base. They emptied their machine guns in a farewell salute to the empty landscape and flew away. Back at Hollandia, Byers said to me, "There is no opposition. We could have landed without difficulty except for the bomb craters."

That's what Byers and Hutch thought then, and I've never ceased to remind them of it.

When the 163rd Infantry, 41st Division, hit the beach the next day there was a different story. The Japs had been living in bombproof bunkers and pillboxes—there were a hundred of them and at least twelve different caves completely invisible from the air. The Jap troops had come safely through the bombardment. They proceeded to put up stiff and well-organized resistance. Wakde is only two miles long and a mile wide, but it took the 163rd two days of continuous and swift action to complete the conquest—even with the use of tanks. One prisoner, a Hawaiian-born Jap marine who spoke excellent English, walked into a supply dump and surrendered. He was the only captive taken at Wakde. More than eight hundred enemy dead were counted.

In the days following General Fuller's departure I was preoccupied with the problems of turning Hollandia into a great military and naval base. I heard very little about Biak, and saw only the usual optimistic communiqués about the progress of the campaign. On June 1 Allied headquarters reported to the press that, after bitter fighting, "Japanese opposition east of Bosnek has collapsed." On June

3 an official spokesman was quoted as saying, "We are mopping up enemy troops." All this looked very promising.

On June 14, however, I received a message at Hollandia requesting that I report immediately at the headquarters of the Sixth Army commander. General Krueger had moved forward from Finschhafen and was now established on the south shore of Humboldt Bay. It was about dark, and I wondered about the urgency of the summons as I motored six miles to Pim Jetty, crossed the entrance of Jautefa Bay in a crash boat, and then took a jeep for five miles more. I remembered an earlier urgent trip to Port Moresby. Had something gone wrong at Biak?

When I talked with the Army commander, it soon became evident that, in his opinion, something *had* gone wrong at Biak. I was to set off by air the next morning at daybreak to take command there. My entire I Corps headquarters was to follow the same day by boat. My mission was to secure and make habitable for American planes the three enemy airfields on the island.

Moving a corps headquarters on fire-alarm notice is no easy job. I immediately called General Byers and told him to start packing. I had brief conversations with members of Sixth Army staff and learned that the Biak task force was having very rough going against veteran Japanese troops armed with big guns and tanks. I got back at my offices late and found the force there busy, efficient, excited.

The cool early morning discovered Byers and my other key officers and me speeding down beautiful Lake Sentani in swift cabin cruisers. At the far end of the lake two Catalina flying boats were warming up and awaiting us. A few minutes later the hulls skipped along the water and we rose into the rising sun and headed toward Biak—three hundred miles away. From my window I could see the Army fighter planes which served as our air escort.

We had a few maps with us but almost no knowledge of what we would find at Biak. I knew, of course, the importance of the island's occupation from a strategic point of view. It would place us within easy bombing range of the Philippines, some eight or nine hundred miles away, and within fighter range of the enemy fields at dot-in-the-ocean Palau. I knew Mokmer drome at Biak had been captured on June 6, and that this was yet a hollow victory. Nearby Japanese forces kept the field directly under fire, so that our planes could not use it.

We came into the bay at Bosnek (where the original landing had occurred) and flopped down on the water in the middle of a squall. And what a flop! For a man as big as myself, transfer from a flying boat to a landing craft is always an adventure. One poorly timed jump in rough weather may mean broken ribs or a broken leg. A small LCM bounced up and down in front of the Catalina, and, astraddle the nose of the plane, I inched my way forward. It was just noon. The young pilot of the Catalina tried to help me and was washed off by a wave. Being a strong swimmer, he got back aboard with only the loss of his braided cap. A little breathless, I finally made the LCM.

Once ashore I went to task force headquarters and promptly set about acquainting myself with the facts of the situation. For the first time I learned of the near-disaster which had marked the second and third days of the invasion. We had landed at Bosnek, one of the two points on the southern coast where there was some flat land between the ocean and high ground. The coastal cliffs, however, were only a few hundred yards away and gave the Japanese perfect command of the approaches. Nevertheless, the enemy had failed to put up a vigorous resistance on D-day, and enemy planes, which were to be a scourge throughout the rest of the campaign, had put in only a token appearance.

Combat troops of the 162nd Infantry immediately swung up the coastal road which the Japanese had built from Bosnek to the air-dromes. They grumbled about the rough footing, the heat, the lack of water but—officers and men—they were in high good humor. There was little opposition. It was going to be, some of them predicted confidently, another Hollandia; the Japs had moved back into the hills, and the Americans would soon be on the airfields with only mopping-up operations ahead. By nightfall the 162nd had traveled eight miles and was within a thousand yards of Mokmer Airdrome.

One battalion crossed a gulley and occupied a ridge. There was only sniper fire that night. But the Japanese trap had been set. The

next morning the enemy opened up. There was artillery, machine-gun fire, the "deadly cough" (the phrase belongs to Spencer Davis of the Associated Press, the only correspondent on the spot) of knee mortars. An avenue of fire divided the American forces, and the forward battalion was unable to withdraw. At the same time Jap tank fire hit the head of the column; if this enemy advantage had been pressed then and there the battalion might have been wiped out.

But eventually the Americans were able to fall back from the exposed ridge to positions within the meager shelter of a cliff along the narrow beach. They had no artillery; they had pushed ahead too fast. Now the Navy destroyers offshore went into action; the Navy fire was not particularly effective against the enemy, secure on the cliffs and in the caves, but it probably prevented a frontal assault. The enemy's six-inch guns were quick to return the fire and knocked a hole in one of our destroyers.

At noon the Amphibian Engineers joined the rescue party. Ten buffaloes appeared offshore and bravely wiggled their way over the coral reefs—while six-inch shells raised twenty-foot geysers around them—to bring ammunition, blood plasma, water, and morphine to the beleaguered troops. Private Albert M. Eshpeter of Fargo, N.D., was the first Amphib pilot ashore. The buffaloes then wiggled back over the coral, and every sea-going tractor was crowded with wounded.

Late that evening a Japanese force, following the line of the cliffs, cut in behind the advance battalion and isolated it completely from the main American forces. At dawn the reinforced Japanese again attacked. There were three determined enemy assaults, and all three were repulsed that day, but with heavy losses on both sides. And while the hot sun beat on the gleaming coral the first tank-against-tank battle of the Southwest Pacific took place. Numbers of tanks involved were small, but the engagement was important in that it demonstrated prophetically the superiority of our armor. Three Japanese tanks advanced from the airstrip. They were met by five American Shermans which destroyed them after the exchange of only a few rounds of fire. Half an hour later the four remaining enemy tanks appeared and were also destroyed immediately.

The Americans had turned back the enemy offensives, but they were under constant fire from the cliffs, and their positions were becoming untenable. That night in the darkness a fleet of buffaloes evacuated them and their equipment and returned them to Bosnek. The Americans had taken a licking. For some days the beach road to the dromes was effectively blocked.

On my first afternoon at Biak, leaving my staff to confer with the task force staff, I went forward along the beach road as far as I could go—about a mile short of Mokmer drome. It was easy enough for me to envisage (with a shiver) what one officer who was there described as the happy-go-lucky advance of the 162nd. On my left was the sea, and on my right were the coral cliffs, which raised themselves skyward like the Palisades along the Hudson. Looking up from my jeep, I could see the openings of caves which had even yet to be cleared of the enemy. Sometimes the cliffs elbowed so far seaward that the narrow road curved around them through shallow water at high tide.

I passed The Narrows, where the Japanese had closed the door of their trap, and saw the wreckage of the Japanese tanks and the aging dead men still in them. I saw the six-inch guns pointed toward the sea, and was glad our original landing had been made at Bosnek and not on the mile-deep flat land at the dromes. On the way back to headquarters I was solemn and reflective. The cliffs made a frowning natural bastion. Inland, I knew, there were no roads and a rising plateau which was as rich in jungle as the seacoast was hard and barren.

There were many conferences at Bosnek that first hot night before I went wearily to bed. Sergeant Dombrowski, my orderly, a man of infinite resource, managed a shower bath by climbing a stepladder and holding above me a big gasoline can punched full of holes. General Byers and I were quartered together in a roomy, sand-bagged tent which had a wooden floor five feet deep in the coral ground. The depth provided a considerable protection against the fire of Japanese snipers who, during most of my stay at Biak, continued to occupy some of the caves near Bosnek and to make nuisances of themselves.

As I went to sleep in this strange country I could hear wind and

rain in the coconut grove around us. The rain stopped about three
A.M. and Japanese planes came over. Byers, Colonel Ken Sweany
(chief of staff of the 41st Division), and I took refuge in a newly
prepared air-raid shelter. I spent a very uncomfortable hour before
I wandered back to bed. This was the first time and the last time I
ever took refuge in an air-raid shelter during the war. My distaste for
shelters isn't a matter of courage. I like my sleep and I'm an enemy
of needless discomfort. And also, perhaps, something of a fatalist.

The next day I started out early, reached Mokmer drome without
difficulty, and found General Doe dug in on the shoreline. It was
his advance command post. Doe was the assistant commander of the
41st Division. I was glad to have Jens Doe again on my team. After
serving with me as a colonel at Sanananda he had led both the
Wakde and Aitape invasions. Doe was a great fighter; he was also a
stubborn, opinionated man, and our disagreements were spirited.
Subsequently Doe became, with my recommendation, the 41st's commanding general.

I was dissatisfied when I returned from the front that Friday night.
I had no clear picture of the military situation, and, after visiting the
command posts of the 186th and 162nd Infantry Regiments, I was
convinced that their colonels were almost as much in the dark as I
was. Everyone knew the Japanese were able to appear and disappear
almost at will because they were housed in caves. But where were
the main caves? How much strength did the Japanese have? We
held Mokmer drome and we held a low ridge immediately back of it.
But the Japanese held a higher ridge immediately behind that. And
still farther back, somewhere to the left, enemy artillery had hidden
positions from which they directed periodic fire on the drome.

It entertained me recently to thumb through copies of the *New
York Times* of 1944. I found there a communiqué from the Southwest
Pacific rear headquarters, dated June 14. It announced, rather triumphantly, that the first American planes had landed at Mokmer
Airdrome. Someplace between the front and the rear, wishful thinking had become a press release. It was on June 14 that I was ordered
to Biak. And certainly no American planes (except the Cubs we used

for observation) landed at Mokmer for a good many days after that.

How had the 41st Division taken the airfield? After the dash up the coast ended in near-disaster, the 186th Infantry had been sent around the back way. Behind the ridges these soldiers moved forward slowly on native trails. This was hard going and steep climbing. At night there was often enemy infiltration, and, next morning, severed communications. Then the 163rd Infantry came in from Wakde as reinforcements, and the 186th was able to drive painfully through to the field.

The inland route was difficult. The jungle at Biak was never as thick as it was at Buna or in the rain-forest at Tanahmerah Bay. But there were evergreen trees which grew as high as one hundred and eighty feet; there were long spidery vines which encompassed the trees like thick cobwebs in a dream, and there was high kunai grass in the open spaces. There was no water. Troops emplaced on the hills had to be supplied with both food and water, and human pack trains did the job. Back at Bosnek the artillery laid it on supposed enemy positions and lived a reasonably comfortable life in daylight. Their troubles started just about dusk when enemy planes began making passes at our rich supply dumps and continued throughout the dark watches. The pack-train lads lived miserable lives—day and night. As they struggled up the hills, Japanese soldiers fired from ambush or leaped out to engage them in hand-to-hand fighting. Men fought with pistols, knives, and fists.

The Japanese at Biak were trained and excellent troops. Captured records show there were nearly ten thousand troops on the island; not all of them in the beginning resisted our invasion. On the southern shore the combat troops belonged to the 22nd Infantry Division (veterans of the China campaign); there was also a detachment of Japanese marines—always bigger and taller and braver than any other enemy troops. The commander of the island defenses was a certain Colonel Kuzume. Documents reveal that in case of invasion he planned to use his service troops to reinforce the infantry, and he did. The Americans invaded with only two combat regiments. Ordinarily, considering the hazards of attack, a 3-to-1 advantage in troop

strength for the invaders is set up by the military textbooks as a fair and equal fight. The 41st Division had not, in my opinion, done badly.

On Saturday General Byers and I found an easier way to get up forward. We took a speedboat to the island of Owi, which lay some four miles off Bosnek. Before the Biak invasion there had been no advance plan to make an airfield on Owi. But when American troops had been unable to capture Mokmer drome, General Fuller, the original task force commander, began three days after D-day the construction of strips on the nearby coral island. The promptness and wisdom of this engineering enterprise saved the lives of a number of American pilots. The very next day after Byers and I were at Owi, a squadron of Lightning pursuit planes, buffeted by a tropical storm until they were out of gasoline, made a gratifying emergency landing there. Owi became a fine field. It was, however, thickly inhabited by the mites which spread scrub typhus, and they made carnival among our engineer troops.

On that Saturday Byers and I were flown from Owi over to Mokmer in Cub planes. As we came in (I believe we were the first to set down at Mokmer) the Japanese opened fire from a distance of two thousand yards. There were no hits then, and there were no hits later when a salvo celebrated our departure. It struck me there was little real danger, but I remembered with amusement General Krueger's farewell message to me at Hollandia: "Now, don't go and get yourself killed."

Byers and Doe and I were driven to the front, and we found we could get quite close. Nastier terrain could hardly have been found. Behind that first ridge there were not only caves and the raw upjutting coral cliffs, but also deep ravines and tangled jungle. A G-2 officer at Doe's command post had shown us maps which presumably established where the troops were located. Things looked a good deal different after we traveled a mile and a half forward.

The 162nd was attacking with two battalions, and a third battalion had been sent on a circuitous route which was expected to deliver them in the enemy's rear. They ended in the rear all right, but it was our rear—and not the enemy's. This managed to get everybody pretty well mixed up and resulted in a dangerous American-American exchange of fire.

A young lieutenant and I climbed a steep hill to an observation post where we had a good view of the battle. Several hundred yards away and running off at an angle was a ridge which the lieutenant said Colonel Archie Roosevelt (son of the late President Theodore Roosevelt) had captured that morning. Down below, so close I could have hit the nearest one with a pebble, were a number of our tanks— all buttoned up and firing. Suddenly it became unmistakably apparent that Colonel Roosevelt's ridge had reverted to original ownership. The Japanese were pouring it on our tanks with rifles and machine guns, while 90-mm mortar fire from someplace in the rear was landing around us. The Japanese fire was understandable, but we were a little surprised when the American tanks began blazing away at us. The answer? There were Japanese caves immediately beyond us and not more than seventy-five or a hundred yards from our small, dug-in perimeter. There was plenty of noise.

I sent for Byers and Doe in turn so they could examine the situation. Looking down, we now could see grenade-armed soldiers running in circles around the tanks. They were Japanese soldiers, and the tanks, roaring and clanking, began to pull out. We certainly had arrived on the battlefield—but this battlefield was a confused scramble. My own exit down the hill was precipitous. I came down the steep side holding to a tropical vine. The vine broke, and I fell twelve or fifteen feet. I landed on my first-aid kit, thus preventing injuries which would have made armchair sitting decidedly uncomfortable during later and less hazardous years.

I had seen enough. That night I gave orders that all fighting be called off the next day—a Sunday—and that the troops be reorganized. The major enemy defenses had been well designed to protect the airfield area from other than a long and costly assault. As yet we did not definitely know the locations of the major caves which hid the main enemy forces and some of their mortar and mountain batteries. The caves obviously had connecting corridors and exits which permitted the Japanese, literally, to disappear from the face of the earth, and to reappear at will in our midst.

I suspected that the Japanese were being reinforced from the other side of the island. (Later it was established that two battalions had been brought in despite the steadfast patrolling of our Navy and our Air. These reinforcements, however, were committed piecemeal by Kuzume, and never operated as an effective force.) I decided to move three American battalions well into the Japanese rear. After we had them closed in, we would fight it out for the cliffs and the caves and the airfields.

My plan called for giving the Japanese a dose of their own medicine. They had won face in the Orient by their successful operations against the British in Malaya. Repeatedly in their progress down the Malay peninsula, the Japanese had got in the rear of the British by the use of assault craft. It won them Singapore. I was to learn at Biak, and subsequently in the Philippines, that Japanese troops, just like Occidental troops, take a very dim and unhappy view of enemy forces in their own rear. It's disturbing.

My orders directed one battalion of the 163rd, which was well up on the distant plateau, to move until it could look down on the Japanese. The orders also directed offensive-minded Colonel O. P. Newman and his 186th to move around behind the enemy. General Doe argued strongly on that point; he said the 186th would be knee-mortared to death. Actually, on Monday, Newman's forces managed a major shift of positions without casualties. The 34th Infantry of the 24th Division came in from Hollandia that week end as further reinforcements and bivouacked along the coast road west of Mokmer drome.

This, in effect, is the message I sent back on Saturday to Sixth Army: "Having arrived here forty-eight hours ago in almost complete ignorance of the situation, I have spent two days at the front. Tomorrow (Sunday), I have called off all fighting and troops will be reorganized. On Monday I propose to put three battalions in the rear of the Japanese, and on Tuesday I propose to take the other two airfields."

It was a bold promise, but that is what we did. The 34th advanced to capture Sorido and Borokoe dromes almost without opposition. Our troubles, however, were just well started. We now had the airfields, but we still did not have the Japanese. Our encirclements were porous, and much of the bitterest fighting occurred from then on. One thing I insisted upon: constant reports on the positions of battalions and companies. All through the day and all through the night I wanted to know where they were. And because I wanted to know, I found out. There was a thin ax handle of a hill which was the highest observation point in the combat area. One company of ours had occupied it, and then, for reasons I never discovered, had moved out. By my command, the hill was immediately reoccupied, and it stayed occupied until the end of the engagement. There would be, if I could help it, no more battlefield scrambles.

My hunger for exact information on one occasion interfered with my lunch. On the day Sorido drome was captured—the Japs had not been able to complete that field before our invasion—I went there with a visitor, General Sverdrup, to determine the amount of construction necessary to put it in working order. Sverdrup, a veritable Samson of a man, was engineer operations officer at GHQ. Everything seemed quiet and peaceable in the Sorido area; at noon we pulled our jeeps to the side of the trail and Sergeants Dombrowski and Ventura produced some K rations.

Sverdrup and I had hardly got our teeth into food when trouble developed. Directly beneath us, in a shore-side cave, Japanese were discovered. Our troops tossed in hand grenades; the Japanese fielded them neatly and tossed them outside again, where they detonated. Dan Edwards, once my aide and now a G-3 officer, was disgusted with this perilous game of catch and suggested that he drop down in the cave and clear it out. I vetoed this suggestion at once; he had enough scars from Buna. Actually the small crisis was handled efficiently. First a phosphorus smoke grenade was lobbed into the cave and then the inevitable TNT. We finished our lunch in quiet.

On another, and more grave occasion, my hunger for information might well have cost Clovis Byers his life. Troops of the 163rd were up against it trying to capture an important enemy position which they called Lone Tree Hill. These men from Montana and Idaho had attempted repeatedly to take and hold the butte. I sent General Byers forward to get a firsthand picture of the situation. Troops at the 163rd's outpost were notified by telephone that he was coming by jeep, and all of us assume, in the light of later events, that Japanese wiretappers heard the message.

Even at the time Colonel Moroney, regimental commander, was uneasy. He had made the phone call forward in code, but he had a feeling someone had listened in. At the last moment he insisted Byers and his party shift, for their own protection, from a jeep to a weapons carrier. Byers proceeded to the forward command post with only one incident: the weapons carrier became mired in a low spot between two small hills. Wheels reversed, spun up a shower of mud, and, on a second fast try at the mudhole, wallowed through without too much difficulty. Byers arrived at the CP with no knowledge there was tragedy immediately behind him.

It was near the mudhole that the Japanese lay in ambush. They were not looking for a weapons carrier. They let it pass. They were looking for a jeep in which they supposed General Byers, Colonel McCreight, and Colonel Collins would be passengers. Not too long after, a jeep did come along. The soldiers in it were signalmen going forward to fix wires.

The Japanese blasted with all they had. Two men in the jeep were killed outright. Three others were badly wounded and the Japs immediately ran forward, bayoneted them, and left them for dead.

Captain Russell Stroup, a chaplain who is now a Presbyterian pastor at Lynchburg, Virginia, was the first to discover the bloody results of the ambush. He had been at the front and was on his way to the rear with the bodies of three American soldiers. He had a truck and three guards. As Stroup came over the brow of a hill he saw the wrecked jeep, and he saw one wounded man—the only survivor—raise himself from the ground and heard him shout, "Get the hell out of here!" The wounded man pointed. "The Japs are over there. A dozen of them. Get going, or they will kill you."

The truck stopped. While the three guards covered him, the unarmed chaplain dashed forward to bring in the wounded man. The wounded man protested. "Don't mind me," he said. "I'm done for. Save yourselves."

That American soldier was Private Earl E. Kueker. Captain Stroup hurried him back to the base hospital, but he died soon after reaching there. I know of no greater bravery and self-sacrifice than his. Alone, in danger and in pain, he had preferred—he had demanded—that his comrades save themselves rather than save him.

The Japs had not fired on the chaplain, but they were there all right. A combat patrol was summoned. At the ambush point the patrol fought it out with the enemy and killed eight of them. The rest fled.

After his fortuitous escape Byers went on to the front. As a result of his report on the combat situation we drew back our troops and put two days of artillery fire and air attack on Lone Tree Hill. In the beginning the hill had been dense jungle. When the artillery and Air finished, it was almost a desert. The Japanese, of course, had retreated into their caves, where the actual fire could not touch them. But in the end we found them to be so shocked by the ordeal that they ambled around like sleepwalkers, and, with a very few casualties, the 163rd was able to take the long-denied promontory.

I have no desire to engage myself in controversies with other sections of the Armed Services. In my various campaigns I found myself deeply in debt to the Navy, to the Air Forces, to the Marine Corps. But, just occasionally, it seems fair to put in a modest plug for the Army. It is difficult for me to believe that the terrain in any other Pacific island was tougher than that of Biak. Of course, I can't know. But I have a sneaking suspicion that our casualties at Biak were kept at a reasonable minimum because we were willing to shoot away tons of ammunition (undoubtedly at great cost to the American taxpayer) when a direct attack promised punishing casualties.

It was plain that Biak could not belong to us before we had captured the caves. The first riddle—no one had solved it before I Corps arrived—was to find the *main* caves. Where were they? Where were the entrances and exits? Aerial photographs were of no help in locating them. Our maps told us nothing.

Colonel Bill Bowen, my operations officer, and his assistants risked their lives on tours of exploration and discovery. For several days, in unarmed Cub planes, they flew repeatedly over the Japanese positions at low altitudes until they sighted and charted the entrances to

the enemy's unbelievable underworld. There were the East Caves directly above Mokmer Village, and there were the caves, farther down the coast, at the Ibdi Pocket. Both were as full of troops as a New Guinea Fuzzy-Wuzzy's unwashed head is full of nits.

Most important of all, however, were the West Caves. (We referred to these as The Sump.) Although we did not know it then, Colonel Kuzume had his headquarters there; it was the arterial center, the heart, of the Japanese defenses. As long as The Sump was occupied, the airstrips were neutralized. The enemy was adequately prepared for siege. The Japanese had plenty of supplies, plenty of ammunition. While our soldiers thirsted, their soldiers filled their canteens at underground brooks. In the adjoining chambers at The Sump there were electric lights provided by gasoline generators; there were wooden floors as insurance against the damp, and deep in the ground there were wooden houses for the comfort of the officer echelon. Ladders and passageways connected the chambers, and troops could be sent in many directions to meet attacks.

There were several frontal entrances to the West Caves. There was also the main sump itself. This was a pothole about eighty feet deep and a hundred feet across. Once it had been a cave, but the roof of earth had worn away and the great hole was open to daylight. Down at the bottom were the caverns which led off to the underground maze. There was another pothole in the immediate region which fascinated me. It was at least a hundred feet deep and so narrow that it had the appearance of a deep well. But a seed had fallen there and taken the principle of growth seriously. From the seed a tree had risen straight toward the sky, and leafy branches now rustled at least twenty feet above the mouth of the well.

The subjugation of the caves presented a problem new to all the commanding officers. It required improvisation, experiment, and trial-and-error tactics. On the Ibdi Caves, for instance, we tried skip-bombing by B-25s. Colonel Dick Ellis's gallant 3rd Attack Group carried out the mission. I'm told that one bomb found its way up a forty-five-degree entrance to a cavern and served its appointed purpose. We used P-40s and A-20s to bomb and strafe the Mokmer

Caves. But at The Sump it was a matter of hard, brutal fighting and persistence which won the engagement.

When the Japanese abandoned the airfields they still kept their troops in the ridge pillboxes which surrounded The Sump, and these pillboxes had to be reduced one by one. Eventually tank fire and mortar fire and grenades drove the Japanese out of the ridges and completely underground. Back up in the far hills Japanese reinforcements tried to get through from Korim Bay and were repulsed three times.

Flame-throwers were now used against The Sump but with only limited success. They could not penetrate far enough in the long, winding caverns to be effective. Also, striking internal walls, they often flashed back with resultant American casualties. We industriously searched out crevices and cracks which led underground and poured hundreds of barrels of gasoline in them. The gasoline was ignited. Eventually a series of dull explosions were heard—the burning gasoline had met up with the enemy's ammunition stores.

The next day infantry captured the lip of the main sump. Under the protection of machine-gun fire and tank-gun fire, engineers lowered an eight-hundred-and-fifty-pound charge of TNT into a cave entrance by means of a winch. The charge was exploded electrically.

Unknown to us, Colonel Kuzume had conceded defeat in the early morning hours of June 22. He assembled his officers around him and ordered all able-bodied soldiers to leave the caves and launch a final counterattack. He distributed hand grenades to the wounded so that they might destroy themselves. In an impressive ceremonial, he burned all documents and the regimental flag. Then, in the Samurai tradition, he knelt and disemboweled himself with his own warrior's sword.

Just at daybreak some of the survivors issued from the cave and launched a banzai attack. They met up with a rear unit of the 186th Infantry. None of the Americans panicked. There were only twelve soldiers on guard at the spot but they stood firm and fought as the screaming Japanese swept frenziedly down the trail. Machine guns, rifles, and grenades were used calmly and effectively—how effectively

the statistics make very clear. Morning light disclosed that one hundred and nine enemy soldiers had been killed. We lost one man; a Japanese leaped into his foxhole and exploded a grenade which killed them both.

It was in the early morning light that I came forward. I had with me in my jeep a visiting observer, Colonel Sam Sturgis, engineer officer of the Sixth Army. We passed over the ridge guarding Mokmer drome and drove along the accustomed trail toward the rear battalion of the 186th Infantry. Abruptly we found our road blocked: there were dead Japanese everywhere. When I say the road was blocked I mean it. When I stepped out the guardian troops were still at their guns. Then I heard the whole story. Eleven enemy officers had been killed by a sergeant with a .50-caliber machine gun. A dead Japanese still lay over the muzzle. In the final close-quarters struggle a redheaded private had killed another onrushing Jap with the butt of his rifle.

Something explodes inside of me, and pleasantly, when I meet up with gallant men. The job of these men was to protect the tent headquarters of their commander, Colonel Newman, and they had done so. I said I would decorate them before the end of the day—and I did. Two men would get the Silver Star and the others the Bronze Star. I hadn't seen the fight, and I suggested they decide among themselves who had honestly earned the Silver Stars. They were startled by my proposal, but it didn't take them long to make up their minds. The sergeant and his redhead partner got the Silver Stars. There cannot be much democracy in an army, but, in this case, the troops there—and not the rear echelon—decided where the ribbons should go.

The banzai attack, perhaps I should add here, has always struck me as military insanity. It is true that it sometimes worked against green and undisciplined troops. Coming home from Japan in 1948, I met on an Army transport a captain who had served in the Philippines. He described a screaming, yelling banzai attack somewhere in southwest Luzon. He said that his whole company had "taken off," and that he too had been tempted to flee. He hadn't. When the Japanese charge had run its course and the attackers had been killed, it turned out that there were just eight of them and only two were armed.

I never saw a banzai in all my Pacific experience, but I know it was never effective against well-trained and well-disciplined troops. Certainly, unless I am misinformed, there was no successful banzai attack against any of the forces under my command. However, it is important to say that the banzai attack may have had a mystical significance to the Japanese soldier himself. I am told it represented the supreme sacrifice of men who preferred to die fighting rather than to surrender or to hide themselves. But the banzai, militarily speaking, is a bust. It is noisy self-destruction and, from the American point of view, just a waste of courageous fighting men.

We didn't enter the Sump Caves for several days and continued to belabor them with explosives. But we knew we had won the fight there. When we did enter the caves on June 27 the stench of the dead was insupportable. Bullets, grenades, gasoline, TNT—each had done its work. It was hopeless in that almost unimaginable purgatory even to attempt an accurate count of bodies. They littered almost every square foot of ground. There were a few of the living still in the far recesses.

This is no place to examine the unfathomable mysteries of Japanese tactics. The near-invulnerability of the cave positions at Biak made our task most difficult and disagreeable. But the decision of Kuzume to stick to a set plan of battle made our victory inevitable. After the task force struck through inland to Mokmer drome, the Ibdi and Mokmer caves were isolated and had only nuisance value. Kuzume, instead of summoning the troops out of the pockets and opposing us with a strong united force, permitted us to reduce their positions piecemeal. I, of course, am glad he was of that mind.

Our mission accomplished, my orders now called for return of I Corps staff to Hollandia on June 28. Reports of that date show approximately twenty-eight hundred Japanese killed in action and thirteen taken prisoner; only one prisoner was a combat soldier. Not all caves had been reduced when I took my departure, and there were still many Japanese in the north of the island. But the victory had been won. There was little more organized resistance.

No one who fought the Battle of the Caves, I suspect, will ever forget the taste of the melted-coral water. Or the suspicion that melted Japanese were in the streams tapped for our canteens. I remember, on my own, going all the way out to a Dutch merchant vessel and climbing a rope ladder to beg a drink of San Francisco water from the ship's tanks. I got the drink of water, but I couldn't talk the skipper out of a five-gallon can of it to take ashore.

The water contamination at Biak was real; I suppose our chlorine tablets (add chlorine to the melted-coral taste and you have something almost unpotable) saved us all from sickness. The American authorities later removed the whole native population and returned them only when Army engineers, after exhaustive tests, took oath that Biak's shallow water table was once more free of pollution.

THE NEW EIGHTH ARMY

Shortly before our departure from Biak, General Spencer Akin, chief signal officer, GHQ, paid us an inspection visit. At dinner he passed on the news that the advance elements of a new army had arrived in the Southwest Pacific—the Eighth Army. I said, "Who is to command it?" (I had not heard from the Allied commander since the Hollandia invasion.) Akin smiled and said, "Don't you know?" After dinner Akin told me that radiograms had been going back and forth between Australia and the United States and that General MacArthur had chosen me for the job. It was some weeks, however, before this information was officially confirmed.

On Thursday, June 29, I took off from Mokmer drome for Hollandia, accompanied by Byers and Brigadier General Horace Harding, artillery officer for I Corps. Our pilot was Brigadier General David W. Hutchison of the 308th Bomb Wing, who was known as Photo Hutch to distinguish him from Fighter Hutch. (To make things more confusing in the Pacific, there was also an Engineer Hutch—General Hutchings.) We were all exhilarated by the quickness of the victory at Biak and happy to be returning to Hollandia so soon. It was a pleasant trip until we ran into a storm off Tanahmerah Bay which tossed the little Beechcraft (C-45) around as if it were a feather; but we landed at Cyclops drome without difficulty.

After a light lunch at I Corps headquarters I learned that General

155

Krueger was returning by air from a visit to Wakde. There was a boat landing near the airfields at Nefaar Village, and I decided to take my thirty-eight-foot cabin cruiser and meet the Sixth Army commander there. Naturally, I was full of the Biak story and anxious to make an informal, verbal report. Perhaps, being all too human, I expected some words of commendation on the successful termina-. tion of the mission he had given me.

General Krueger was at Nefaar. When I got off the boat and saluted him, he said only, "I didn't know you were back." During the half-hour cruise down Lake Sentani to my headquarters I sat beside my superior officer. During all that time he addressed only one remark to me. As we passed a native canoe which had been rigged with a picturesque sail, General Krueger asked me what it was. I said the sail was made of palm fronds which had been raised to catch the wind.

There was a jeep waiting for General Krueger when we reached the I Corps dock. As he left the boat he turned and said, "Congratulations on the fine work you did." A moment later he went into a tirade against General Fuller (who had asked to be relieved at Biak, despite my own earnest endeavors to persuade him to change his mind). Then Krueger inquired if I would recommend Jens Doe to succeed Fuller as commander of the 41st Division. Both Fuller and I had previously suggested the tough, fighting Doe for some division command. I said that I would recommend Doe for command of the 41st Division without any qualifications whatever.

I invited General Krueger to come up to my house. He said he did not have time. As he got into his jeep I said, "Whenever you want to talk to me I will be glad to come down to your headquarters and report on the Biak operation."

"I shall be too busy to talk to you," General Krueger said and departed in a cloud of dust.

The Army teaches men to be philosophical. I took General Krueger at his word and stayed away. But I was puzzled and confused. The next day I got a little light on the situation. Brigadier General Bob Shoe, acting chief of staff of Eighth Army, came to see me. He and several other officers of the advance echelon had flown to Hol-

landia by way of Brisbane. In Brisbane, General MacArthur told
Shoe (as Akin had told me) that I was to command the new army.
I asked Shoe whether he had passed this news on to General Krueger, and he said that he had. Now, for the first time, I began to
understand the strange and silent trip across the lake, the curtness of
my reception after a desperate but successful battle assignment.

I did not learn the whole story, however, until several months
later, when General MacArthur informed me that Krueger, as head
of Sixth Army, had steadfastly opposed the creation of another Army
headquarters in the Pacific. He made no objection, General Mac-
Arthur reported, to the selection of me as commander of Eighth
Army. It was Eighth Army itself to which he objected. My own
position, of course, was just that of the man in the middle.

Perhaps the lay reader should be warned that when military men
speak about First Army or Third Army in Europe, or Sixth Army or
Eighth Army in the Pacific, they are not necessarily referring to the
troops who fight the battles. They may be referring to the organiza-
tional setup. An Army in war is like a big corporation in the world
of business. An Army has its planning staff, its administrative staff,
its bookkeeping staff, its legal department, its police officers, its signalmen, its engineers, even its chaplains. All are trained for the job.
All are members of the Army headquarters.

Bob Shoe told me that Eighth Army headquarters was already on
the water headed for Hollandia. It then consisted of five hundred
officers and twelve hundred enlisted men, and it was coming to me,
ready-made and intact, all the way from Memphis, Tennessee.
There, commanded in turn by Generals Ben Lear and Lloyd Freden-
dall, it had been called Second Army and had functioned as a unit
for several years. The main elements of the headquarters were at that
moment aboard the big Army transport *General Pope*, which was
scheduled to dock at Hollandia in about three weeks' time.

It was plain that preparations must be made to house these troops.
Eventually General Krueger and I discussed the matter and he
agreed to let me go ahead with a construction job despite the fact
that my command had not yet been confirmed. The Philippines
campaign was in the offing, and I knew that I Corps was scheduled

to make the landing at Sarangani Bay in southern Mindanao; indeed, my staff was already doing its planning. That meant the Corps' stay at Hollandia would be brief. I found a new location for my long-time companions and then worked on the enlargement of our old I Corps camp to make it suitable for an Army staff and attached troops.

The beauty of that campsite will never grow dim in my memory. We were on the shore at the east end of Lake Sentani. Above us and to our right rose the towering Cyclops Mountains, seven thousand feet high and splendid at dawn and at sunset. The calm blue water of Lake Sentani was our lovely front yard. I have never been accused of being a poet, but there were clear blue mornings when I felt like one.

For generations—long before the Dutch or the Japanese or the Americans came—tribal life in that section had centered around the lake. It provided fish for food and peaceful water for travel. Lake Sentani was only twenty miles long, but who wanted to go farther? On the thin peninsulas which pushed into the water there were native villages with houses on stilts. And, when the sun came up, the mirror-like lake was busy with long native canoes, propelled by paddles stroked in unison. Many of the tribesmen were working for us on construction jobs, and they took off from our dock (like idyllic commuters) when the day was done. The prevailing wind was from east to west, and men of the great fleet of native canoes would lift palm-frond sails to puff them home. Then the sun would go down swiftly over Lake Sentani with one sail still caught in the last ember of its fire.

The natives liked the new Times Square activity on the lake. They had seen Japanese landing craft, but they chattered excitedly over the sleek cabin cruisers which we transported overland from the harbor by eight-wheel Air Corps trailers. I wonder what they think about now? Life must be more dull. In those days cabin cruisers cut through the waves, seaplanes dipped down from the clouds and landed smoothly on the water, and each day had a new surprise. The 24th Division was still setting roadblocks in the jungle and capturing straggling Japanese troops from the southwest who tried

to by-pass the area. Occasionally the natives themselves would en-
trap some poor starving devil in their taro patches, truss him up like
a chicken, and transport him by canoe to our prison compounds.

The first reaction of the experts after the invasion had been that
Hollandia was nothing but a mudhole and impracticable as a base.
Our quick engineering job, both in the making of airfields and the
making of roads, changed their minds. By midsummer the Hollandia
area was full of troops and full of Army, Air, and Navy headquarters.
During this period I was a very busy man, but I did have the opportunity, particularly in the early days, to observe how poorly the
infantry usually seems to fare in the matter of obtaining physical
comforts when contrasted with other more specialized services. The
Air Forces and the Navy had transport over water. I am blaming no
one; it is only natural for a service to look after its own. I merely
comment on the contrast.

After the infantrymen captured the airfields they slogged on into
the jungle and wilderness. My engineers rebuilt the strips, and the
Air Force took possession. They arrived with their wire screens and
their iceboxes. George Kenney, as early as Buna, had demanded and
won permission to fly in fresh vegetables for his pilots and ground
crews. Fresh vegetables were delivered to Air Forces personnel at
Hollandia from Australia. Carrier planes known as "fat cats" brought
in perishables from a civilized continent that was far behind us.

In the vicinity of Hollandia Town on Humboldt Bay we had laid
aside a section for the Navy. Seabees—a Navy engineering group—
landed and constructed a beautiful village there and an excellent pattern of roads. Modified Quonset houses were thrown together, and
when the electric refrigerators were installed and the time was right,
the Senior Admiral Ashore took tenantry.

But what about the infantry? Because of the original necessity for
speed—a necessity which has always seemed odd to me since there
was a year for the planning—the decision was made before embark-
ing on the Hollandia invasion to leave barracks bags behind. They
were to be brought up by what is described politely in wartime lingo
as "ships of the rear echelon"; those are the ships you *hope* will get
there soon. The barracks bags did not arrive forward for six weeks.

As a result, for his first six weeks at Hollandia the infantryman was forced to live in his jungle uniform and to get along with the single pair of shoes in which he had landed. Food was C ration. The GIs did not complain about that; but the swamp rotted their shoes, and there were no shoe replacements. Everyone concerned with the Hollandia operation prospered except the combat troops who had made the quick victory possible. Air Forces personnel were ferried to Australia for rehabilitation, but we couldn't spare the infantrymen. It was never convenient for them to have a leave of absence. Anyway, there was no place for them to go.

The transport *General Pope,* which carried my headquarters staff, poked its nose into Humboldt Bay late in the month of August. Thanks to the feverish activities of Colonel Dave Dunne and others, there were roofs to shelter the personnel. Some people have given me the credit for this quick construction. Actually the credit belongs to Dunne, engineer officer of Eighth Army, and his efficient chum, Colonel John R. Jannarone. And to the strong-backed boys who lifted the stringers. It is true that I rallied around every day to praise or decry, but they did the job, and inventively. When something was short in supply, they managed with makeshift. It turned out, makeshift or not, to be an excellent camp.

Finally came the morning when I assembled the headquarters troops for the first time. I think I burdened them with a speech, but it was well meant. Actually, they impressed me more than my oratory could have impressed them. In civil life or the Army, I had never seen a finer group of men, and I knew, for a certainty, that we were going places.

This seems a proper time to call the roll. Colonel A. E. Schanze was G-1, Colonel G. A. A. Jones, G-2, and Colonel H. C. Burgess, G-4. After a spirited wrestle with GHQ I brought with me from my previous command General Byers as chief of staff and Colonel Bowen as G-3. (They were to be promoted respectively to major general and brigadier general somewhat later.) When the firsthand experience in jungle fighting of Byers and Bowen—and I had been there too—augmented the know-how of the expertly trained technicians from Memphis, I felt that Eighth Army was well heeled. I never changed my mind. I have not mentioned one of the strongest members of the team, Colonel Art Thayer. Arthur Thayer was assistant chief of staff and a man of invaluable talent and energy. I know that Clovis Byers joins me in this encomium. From Hollandia to Yokohama, we profited by Art Thayer's sound and sensible advice.

During July and August the American advance continued along the coast of eastern New Guinea in preparation for the Philippines campaign. On July 2 the 158th RCT under General MacNider landed on the island of Noemfoor, not too far from Biak in Geelvink Bay, and was reinforced by the 503rd Parachute Regiment. Possession of the airfield at Noemfoor gave needed breadth and depth to air deployment, permitting further penetration and dislocation of enemy supply lines.

Later the 6th Division, under Major General Franklin C. Sibert, son of the General Sibert I had known earlier in Panama, made several landings on Vogelkop, the peninsula at the far eastern extremity of New Guinea. These landings were at Cape Opmarai, Amsterdam, Middelburg Island, and Sansapor. The latter became division headquarters, and my good friend General Ed Patrick, who had been General Sibert's chief of staff, succeeded to command of the 6th when Sibert was given a corps.

I visited Ed Patrick at Sansapor on several inspection trips. I remember one occasion when he showed me the scene of his own narrow escape from death. He was asleep on a cot in the far end of a native hut when a Jap bomb landed. Roof, walls, scant furniture, everything but the cot on which he slept was fragment-pierced. He escaped injury. But on another day gallant Ed Patrick was not so lucky. He was killed in action by a machine-gun burst in northern Luzon some months later.

In July the Americans down at Aitape came in for rough handling. I have described the comparatively easy capture of the airdrome there in April. Subsequently, the 32nd Division, under Bill Gill, moved inland. The purpose of the move was to prevent Japanese

troops under General Adachi from making their way out of the now isolated stronghold at Wewak and by-passing Aitape from the landward side.

The 32nd's beachhead extended inland to the Torricelli Mountains. The main line of resistance, however, was established along a natural barrier made by the Driniumor River, seventeen miles from Aitape. Adachi probed cautiously, seeking a way to get around the Americans, and found none. So, on July 10, he threw the Japanese Eighteenth Army against a narrow segment of the 32nd's lines and forced a crossing of the river. It was a breakthrough. What had been a campaign of uneventful patrolling now turned into a full-scale battle. Before it was finished the 127th and 128th Infantry of the 32nd, the 112th Cavalry RCT, the 124th Infantry of the 31st Division, and elements of the 169th Infantry of the 43rd Division were engaged.

General Gill pulled his men back two miles, reorganized, launched a counterattack. The Americans pocketed three Japanese regiments and reached the west bank of the river. For three weeks Adachi sent battalion after battalion across the shallow Driniumor in an effort to rescue his pocketed forces but never again managed (in the face of torrents of machine-gun fire) to establish himself on the other side. Meantime, the Americans methodically destroyed the three regiments of Japanese which had been cut off.

I visited this battlefield when Aitape came under Eighth Army command, and General Gill told me the whole story. The XI Corps directed operations, but Gill was the field commander. After Adachi had been repulsed in frontal assault, he attempted an end run into the Torricelli Mountains. Gill's force at the right end of the Driniumor Line held the position against Adachi's last assault, which took place at a point called Afua. Meanwhile, Gill sent a force across the Driniumor which circled into the rear of the attackers.

Cub planes—the same Cub planes which would have been so valuable to the 32nd at Buna and Sanananda—directed the movement of this force by flying directly over troops. Nine days were necessary to move ten miles in the dense jungle. When the Japs failed to break through at Afua and began to retreat, they found four battalions of the encircling force directly across their path. Few of the Japanese

survived. Those who did, pursued by artillery fire, retreated toward Wewak. Seven of Adachi's nine regiments were cut to pieces. There are reports that Adachi lost ninety-three hundred men, but these reports of enemy casualties probably are exaggerated.

Anyway, it was a famous, if insufficiently reported, battle, and it was a tough and unexpected campaign. Sometimes I wonder what would have happened if Sixth Army had been content at Aitape with the coastline and the airfields and had not gone inland to seek out the enemy. Would the Japanese have attacked at Hollandia? Would they have reached Toem-Sarmi? Or would they—hopeless, disciplined wretches—simply have starved to death along those uncharted back trails in mountains and jungles?

Originally there had been eighteen thousand Japanese in the Vogelkop peninsula alone. Because of the magnificent efforts of our Navy and Air Forces, their sources of supply had been cut off. With Sansapor captured, even the menace of Japanese Air almost disappeared from the New Guinea area. General Marshall in his official report has written:

"In a little over twelve months American forces in the Southwest Pacific, with the assistance of Australian forces, had pushed thirteen hundred miles closer to the heart of the Japanese Empire, cutting off more than one hundred and thirty-five thousand enemy troops beyond hope of rescue. The operations had been performed under adverse weather conditions and over formidable terrain, which lacked roads in almost every area occupied, and made troop movements and supply extraordinarily difficult. Malaria was a serious hazard, but with suppressive treatment and rigid mosquito control, it was no longer a serious limitation to tactical operations."

In late August I was formally relieved as commander of I Corps and was succeeded by Major General Innis P. Swift. There was a real emotional wrench when I went to corps headquarters and bade good-by to the officers who had been with me so long and who had served so efficiently and so well. I was leaving old and loyal friends. We had been through a lot together.

The clans were gathering at Hollandia, a sure sign always that a major campaign is ahead. Army engineers constructed a fine head-

quarters in scenic country for General MacArthur's staff, and one by one the high-ranking officers of GHQ began to arrive by air from Brisbane to take up residence. The Hollandia airfields were now like Grand Central Station, and my camp was an intermediate stop on the way to the coast camps on Humboldt Bay. Generals, civilian dignitaries, and correspondents moved through like letters in a mail drop; most of them stopped for a chat or a conference. General William F. Marquat came, and General Pat Casey of the Engineers, and Dick Sutherland and Steve Chamberlin and Jack Sverdrup. In retrospect, the two biggest men I knew in the Army, Sverdrup and Colonel Roger Egeburg, seem to me like Viking twins. Egeburg was a Cleveland doctor; like Sverdrup, he was a man of inexhaustible energy. He too chose to walk over the mountains to Buna in the early days. I do not believe Egeburg ever understood the smaller vitality of lesser men. He arrived at Buna in good temper and presented me with a Japanese knife he had taken in a hand-to-hand fight. He put no store by the knife; his adversary in the struggle had been, by his standards, too puny. I carried the knife for many months.

The Seventh Fleet under Admiral Kincaid—the fleet assigned to General MacArthur—had once been the orphan of the Pacific, but the number of fighting ships steadily swelled in Humboldt Bay. Ground Forces, Air Forces, and the Navy now had the pleasant experience of feeling their own fat. After two years it was a pleasant experience not to feel their own lean.

The Eighth Army was officially born September 9, 1944, and outgrew swaddling clothes with great rapidity. It was to have an adventurous life if not a merry one. Four months elapsed before major amphibious operations were undertaken, but the Eighth almost immediately assumed command of two hundred thousand troops dispersed between Morotai Island and Australia and began preparing itself for the Big Show. The Big Show was the Philippines campaign and, ultimately, the occupation of Japan.

LEYTE CAMPAIGN

Few non-military people know the invasion of the Philippines almost didn't happen. In July of 1944 a message from General Marshall in Washington summoned General MacArthur to a conference at Pearl Harbor. When the latter inquired about the identity of the conferees and their purpose, he was told that no further information was available. Not until he arrived in Hawaii did he know the reason for his mysterious mission. President Roosevelt was there, and so were many high-ranking naval officers.

It seemed evident to General MacArthur, as the conference proceeded, that the President had been won over irrevocably to a strategical plan which would by-pass the Philippines. The Navy wanted to leapfrog the islands, attack Formosa, and seek air bases on the Chinese mainland for the final drive on Tokyo. Admiral King had already departed, but Admiral Nimitz presented his case. Now the President called on General MacArthur for comment.

Because of his ignorance of the purpose of the conference, the Southwest Pacific commander had brought no documentation with him, but he bespoke the military argument for the Philippines with eloquence. Then, in a ten-minute private interview with the President, he presented another argument. The United States had moral commitments which should be carried out. Was Mr. Roosevelt, he asked, willing to accept responsibility for breaking a solemn promise

165

to eighteen million Christian Filipinos that the Americans would return?

The interview over, General MacArthur bowed and started to leave. He felt sure his was a lost cause. The President stirred.

"Wait a minute, Douglas," he said. "Come back here."

And the Philippines invasion was on again.

The President's decision was one of paramount importance, both to the war and the men fighting it. I am convinced (with, to be sure, the advantage of hindsight) that landings on Formosa and the Chinese mainland without the clearing of the Philippines and Borneo would have been almost disastrously costly. Japanese planes would have attacked both from China and the scores of nearby airfields and made our positions untenable.

Before the invasion of Leyte and after, Army and Navy planes indefatigably, day after day, week after week, plastered the Japanese air bases in the Philippines. Yet as late as the American landing on the island of Mindoro—almost two months after the original invasion—Jap Air was still strong enough to keep Mindoro harbor clear of our shipping. If the enemy could do that with our Army planes already cozily based on Leyte, it gives any reasoning man a shudder to envision what might have happened at Formosa with the sinister network of Japanese airfields and bases intact.

There was still another reason for capture of the Philippines. If we were to undertake an armed invasion of Japan—and all planning, necessarily, in 1944 looked forward to that objective—we needed the deep-water harbors, the great bases, and the excellent training areas available in those islands, which, in the main, had a friendly and loyal population. We had no knowledge of the atomic bomb; indeed, it was not until almost a year later that the first atomic bomb was exploded experimentally in New Mexico. Up until then even the scientists weren't sure it would work.

I have heard the story of the Pearl Harbor conference from several persons who were present, including General MacArthur himself. He told me about his experience when he visited Hollandia on his way aboard a cruiser to observe the landing at Morotai, the northernmost of the island steppingstones deemed strategically essential to the Philippines operation. Morotai was taken without much difficulty.

Now preparations went into high gear. At that time, as many people know, we had the firm intention of striking in force at Mindanao, the southernmost island of the Philippines. It was the nearest point of contact, and the second largest island of the group. Sarangani Bay had shelter for all except the largest of warships, and there were guerrillas there who professed to have knowledge of Japanese strength and who promised they would push against Japanese garrisons from the rear.

Circumstances altered the plan. On September 9 and 10 Admiral Mitscher's carrier planes hit Sarangani Bay and reported that the Fifth Air Force had already so flattened enemy installations that only a few Jap planes rose to intercept. Then Admiral Halsey's carrier planes struck the central Philippines from a position within sight of the mountains of Samar. They flew twelve hundred sorties on one day and twelve hundred sorties on the next.

Opposition was so weak that Admiral Halsey took a bold step. It was a courageous decision because it threw a monkey wrench into the long-time planning of both Army and Navy. Halsey recommended that the central Philippines be attacked as soon as possible. The Mindanao invasion had been planned for November 15. Halsey, in his message to Admiral Nimitz, his superior, suggested that General MacArthur hit Leyte, the mid-rib of the Philippines, well ahead of that date. It just happened that the Joint Chiefs of Staff were meeting at Quebec to consider, principally, European matters. Here is General Marshall's report on the Halsey recommendation:

"The Joint Chiefs of Staff received a copy of a communication from Admiral Halsey to Admiral Nimitz on 13 September. He recommended that three projected intermediate operations against Yap, Mindanao, and Talaud and Sangihe Islands to the southward be canceled, and that our forces attack Leyte in the central Philippines as soon as possible.

"The same day Admiral Nimitz offered to place Vice Admiral Theodore S. Wilkinson and the 3rd Amphibious Force which included the XXIV Army Corps, then loading in Hawaii for the Yap operation, at General MacArthur's disposal for an attack on Leyte.

"General MacArthur's views were requested, and two days later he advised us that he was already prepared to land on Leyte 20 October, instead of 20 December as previously intended. It was a remarkable administrative achievement.

"The message from MacArthur arrived at Quebec at night, and Admiral Leahy, Admiral King, General Arnold, and I were being entertained at a formal dinner by Canadian officers. It was read by appropriate staff officers who suggested an immediate affirmative answer. The message, with their recommendations, was rushed to us, and we left the table for a conference. Having the utmost confidence in General MacArthur, Admiral Nimitz, and Admiral Halsey, it was not a difficult decision to make.

"Within ninety minutes after the signal had been received in Quebec, General MacArthur and Admiral Nimitz had received their instructions to execute the Leyte operation on the target date 20 October, abandoning the three previously approved intermediary landings.

"General MacArthur's acknowledgment of his new instructions reached me while en route from the dinner to my quarters in Quebec."

Both Army and Navy did themselves proud in quick preparations for the new enterprise. On October 19 an immense armada approached Leyte. In the covering naval forces were the battleships *California, Mississippi, Maryland, Pennsylvania, Tennessee,* and *West Virginia* with a screen of cruisers and destroyers. There were two assault forces: Admiral Wilkinson's and Admiral Barbey's.

The land forces were under the Sixth Army, and two divisions of Sibert's X Corps were the first to hit the Leyte beaches: the 24th Division, which had done such an excellent job at Tanahmerah Bay, and 1st Cavalry, which had made the best of a difficult situation in the Admiralties. In support they had 53 assault transports, 54 assault cargo ships, 151 landing ships (tanks), 72 landing craft (infantry), 16 rocket ships, and 400 other amphibious craft. Air cover was furnished by 18 Navy escort carriers.

A day or so later General John R. Hodge's XXIV Corps, shipped from the Central Pacific, landed just above Dulag. This consisted, then, of the 7th Division under Major General A. V. Arnold and the 96th Division under Major General James L. Bradley. After meeting moderate resistance on the coast, the American troops proceeded inland.

Leyte was to be a long and stubborn campaign, but after a few days the progress of the Ground Forces became less important, from a world viewpoint, than events upon the sea. A climactic naval engagement began. It was the Battle of Leyte Gulf, one of the decisive battles of the war. A single Japanese search plane had sighted the great American amphibious force and reported its presence to Admiral Kurita's Singapore fleet. Approximately sixty per cent of Japan's naval units were under Kurita's command. For a period of many months our Navy had endeavored to entice Kurita into combat. He would not be enticed. With great good sense, he had harbored his carriers and battlewagons.

But now the warlords in Japan made their decision to commit the fleet in a final gamble to prevent America's return to the Philippines. I shall not repeat here the story of the Battle of Leyte Gulf. Admiral King described it in his official report, and Admiral Halsey, who was in command, has given a detailed report of that complex engagement in his own book. The Americans gambled also, and at one time the progress of a section of the Japanese fleet through the San Bernardino Strait threatened the whole security of the Leyte landing forces. But in the end it was a glorious victory. By October 26 it was evident that Third and Seventh Fleets had virtually eliminated Japan as a sea power.

Field Marshal Count Hsaichi Terauchi, with headquarters in Manila, was Japanese commander of most of the conquered areas— New Guinea, the Netherlands Indies, Borneo, Thailand, French Indo-China—and for a considerable time he had watched his empire shrink. He had no intention of giving up the Philippines. Terauchi, a jingoist, had been Minister of War, and he had commanded the forces which in 1937 assailed China. In 1943 he assumed command of all southern armies, with headquarters in Singapore, and, a few months later, transferred his headquarters to the pleasant

environs of Manila. At one time Terauchi commanded seventeen Japanese armies and more than nine hundred thousand men.

The naval defeat added greatly to Terauchi's difficulties in transporting troops from one island to another. It did not reduce his stubbornness and determination. He intended to fight, and he decided he would do a lot of his fighting in the rice paddies and mountains of Leyte. He relieved Lieutenant General Shigenori Kuroda, and put General Tomoyuki Yamashita in charge. This was the same Yamashita who had conquered Singapore and who had taken over the Philippines early in the war when General Homma could not capture Bataan. For his victories Yamashita had been given the First Area Army in Manchuria, one of the most important Japanese field commands.

When Yamashita took over from Kuroda, he sent this message to General Makina, head of the Japanese 16th Division on Leyte: "The Army has received the following order from His Majesty, the Emperor: 'Enemy ground forces will be destroyed.'"

The American XXIV Corps captured Dagami and Berauen in the center of the island; X Corps moved across the narrow San Juanico Strait to take the south coast of the adjoining island of Samar and, after a brief voyage by water, landed on the north coast of Leyte. Now the fighting became more difficult.

The 32nd Division, the 11th Airborne, and the 77th Division came in to reinforce the troops already engaged in a bitter campaign. Despite the efforts of General Kenney's land-based fighters and Admiral Halsey's carrier planes, the Japanese continued to land formidable reinforcements. One of the outfits which came in was the Japanese 1st Division, a crack aggregation from the Kwantung Army. This made it obvious that Yamashita was committing his finest troops. The 1st Division had been in China when Sixth Army's expedition against Leyte was discovered; it had been speeded by transport from Shanghai to Manila and then on to Leyte.

Back in Hollandia, I was shaking down the new Eighth Army and awaiting the summons to Leyte which was part of GHQ's plan. Shortly before this the Air Forces had provided me with my own Flying Fortress. The crew was headed up by Major Chuck Downer, who was to remain my personal pilot until the end of the war and after. I named the plane *Miss Em* for my wife. The *Miss Em,* a hardy traveler, was to put down on many far-flung airstrips during the coming months, for I made it a rule to keep in close personal contact with even my most advanced outposts.

I cannot estimate how far I traveled in that B-17, but there was rarely a week when Downer and I did not clock off thousands of miles of travel. From Hollandia I made regular trips of inspection, to Aitape and Wakde and Noemfoor and Sansapor, and back to Buna, Finschhafen and Cape Gloucester. The constant two-way flow of GHQ officers between Hollandia and Leyte kept me pretty well informed on the fighting forward. Generals Sutherland, Chamberlin, Frink, and others often shared a meal or an evening with me. I saw General Kenney and Admirals Barbey and Wilkinson frequently. I knew that progress at Leyte was much slower than had been anticipated in the beginning.

American troops controlled the coastline on three sides of Leyte, but the fighting constantly increased in intensity. In some places no forward progress was made in many days. Japanese reinforcements continued to pour in. By November 5 American troops had proceeded overland to the vicinity of Limon, at the northern end of the valley road leading to Ormoc, the principal Japanese installation on the island. Jap Air was extremely active. On November 3 three Jap transports unloaded at Ormoc. On November 7 three large transports and four small transports landed. On November 9 ten destroyers and two heavy cruisers brought in four more large Japanese Army transports. On November 11 another convoy headed into Ormoc Bay. Kenney's planes made inroads on all these expeditions, but the Japanese accomplished landings anyway. The chips were really down, and the fighting was for keeps.

General MacArthur's plan had anticipated a quick conquest of Leyte and then a reasonably early assault on Luzon with the assistance of Halsey's great fleet. Eighth Army was to take over from Sixth Army, finish the job on Leyte, and then hold itself available for a conquest of the southern Philippines.

On November 15 I received news of the death of Frank Prist, the handsome young Acme photographer I had known since he shared quarters with Barney Darnton and Bob Sherrod in the early days of the Australian period. Frank Prist had been at Buna and Hollandia. Prist was killed in the Ormoc area where Colonel Red Newman, another close friend, was wounded at about the same time.

Exactly a month after the original Leyte invasion the advance members of my staff and I left Hollandia, headed for our future headquarters. We stopped at Noemfoor to visit General MacNider and took off again at two-forty-five A.M. Flying steadily through the darkness, we came down in the early dawn—by error—on the island of Angaur, where the 81st Division under Major General P. J. Mueller had experienced severe combat. This was only a short distance from Peleliu, where we expected to take on gasoline. We flew on to Peleliu, had breakfast there, and were shown over gaunt, desolated battlefields by troops of the 1st Marine Division. The Japanese still held caves on one side of the island.

I learned later that Admiral Halsey had opposed a Navy amphibious strike against the group of tiny islands known as the Western Carolines. They included Angaur, Peleliu, Babelthuaup, the island of Yap, two hundred and eighty miles northeast, and Ulithi atoll, one hundred and twenty miles beyond Yap. Halsey believed Ulithi was a useful anchorage, but he was convinced the others were not worth much of a price in casualties, and that there was a strong possibility the price—as at Tarawa—might be excessive. Halsey was overruled. By mid-September the strike had been made.

It seemed to me that November morning, as I toured the ravaged landscape, that there was little at Peleliu worth fighting for. There were evidences everywhere which told experienced military men how savage the battle had been. I had a personal interest. Brigadier General Julian C. Smith, a long-time friend, had been the Marine commander ashore.

To me Peleliu seemed like a dot in the ocean. I was used to more varied terrain. The hills of Peleliu were two abrupt chalk ranges about two hundred feet high which looked down on flat coral. The hills were thoroughly fortified; they were full of caves and dugouts of concrete and steel, and had been garrisoned by ten thousand excellent Japanese troops. There was no protection or concealment for an invading force. To be sure, the battleships had set up a terrific bombardment—I examined one hole made in concrete by a sixteen-inch shell from the old *Mississippi* which must have killed every Jap in the dugout. But bombardment in such terrain is relatively ineffective.

A rugged struggle but a quick decision had been predicted before the Peleliu landing. Actually, it was not until several days after I passed through that the senior Japanese commander burned his colors. To defeat the enemy there, the gallant fighting men of the 1st Marine Division suffered these losses: 1121 killed in action, 73 missing in action, 5142 wounded in action. It is interesting that in April of 1947, long after the end of the war, twenty-seven Japanese, apparently well fed, came out of their caves at Peleliu and formally surrendered to an astonished American garrison officer.

Just before lunchtime that same day my party landed in Leyte. When Chuck Downer eased the *Miss Em* down on the airstrip at Tacloban there was hardly a bump, and I marveled at the engineering skill and courage of the American Army engineers who had built that runway between persistent Jap bombing and strafing raids. General Irving and other old companions were at the field to meet me. In earlier discussions it had been agreed that Eighth Army headquarters would be constructed at Telegrafo, about twenty miles down the coast from Tacloban. Immediately after lunch I crawled into a jeep and asked to be driven there.

The rainy season had already begun on Leyte, and my first visit to Telegrafo was mostly disenchantment. My jeep bogged down in mire. The only construction in evidence was a dugout for protection against air raids—and I never did use that. In brief, Telegrafo was a swamp and a mudhole and nothing more. Nevertheless, we moved in that day. Shacks were erected, boards provided foothold in the soft mud, and in the evening we went to bed amidst a cloud of insects. Next morning, however, Dave Dunne and his lads began the rude preparations for a miracle; first of all, they cut a drainage ditch six feet deep squarely through the center of the camp. In the end, what with drainage, DDT, and gardening, the

eyesore at Telegrafo became the finest camp (or at least I thought so) along the Leyte east coast.

The next day was eventful. I went by boat to Tacloban early, and participated in a long General Staff conference about the taking over of the Leyte show. Just after lunch I had an interview with President Osmeña of the Philippines, and there was an earthquake —seismological variety—while I was in his office. Then I spent an hour or so with General MacArthur. It was at this meeting that General MacArthur first proposed that I undertake a daring expedition against Manila with a small mobile force. I shall discuss this operation—called Mike-6 in code—more fully later. It is significant that General MacArthur, whose knowledge of Civil War tactics and Civil War personalities is almost as encyclopedic as that of the eminent Dr. Douglas S. Freeman of Richmond, described the venture as one that "would have delighted Jeb Stuart."

In the meantime, he filled me in on his general plan. Sixth Army, as soon as it could dispose of the Leyte campaign, was scheduled to make a massive invasion of Luzon at the top of Lingayen Gulf. The Japanese had come in through the Lingayen valley at the start of the war, and we would too. For the original landing Sixth Army would not utilize troops then fighting in Leyte. My old I Corps (now Swift's) and Griswold's XIV Corps would do the job.

Yamashita, the rainy season, and evil terrain made Leyte hard going for the military calendar-keepers. When GHQ set December 7 as the date when command would be taken over by Eighth Army, General Krueger came to see me. He expressed, with considerable eloquence, his concern at handing me what the younger members of my staff might have called a "hot potato." Certainly, the results at that time were indecisive. And the opposition was rugged: the experience of the 24th Division offers convincing evidence. A combat force of the 24th, then and later excellent fighters, landed November 7 at Carigara Bay on the north coast of Leyte. The force struck south from Pinamapoan and ran into the 1st Japanese Division at a circle of hills ideal for defense. This position became known as Breakneck Ridge. After several weeks of fighting the ably commanded 24th had got only two or three miles inland. Later the

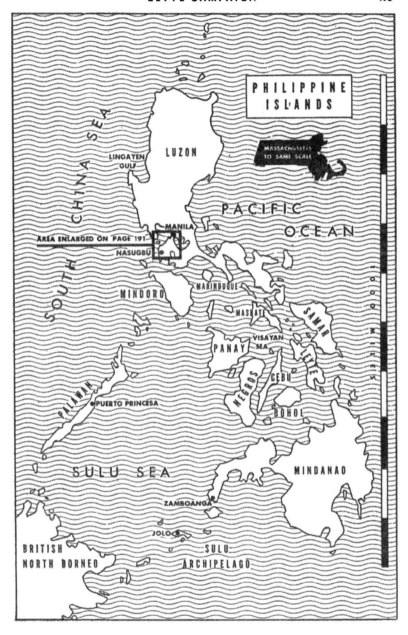

32nd Division took over the same positions and found forward movement equally slow.

In the end, GHQ set a later target date for the Lingayen Gulf assault and asked General Krueger to finish his Leyte campaign by December 25. By this time the 32nd Division was pressing south, the 1st Cavalry was attacking Jap positions in the neighborhood of Breakneck Ridge from the flank, the 7th Division had cut through the narrow waist of Leyte and was trudging up the coast of the Camotes Sea toward Ormoc.

Now the 77th Division—the talented group I had helped to organize back in South Carolina—was summoned into action. These troops called themselves the "Old Buzzards"; as I have said, they were family men from Brooklyn, Manhattan, and Jersey City, and, unique among combat soldiers, their average age at induction was thirty-two. Under Major General A. D. Bruce they made a furious amphibious assault just south of Ormoc on December 7. Three days later, after weathering intense air attack and beating down fanatic opposition, they entered the town. Casualties were severe. The 77th now penetrated inland and on December 21 achieved contact with elements of X Corps sweeping down from the northeast.

One of the most rigorous battles was fought at Cogon, north of Ormoc, where the 77th made a four-day assault. Most of the enemy were in covered foxholes, and some of the foxholes had armored lids. Colonel Max Myers, who wrote the 77th's story, reports that American soldiers there called artillery air bursts to within twenty-five yards of their own front lines to beat back Japanese charges. He also reports brilliant improvisation on one occasion, with an armored bulldozer. As the blade of the bulldozer uncovered foxholes, Captain James F. Carruth of the 302nd Engineer Battalion leaned from his cab and blasted the occupants.

In late November I attended an important conference which was concerned with planning for the landing on Mindoro Island. Mindoro lies immediately south of Luzon, and possession of it was vital to the success of any Luzon operation. It was at this meeting that General Kenney admitted to General MacArthur (despite previous bold promises) that his Leyte-based planes would not be able to protect an amphibious landing if the day were overcast. This came as somewhat of a surprise to those who earlier had heard General Kenney argue that Admiral Halsey's carrier-based planes were no longer necessary to the Leyte operation.

Surprises are a commonplace of war—and reconsidered opinions too. As a result of Kenney's testimony, General MacArthur urged Admiral Kincaid of the Seventh Fleet (under MacArthur command) to wheel his old battleships and baby flattops through the narrows to cover the invasion. Kincaid objected violently. He pointed out that to get to Mindoro his fleet must pass through Surigao Strait and the Sulu Sea, where the vessels would be clay pigeons for Jap land-based planes. In the end, of course, Kincaid accepted the assignment, and Seventh Fleet did its usual fine job.

There were repeated Jap air raids during this heated conference. The finer points of the discussion were frequently blurred—to me, at least—by the persistent roar of American ack-ack. I was interested and somewhat entertained by the fact that General MacArthur chose to ignore the air raids. Since the Supreme Commander was deaf to the violence around him, the rest of us maintained the elaborate pretense that we couldn't hear any bombs falling either.

Rain and raids were now everyday occurrences. There was little in the way of recreation even for troops not immediately in the line. Tacloban, capital of Leyte, had a population of about thirteen thousand and was the only town of any size or modernity on the island. Few combat troops got there, and it wasn't very exciting for them when they did. So, in camps and headquarters along the coast, privates and generals alike often sat gladly in a pouring rain to watch an outdoor movie. There was a recognized technique for a rainy night; you adjusted your poncho around yourself and your chair and put a helmet liner on your head so the water wouldn't drain down in your eyes. Thus, with vision clear, you were a proper and appreciative audience for the artistry of Gloria Gumm in *Passion's Darling*.

The Americans had developed a device which protected the movie screen and the movie projector so they could not be seen from aloft. This, of course, was a precaution against raids. One night

when General Byers and I and innumerable soldiers sat contentedly
in the moist darkness, a covey of our planes came in all lighted up
from some strike. It was an old story to us. Our planes always came
in lighted because the pattern of light made their identity clear.

That evening an ingenious enemy pilot made capital of the custom. All of us saw one straggler plane come in belatedly, circle
over us a number of times, and ease out of the spiral at two hundred
feet. Then—boom, boom—we heard a series of explosions, and the
lone plane was quickly away. Tenuan Airstrip, a few miles up the
coast, had been bombed without a round of American ack-ack being
fired. It was a bad bombing too. The enterprising Japanese had got
on the tail of our homeward-bound ships, and, all lights burning,
had unscathedly followed them in.

A quite different sort of an air raid was the one which threw a
surprise into the 11th Airborne. This was a parachute drop. The 11th
Airborne, trained and designed for just such operations itself, was
on the receiving end. The division arrived in Leyte just two days
before I did. It was sent up into the mountains near Berauen to relieve the 7th Division and shared with the 96th Division the task
of pushing through Leyte's central mountain range. The object was
to cut the Japanese fighting force in half. Jungle warfare was extremely irksome to these soldiers who had had modern specialized
training which was not then utilized. They were trained to the
hazardous parachute landing, to the quick advance. And then they
found themselves in wet country where not even artillery could be
advanced. Called airborne, they were only infantry, and, indeed,
their supply was a combination of the new and the old. Cub planes
brought in urgent supplies; other supplies came in by the ancient
animals of Philippine transport—carabao.

Major General Joe Swing set up his 11th Airborne headquarters
not too far away from mine, and I saw him frequently. My diary of
December 6 simply says: "Raids again." But Joe Swing had a different story, and I heard it next day. Swing had eaten his supper
and, looking for a breath of cool air, was sitting outside his tent in
his underwear. It was dusk. Indifferently he watched a flight of

Japanese bombers flying high over three nearby airstrips. Then two flights of Japanese transport planes came in slowly at seven hundred and fifty feet. Japanese parachutes began to swell and float in the Leyte evening. It was an all-out attack on our strips and Swing's headquarters. Several miles away were the 44th General Hospital and the Signal Center which controlled Fifth Air Force communications throughout the Philippines.

The 11th Airborne never had a more confusing night. The attack was, of course, a complete surprise, but the confusion of our troops was hardly a patch on the confusion of the Japanese; in the growing darkness it was hard to tell friend from foe. Anticipating this, the enemy had devised a system of identification for assembly on the ground which included bells, horns, whistles, and even distinctive songs for each small unit. This was ingenious but not too effective. Many of the Japanese were killed before they could take up fighting positions.

We know now that the parachute drop was part of a coordinated plan of attack which involved the Japanese 26th Division and the remnants of the Japanese 16th Division. Some four hundred and fifty paratroopers were airlifted from southern Luzon. They were supposedly crack troops, and they were provided with bottles of liquor to sharpen their morale. Labels on the bottles gave the firm instruction that the contents were *not* to be drunk until the planes were in the air.

Many men were killed on both sides during that bedlam night. Flames leaped high in the sky as the Japanese burned American planes and supply dumps. The attack was upon the headquarters, and two artillery battalions and an engineer battalion functioned as infantry that night. In other sections of the dark battlefield cooks and clerks were the fighting men. Eventually dawn came. Some three hundred Japanese were killed the next day, and the remainder were hunted out in surrounding areas and killed over a period of three days. The enemy attack failed completely. Only a part of one regiment of the Japanese 26th Division ever reached the concentration area—and too late.

This long after I think of the Japanese parachute attack as a near thing. It had no military importance, but, with better luck, it might have had.

There is a memento of this struggle now at the Military Academy at West Point. Joe Swing gave it to me, and I sent it on from the Pacific. During the fighting on an airstrip two ducking and dodging American GIs—Allen W. Osborne and Eustis A. Jolly—were hand-carrying ammunition to the troops under fire. They noticed a large Japanese flag fluttering in a tree and, being incorrigible souvenir hunters, decided to acquire it. Each time they attempted to shinny up the tree they were met by a fusillade of Japanese bullets. So they changed tactics. They got an ax from their truck and, still under fire, chopped down the tree. That hard-won Japanese flag now hangs in the West Point museum.

How can you explain youngsters like that? Despite the calamity howlers they continue to exist. Whatever challenge the future holds, I think America can meet it.

THE DASH FOR MANILA

Eighth Army took over Leyte on Christmas Day. There were eight divisions fighting there when I assumed command. When the 32nd Division and 1st Cavalry broke through on a narrow front, GHQ described the Leyte campaign as officially closed and future operations as "mopping up."

Actually the Japanese Army was still intact. I was told that there were only six thousand Japanese left on the island. This estimate was in serious error, as subsequent events proved. Soon Japanese began streaming across the Ormoc valley from eastern into western Leyte, well equipped and apparently well fed. It took several months of the roughest kind of combat to defeat this army. Between Christmas Day and the end of the campaign we killed more than twenty-seven thousand Japanese.

Many others, evacuated safely by *bancas* (small boats), reappeared to fight Eighth Army on other islands in later campaigns. I called these singularly alive veteran troops the Ghosts of Leyte. It should also be noted that after the atomic bomb fell and Japanese troops surrendered en masse on many islands, there were almost none left to surrender on Leyte. As I recall, only four Jap soldiers presented themselves.

I am a great admirer of General MacArthur as a military strategist; his plans were always fundamentally sound. But I must admit

that, after serving under him for over six years, I never understood the public relations policy that either he or his immediate assistants established. It seemed to me, as it did to many of the commanders and correspondents, ill advised to announce victories when a first phase had been accomplished without too many casualties.

Too often, as at Buna and Sanananda, as on Leyte, Mindanao, and Luzon, the struggle was to go on for a long time. Often these announcements produced bitterness among combat troops, and with considerable cause. The phrase "mopping up" had no particular appeal for a haggard, muddy sergeant of the Americal Division whose platoon had just been wiped out in western Leyte. Or for the sweating, bearded, stone-dusty GIs of 1st Cavalry and the 37th Division as they engaged in building-to-building, and sometimes room-to-room, fighting around the Walled City weeks after the announcement that Manila had been secured. Or to the historian of 11th Airborne who wrote:

"Through mud and rain, over treacherous, rain-swollen gorges, through thick jungle growth, over slippery, narrow, root-tangled, steep foot trails, the Angels (as they called themselves) pushed west to clear the Leyte mountain range of its tenacious defenders. It was bitter, exhausting, rugged fighting—physically, the most terrible we were ever to know."

The combat infantryman, in this last war, deserved the best and usually fared the poorest in the matter of sugar plums, luxuries, and mail from home. The rear echelons fared the best. The home folks in America were vastly generous, but transport to the front could not always carry out their good intentions. Ammunition and rations came first. This the GI could understand. But after the unutterable boredom and danger and discomfort of fighting at the front, he expected kudos when he was relieved. It was disconcerting to find out he had only been "mopping up." Was that why his outfit had taken its casualties?

If there is another war, I recommend that the military, and the correspondents, and everyone else concerned, drop the phrase "mopping up" from their vocabularies. It is not a good enough phrase to die for.

In addition to the direction of fighting on Leyte and Samar, the
Eighth Army now had multitudinous jobs in housekeeping. The
XXIV Corps belonged to the Central Pacific Command and had
been loaned (under the complicated protocol of the time) to General MacArthur by Admiral Nimitz. There was a time limit on the
loan and the commitment was firm. The XXIV Corps had to be
withdrawn from my command in time to be re-equipped and sent
into Okinawa on the date set by the Navy and the Combined Chiefs
of Staff.

Eighth Army, of course, staged the departure of the XXIV Corps,
just as it staged the departure of many units of the Sixth Army for
the Luzon operation. The re-equipping of General Hodge's troops
was something of a revelation to the veterans of the old Southwest
Pacific Area. Our troops unloaded the cargo vessels that came in
from the Central Pacific, and, as the stores were brought ashore on
the beaches of eastern Leyte, all of us marveled. We had never seen
such wonderful gear!

But what astonished the old jungle fighters more was the fact
that the Central Pacific Command meant what it said by re-equipment. Re-equipment meant *everything* new for those three divisions.
Every soldier received a completely new outfit from his helmet to his
shoes. He had, whether he needed them or not, new underwear,
new pistols, new guns. His outfit had new jeeps and trailers, new
machine guns and mortars and tanks, and even brand-new .105
howitzers. I joked with Johnny Hodge about this purse-proud
wealth and told him that most of the divisions I had served with
would be glad to accept his "old clothes."

As a matter of fact, we did. Equipment turned in by the XXIV
Corps was stockpiled and the serviceable items were later issued to
various Eighth Army units. In the Southwest Pacific Area we were
never able to re-equip a division completely. Even in the case of
the 24th Division, which had fought two hard campaigns and was
even then being prepared for a further campaign in Mindanao, the
best we could do was to replace equipment and clothing which
were worn out.

Also, when the 81st (Wild Cat) Division came into Leyte from

the fighting on Angaur, the mouths of a good many regimental commanders watered. The 81st, which formerly had been under Halsey in the South Pacific, had the latest type of mechanical equipment and it was all brand-new. Seeing is believing, and my eyes told me that General MacArthur had been fully justified in his frequent and repeated complaints that the SWPA was at the tag end of the American supply line.

Sometime in January I attended a conference at General MacArthur's headquarters at Tacloban where all the principal Army and Navy commanders were gathered. General MacArthur introduced Admiral Nimitz, who had flown in from Pearl Harbor and who had an important announcement to make. Pointer in hand, his handsome white hair smoothly brushed, Nimitz turned to the large maps of the Pacific which hung on the wall. The Great Fleet, he told us, was now driving into the shore-bound China Sea to destroy Japanese shipping. From this rich region came the oil, rubber, rice necessary to Japan's survival. The announcement brought applause.

After long miles and weary months of The Hard Way Back, all of us had the heartening news that Japan's stolen marine empire had been broken asunder. During the next weeks the Great Fleet roamed at will from Hong Kong to Indo-China, pounding away at shore facilities and shipping. It destroyed almost everything in the way of war vessels which Admiral Kurita had been able to salvage from the disaster of Leyte Gulf.

Despite this triumph, however, there were grave days ahead for the American Navy, tragic days. The expedition against Okinawa witnessed the deadly, full-blown kamikaze campaign against our fleets. These Japanese suicide planes struck more than two hundred and sixty American ships. Our loss of life and shipping was appalling. I have always believed that the kamikaze campaign provided final factual evidence on the strategic wisdom of not by-passing the Philippines. If we had not destroyed airfields, bases, and planes in the Philippines, the impact of the kamikaze campaign probably would have been too great for the Navy to withstand.

Admiral Nimitz, the day after the historic conference at Tacloban, came down to Telegrafo to lunch with me, and he was only the first of a procession of interesting men who managed to pay a visit. As at Hollandia, everybody passed through—correspondents, newspaper editors from the States, former Secretary of War Pat Hurley, supply officers with Pentagon pallor, guerrilla commanders from many of the islands, theatrical people from the USO groups. Lieutenant General Simon B. Buckner, who commanded Tenth Army's expedition against Okinawa, and who was killed there by a Japanese shell almost as victory was at hand, had his last dinner ashore in the Philippines with me.

Later I took Uncle Joe Stilwell, who ultimately succeeded Buckner, on an aerial tour of Eighth Army's combat areas. I had known the colorful Stilwell for many years, and he was pleased by the idea of covering a lot of island territory in my B-17. One night, after watching front-line fighting, we slept in the same tent under a palm tree. Before we drifted off to sleep, disturbed only by the usual night sounds—the dropping of coconuts, the scuttling of land crabs, and an occasional burst of fire—Stilwell took out after Chiang Kai-shek and others he believed had thwarted his mission in China. Uncle Joe, reclining on his cot, used some of the choice rhetoric which had made him famous in the Army—and thus I had an interesting preview of a controversial book which was published as *The Stilwell Papers*.

The withdrawal of the XXIV Corps complicated my job at Leyte. This meant the loss of the 7th, 96th, and 77th Divisions. Now the Americal Division came in. The Americal was unique. It was the only division in the United States Army which had a name and not a number. It had been assembled and dispatched to the South Pacific at the start of the war to garrison the Free French island of New Caledonia. The division name was a simple elision: Americal —Americans in New Caledonia. The Americal had taken over from the Marines at Guadalcanal and hung up a good record for itself. They had also fought well in Bougainville.

I had hoped to save the Americal and rest it for a later campaign in the central Philippines, but now I sent it into the line. The division had had a distinguished series of commanders since its formation, and at this point was led by Major General William H. Arnold.

"Duke" Arnold then was the youngest division commander in the Pacific. He and his men accepted their unexpected assignment and carried a great part of the burden of the final clearing of Leyte. They took fourteen hundred casualties before going on to the invasion of Cebu.

From the broad viewpoint, it had become evident already that Japanese control of the Philippines was cracking. They had lost control of the sea, they were losing the duel in the air, and Marshal Terauchi had fled with his headquarters to the more secure environs of Saigon, Indo-China.

As the year 1945 was ushered in—with, I might add, a minimum of joy and jollity on the combat fronts—a new American assault force was assembled at sea east of Leyte. It moved through the Surigao Strait and into the Mindanao and Sulu Seas and then swung north to pass through the very heart of the Philippine Archipelago. Two years before, the Japanese Navy and Air Force had maintained unquestioned control of those land-surrounded waters. Sixth Army with air cover and fleet protection was on its way to Lingayen Gulf, which had always been considered Luzon's point of greatest vulnerability.

On January 9, I Corps and XIV Corps hit the beaches. General Marshall has written: "Japanese forces on the island, harassed by guerrillas and by air, drove north, south, east, and west in confusion, became tangled in traffic jams on the roads, and generally dissipated what chance they might have had to repel the landing force. . . . By nightfall 68,000 troops were ashore and in control of a 15-mile beachhead, 6000 yards deep."

These divisions made the landing: the 37th, the so-called "Ohio Division" under my friend Major General Robert S. Beightler; the 40th, under Major General Rapp Brush; the 6th under Ed Patrick; and the 43rd under that excellent Vermont National Guard commander, Major General Leonard F. Wing. The 13th Armored Group, the 158th RCT, and the 6th Ranger Battalion went ashore two days later. The 25th Division, under Major General C. L. Mullins, was held in reserve at sea.

Because I was not on the scene and have no firsthand knowledge

of that phase of Sixth Army's campaign, I shall resort again to General Marshall's terse report, as Chief of Staff, to the Secretary of War:

"The landing had caught every major hostile combat unit in motion with the exception of the 23rd Infantry Division to the southeast of the beachhead in the central Luzon plain and its supporting 58th Independent Mixed Brigade twenty-five miles to the north of Lingayen Gulf. Yamashita's inability to cope with General MacArthur's swift moves, his desired reaction to the deception measures, the guerrillas, and General Kenney's aircraft combined to place the Japanese in an impossible situation.

"The enemy was forced into a piecemeal commitment of his troops. The Japanese 10th and 105th Divisions in the Manila area which were to secure Highway No. 5 on the eastern edge of the Luzon plain failed to arrive in time. The brunt of defending this withdrawal road to the north fell to the 2nd Japanese Armored Division, which seemingly should have been defending the road to Clark Field.

"General MacArthur had deployed a strong portion of his assault force in his left or eastern flank to provide protection for the beachhead against the strong Japanese forces to the north and east.

"In appreciation of the enemy's predicament the Sixth Army immediately launched its advance toward Manila across the bend of the Agno, which presumably should have been a strongly held Japanese defense line.

"The troops met with little resistance until they approached Clark Field. The I Corps, commanded by Major General Innis P. Swift, had heavy fighting on the east flank, where the Japanese were strongly entrenched in hill positions. For the time being they were to be held there to keep the supply line for the advance on Manila secure."

During the period of the Leyte take-over, Eighth Army staff had also been planning for two post-Lingayen landings of our own on Luzon. On January 29 the XI Corps, commanded by Lieutenant General "Chink" Hall, went ashore on the west coast of Luzon just above Subic Bay. Troops involved were the 38th Division reinforced and the 34th Infantry RCT. Hall's mission was to seize Olongapo and open Subic Bay to American shipping, to cut off Japanese on

the Bataan peninsula where the Americans had made their stand three years before, and to press forward speedily to make junction with Sixth Army forces moving ponderously down the rich central valley. Hall did his job efficiently and with speed; on the second day our Navy minesweepers were already preparing Subic Bay to receive transports and Army supplies. On February 5 contact was made with Griswold's XIV Corps. Meantime, by orders of GHQ, operational control of Hall's troops passed over to Sixth Army.

Now the stage was set for what I regard as one of the most thrilling exploits of the Pacific War—the 11th Airborne's dash for Manila. This included an airdrop on Tagaytay Ridge.

I have reported that General MacArthur told me late in November that I was to command a landing in southern Luzon. At worst this would be a diversionary attack which would cut Japanese communications and pin down a sizable number of the island's defenders; at best, it might be a decisive maneuver in the Luzon campaign and hasten the capture of Manila.

My staff prepared a plan which called for the use of three divisions. In the end, because of shortage of water transport and unavailablity of combat troops, I made the landing with 11th Airborne alone—reinforced by a few service supply units. No one could have asked for finer fighting men. Elements of the 24th Division later took over the rear area.

There were times in January when it appeared that the expedition would be abandoned. A young captain from a parachute regiment had been smuggled ashore by submarine; he returned from guerrilla headquarters near Nasugbu, a port in southern Luzon, with dire reports of the situation. He said there were two thousand Japanese around Nasugbu, twelve thousand back of those with heavy artillery and tanks, and fifteen thousand on Tagaytay Ridge. If these reports were true, they negated the chances for a successful expedition, since a hazardous advance up a narrow defile between high mountains was contemplated.

I did not believe the reports. Still, in war, you never know, and GHQ was entirely justified in taking a gloomy view of the enterprise. This solution was worked out. The expedition would be considered a reconnaissance in force. If the original landing troops ran into serious difficulties I would order their withdrawal, and the Navy would remain to take them off. The Air Forces were also worried. Our plan called for land advance to Tagaytay Ridge, overlooking beautiful Lake Taal, and reinforcement there by the airdrop of the 511th Regimental Combat Team, which consisted of three parachute battalions and an artillery battalion. These paratroopers were already at fields on the adjoining island of Mindoro, but they were not to be given airlift until I was satisfied with the land advance—and personally gave the order.

In other words, it was up to me to decide whether to hit or run; and also whether to advance on Manila. At dawn on January 31 I was aboard the command ship *Spencer* with General Swing and Admiral Fechteler. Visibility was excellent, and from deck we could see both the white beaches of Nasugbu and the green mountains of Luzon. Destroyers and rocket-firing LCIs pounded the shore for an hour, and on the landing craft, to quote the graphic phrase of a service reporter, "stomach butterflies nervously flapped their wings."

Then the landing craft went in, and the troops waded ashore in shallow water. There was sporadic machine-gun fire and some artillery fire. But it was quickly evident the Japanese intended to follow their usual pattern—little defense at the beachhead and tough defense at prepared positions in the hills. By nine-forty-five that morning the town of Nasugbu and the important airstrip were in our hands.

The 11th Airborne troops must have dragged their feet as they passed through the town on their way to the hills. Nasugbu was almost untouched by war, and it was the only town of any consequence they had seen in the Pacific. There was a tremendous welcome; Filipinos lined the streets and gave away such precious and hoarded food stocks as eggs, chickens, bananas, papayas. There was a village square and a bandstand, and a lot of cheering and chatter. But 11th Airborne moved on and reached a huge, sprawling sugar *central* about six miles to the east. The Japanese had intended to destroy this combined industrial plant and warehouse, and a seven-man demolition squad was assigned to the job. A stray destroyer

shell discouraged them, and they retired without setting off their explosives.

At the *central* the Americans found a Lilliputian railroad. It had narrow tracks and cars about the size of a living-room sofa, and it had been used, in peacetime, to transport sugar to the coast. The tiny locomotives burned alcohol, and we captured six thousand gallons to fuel them. The miniature railroad was immediately put to work hauling supplies and soldiers inland.

Three hours after the initial landing I decided, because of the limited resistance, that we would hit and not run, and ordered the floating reserve put ashore. Indeed, so speedy was the advance inland that the Navy had to chase the Army to turn over command. General Swing remembers that in the afternoon he espied a very dusty jeep approaching his command post near the Palico River bridge. A very dusty Admiral Fechteler was the passenger.

"Thank God I've caught you, Joe," said the Admiral. "Thought I might have to chase you all the way to Manila. I'm tired of playing hare-and-hounds in a jeep. Please take over and let me get back to my ships."

Palico River bridge, eight miles from the coast, was one of the reasons for our speed. If this steel-trussed span were destroyed, forward progress would be seriously impeded. Our engineers didn't have the equipment to replace it, and by-passing would be difficult because the Palico River—like most of the rivers of Luzon—flows through a deep, steep-sided canyon.

The bridge was mined, but our advance was so swift that the unwarned Japanese guards were caught on the far side of the river. They attempted to get to their detonator, but our devastating fire from the west bank forced them to withdraw, leaving their dead and wounded. The bridge was saved.

My orders to General Swing called for advance all day and advance throughout the night. Enemy troops were confused and retreating, and a halt at dark would have permitted them to reorganize. So by the light of a tropical full moon the Americans shoved on. Beyond Tumalin the road began to climb more steeply and to cut through the hills. These narrow defiles, with precipitous wooded banks on

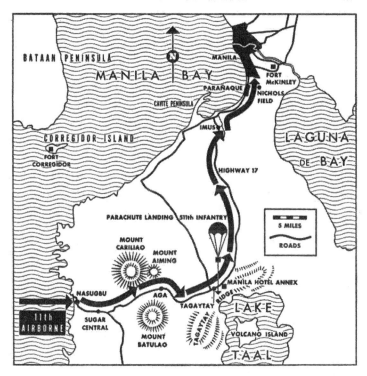

either side, were natural troop traps which the Japanese could have
—and would have—defended if we had not achieved surprise. All
bridges over river gorges were intact.

That night I went back to the *Spencer.* It was not a restful night
because there were a number of attacks by explosive-laden Japanese
suicide crash boats. Just after daylight, a little worn, I went on deck
and watched a curious cat-and-dog encounter between an American
destroyer and a suicide boat. The destroyer was trying to sink the
Jap craft with five-inch guns and pursued it assiduously. Whenever
the enemy wheeled and made a direct run at the destroyer, the destroyer zigzagged and took to its heels. In the gay morning sun it

seemed like a crazy version of you-chase-me and I'll-chase-you. But it wasn't a children's game, even though the fluffy white clouds and the clean blue sea were like the illustrations in children's books. After about fifty rounds of firing, a shell from the destroyer found its target. The boat did not sink: it disintegrated.

Highway No. 17 is a two-lane road which leads all the way from Nasugbu to Manila. The roadbed is rough and rocky as far as Tagaytay, but it is durable and it is dry. The 11th Airborne (they now called themselves the "Mud Rats of Leyte") found the terrain to their liking. Dust was better than mud. After Leyte's moist heat they welcomed the distinct chill of Luzon's upland nights.

I went ashore early on the second day and motored to the front. I found the troops fighting at the picturesque Cariliao-Aiming-Batulao defile. Here the highway passes between three mountain peaks— Mount Cariliao, Mount Batulao, and Mount Aiming, and the Japanese had prepared this ideal defensive terrain for their first determined stand. The battle had begun in the moonlight, and was being waged hotly at midday. The highway was bracketed by enemy artillery fire. There were dugouts and caves in and between the three wooded mountains, and they were interconnected by trenches. There were deep tank traps across the road; our adversaries did not realize how quickly bulldozers could fill the excavations.

The 11th Airborne was living up to its reputation. The troops stood up unflinchingly under artillery fire and performed flawlessly. In twenty-eight hours ashore they had advanced nineteen miles on foot. All combat equipment had been unloaded, a port and an airstrip had been established. I was satisfied that the dash on Manila should be undertaken and, after a conference with General Swing, personally gave the order for the parachute drop on Tagaytay Ridge. I set it for February 3, two days away.

The Battle of the Peaks was to continue through February 2 and 3. This engagement was of vital importance to the monumental bluff we were running against the Japanese. Our vehicles went roaring up and down the road, raising never-ending clouds of dust. By the generous use of what artillery we had, by our heavy and confident assaults, by repeated strikes from the air, we gave the enemy the impression that a force of army proportions—complete with an armored division —was invading southern Luzon. This impression was not lessened by the fact that American radio announced the news that the "Eighth Army" had landed there.

We numbered, even when four more battalions later joined us by air, only about seventy-eight hundred men. Actually the task force was a small light division, understrength and even undermanned. There had been no replacements for our Leyte losses. But if we were to capitalize on our bluff we had to crack the line in front of us. Otherwise the confused Nipponese would come back out of the hills, cut our supply route, and isolate us.

Air support at this time—it was to dry up when we were engaged in even heavier fighting at the outskirts of Manila—was expert and heartening. A-20s of the 3rd Attack Group were coming over low and dropping parachute bombs just ahead of our soldiers. P-38s were blasting enemy positions near the village of Aga. I remember an unidentified and mysterious civilian, wearing a handsome monogrammed silk shirt, who warned me he had recently visited Aga and that there were thirty thousand troops there. I asked him, somewhat acidly, if he recommended I retreat. My answer was a blank look. It should be remembered that at this time I had four small battalions—and one of them was at the rear guarding the base at Nasugbu.

Late in the afternoon Aga was ours, and I inspected the ruins. I was the first man to enter the abandoned quarters of Colonel Kobayashi Shimaji, commander of the 31st Infantry. I found there the regiment's battle flag, and it was only when I had the flag in my hand that it occurred to me I had violated the instruction endlessly hammered home to my troops: "Never enter an enemy installation without proper precautions; it may be booby-trapped." The good Lord gave me a raincheck that time.

On the morning of the 3rd there was a coordinated attack on the last enemy mountain position which had survived our assaults. Forty-five minutes later the parachutes of the 511th Parachute blossomed in the clean sunlight of Tagaytay Ridge. The Air Forces could spare only forty-eight C-47s for this vital project, so the planes ferried back and forth from Mindoro that day for three separate drops.

Artillery for the paratroopers was dropped the following morning. All these parachute landings were made without battle casualties.

Nevertheless fighting on the slopes was furious until midafternoon. There was a time at the front when four generals were pinned down by Japanese fire—General Swing and I and two of his brigadiers. Not long after, Colonel Rinaldo Coe, my efficient headquarters commandant, was killed by shell fragments, and Colonel Robert Soule, of the 188th Glider Infantry, was wounded. Shortly Soule was up with the advance guard of his regiment. He analyzed the situation and directed the attack. He crawled back under Japanese fire toward his radio transmitter and was then shot. Finding the transmitter damaged, he crawled to his jeep and gave instructions over the jeep radio to his executive officer to lead the attack. Then he went to an exposed position for better observation and, by walkie-talkie, directed the attack.

I watched a doctor dig the slug out of Soule and fill the hole with iodine. Then I saw Soule take off through the high, coarse grass to cheer on his troops to the conquest of Tagaytay Ridge. They made it. They renamed the spur they fought over "Shorty Ridge." I recommended Soule for promotion to brigadier general and for the DSC.

Tagaytay Ridge was by all odds the most important military position in southern Luzon. It was twenty-four hundred feet high and a concrete road led downhill. We were ready for the dash on Manila. Thousands of Japanese remained in the hills around us, but they were so demoralized they did not attempt aggressive action for many days. I pressed forward with the infantry, and my headquarters was set up in what had once been the annex of the Manila Hotel. It was a bare and looted building, but the view was just the way I remembered it. And just as beautiful.

I could see the city of Manila gleaming whitely in the sunshine. I could see Corregidor, and the hook of the Cavite peninsula, which curves into Manila Bay. In another direction I could see Balayan and Batangas Bays on the sea, and, inland, Lake Taal in the crater of an extinct volcano and the shimmer of Laguna de Bay. It was strangely like a homecoming. But soon tall plumes of smoke began to rise in Manila, and at evening the tropical sky was crimsoned by many fires.

The Japanese were deliberately destroying the magical town which had been traditionally called "the Pearl of the Orient."

Swing pushed troops forward that night in preparation for the advance the next day. His reconnaissance platoon reported at four A.M. that the road was secure as far as the village of Imus, where the Japs had blown up the bridge and set up a defense line. The platoon had discovered a dirt road through Imus which by-passed the bridge and returned eventually to the main highway. Bridge or no bridge, our soldiers would be able to cross the Imus River single file on the ledge of a narrow dam.

Two regiments were squeezed into trucks and sent down the road at daylight on the 4th. Other troops followed on foot. There was trouble at Imus, and I got into it. But before that, I had important news. From the day we landed at Nasugbu I had been trying unsuccessfully to get information about the advance of the Sixth Army toward Manila from the north. On the morning of the 4th I received a brief radio communication that the 1st Cavalry Division had reached Grace Park in north Manila the afternoon before. Until then I had not known that any American troops were south of Clark Field and had assumed that the 1st Cavalry was still at Lingayen Gulf.

The 1st Cavalry was to enter Manila with little opposition. The 11th Airborne was to run into desperate opposition, which resulted in a severe casualty list. The reasons now are clear. The Japanese, before the Lingayen invasion, had believed that a major thrust was coming from the south. As a result, twelve thousand five hundred of the sixteen thousand Japanese marines guarding Manila were entrenched in a protected corridor in the area of Nichols Field and Fort William McKinley. The Japanese called this narrow southern network the Genko Line. I have always thought that the American civilian prisoners released from Santo Tomas by the 1st Cavalry owe a hitherto unacknowledged debt to the blood and bravery of the 11th Airborne Division.

The trouble at Imus started near the destroyed bridge. Our by-pass carried us directly around an old wall-enclosed Spanish barracks. Japanese marines were firmly ensconced there, and we were held up for some time. The barracks walls were five feet thick, and the Japs

had all avenues of approach covered with mortar and machine-gun fire. Colonel Bowen and I arrived there about midday and were forced to leave our jeep and shelter ourselves against the outside wall to avoid being hit by flying bullets. Some of our self-propelled guns were already in action, however, and pretty soon we were able to get by. A tech sergeant was largely responsible for the reduction of the barracks. Robert C. Steele, of the 511th, ordered covering fire from his platoon, advanced alone, and climbed to the roof of the barracks under fire. He tore a hole in the roof, poured gasoline inside, and ignited the gasoline and the enemy with a phosphorus hand grenade. When the enemy rushed to the open air, Steele's platoon mowed them down. Steele was awarded the DSC posthumously; he died in the Manila fighting a few days later.

At ten o'clock that night, after an exciting jeep ride, I set up my headquarters in Parañaque, the entrance to Manila. Our gamble had been successful. Four days after landing at Nasugbu we had a beach-head—as someone has described it—"sixty-nine miles long and five hundred yards wide," and we had penetrated the right flank of the Genko Line.

At five the next morning we crossed the partially destroyed bridge at Parañaque, and I made the official announcement to GHQ that we were in Manila. There had been fighting all night near the bridge, and Colonel I. R. Schimmelpfennig, the 11th Airborne's beloved chief of staff, had been killed by machine-gun fire. Earlier that day he had promised amiably to bring my toilet kit forward from the Manila Hotel annex. He kept his promise. When they found him, my safety razor was still in his pocket.

For an outfit without the heavy guns and heavy equipment necessary to breach a line, there was hard fighting ahead. My headquarters was a building on Manila Bay which had been used as a Japanese hospital and is now the Malibu Beach Club. During my five days there, when not actually up forward, I could watch the fighting at Nichols Field from the building's cupola. All the Japanese guns along Dewey Boulevard down to the Manila Hotel kept us under constant fire, and there was never a quiet moment.

On February 7 General MacArthur announced that Manila was secured—although some weeks of fighting were to follow before the last Japanese defenders could be liquidated. On February 9 I returned to the Eighth Army headquarters in Leyte to push the campaign in the central and southern Philippines. Next day, command of the 11th Airborne passed to the Sixth Army.

I like to recall one story about the spirit of Joe Swing's irrepressible paratroopers. In the thick of the struggle for Manila they found that the outer rim of the enemy's position was protected by five-inch naval guns, removed by the Japanese from warships and mounted at strategic spots. Hard pressed and under heavy bombardment, a company commander passed on the information to headquarters in this message:

"Tell Bill Halsey to stop looking for the Jap fleet. It's dug in on Nichols Field."

Although I no longer led them, I followed the subsequent exploits of the 11th Airborne with pride and interest. I heard the story of the bold and temporarily imperishable Private Manuel Perez, Jr. This amazing youngster, who won the Congressional Medal of Honor, singlehandedly stormed a dugout in the drive on Fort McKinley, killed eighteen Japanese soldiers, and neutralized a position which had held up the advance of an entire company. Unhappily, a week later, still fighting before Manila, he died a hero's death.

I read the communiqués as the bitter struggle went forward. The defending Japanese marines fought furiously and bravely, and the 11th Airborne took substantial casualties. Initially, the seriously wounded were flown to Nasugbu in Cub planes. Later, when an airstrip had been hastily constructed at Imus, C-47s evacuated casualties directly to Leyte. Fort McKinley fell on February 17. The ancient and important naval base at Cavite was taken February 21.

Then came the celebrated raid on Los Baños, which was led by Colonel Shorty Soule. It was an excellent example of the imagination, military coordination, and discipline of a fine division. As early as February 3, when we were just arriving on Tagaytay Ridge, General

MacArthur had ordered an attack—as soon as feasible—on a Japanese internment camp near Los Baños, where more than two thousand American and European civilians and prisoners of war were held.

It was a complicated problem. Los Baños was on the southern tip of shallow Laguna de Bay, and thus some fifty miles behind enemy lines. It was estimated, and accurately, that there were between eight and fifteen thousand enemy troops available for counterattack within four hours' march of the camp. Past history had given us reason to fear that the Japanese camp guards, if they knew attack was imminent, might execute their prisoners and thus clean the slate. I knew the problem because I had taken part in the early planning.

Trusted guerrilla spies were sent into the area. Five days before the operation they brought back a gentleman named Peter Miles who had recently escaped from the camp and gone into hiding. Miles had been an engineer in the Philippines before the war, and his careful information was invaluable. Miles drew up an exact map of the camp, which included a detailed blocking out of the arrangement of the interior, the positions of pillboxes and blockhouses and sentries, and the quarters of the internees. Engineer Miles also reported on the physical condition of the internees and accurately estimated the number of the sick and helpless who would require evacuation by litter.

All of the planning was highly secret, and few of the troops involved knew anything about their mission until they were plucked from their positions near Fort McKinley under the cover of darkness and moved to the positions from which they would make their attacks. Fifty-nine ungainly amphtracs—amphtracs walk on the land and swim in the water—moved noisily into Parañaque from the north. Nine C-47 planes of the 65th Troop Carrier Squadron landed on Nichols Field and picked their way hopefully along the pitted runways. A company of paratroopers moved to Nichols Field and slept under the wings of the planes.

Joe Swing and his boys of 11th Airborne had planned, for the sake of surprise and the safety of the internees, one of the oddest expeditions in military history. It was to include a ground force advance, an amphibious expedition, and a parachute drop. A great deal of faith, too, had to be placed on a reconnaissance platoon. This platoon consisted of one American officer and thirty-two Americans and about eighty Filipino guerrillas. They departed in *bancas* two days before the operation and, after reaching the southern shore, went into hiding. In the darkness of February 22 it took each man about seven hours of plodding over flooded rice paddies to reach his position. At seven A.M. on February 23 two columns of phosphorus smoke rose near Los Baños to guide the paratroopers to their drop zone, and two columns of phosphorus smoke rose from the beach at Los Baños Village to guide the amphtracs in. After the signal fires were satisfactorily started the reconnaissance platoon went seriously about the job of killing Japanese sentries.

The overland expedition by the 188th Glider Infantry began when troops waded the San Juan River and ran up against stubborn enemy opposition. The 1st Battalion had taken off in the darkness from Mamatid aboard the amphtracs—which were slow and so noisy that they could not be counted upon for surprise. The amateur skippers were ordered to drive out into the tepid lake and then turn directly south. This meant navigation by compass, and the skippers were full of cuss words and confusion. There wasn't a real seaman among them. It was a moonless night and they had seven and a half miles to go. Somehow the grumblers solved their mathematics.

The reconnaissance platoon did away with the sentries, the paratroopers hit the jump area precisely, the amphtracs came ashore and thundered down to Los Baños. Nearly two hundred and fifty of the Japanese garrison were killed, and the amphtracs took out all of the internees by water. There were many litter cases, but the sole casualty among the internees was one slightly wounded man. The 11th Airborne's casualties were two dead and one wounded.

It was a memorable job.

FIFTY-TWO D-DAYS

The Eighth Army set an all-time record for swift amphibious movement during its Victor Operations. There has never been another army
just like it. Eighth Army took over the island of Leyte on Christmas
Day. It had fifty-two D-days between that date and the Japanese
surrender. In one forty-four-day period alone these troops conducted
fourteen major landings and twenty-four minor ones, thus rolling up
an average of a landing every day and a half. There was never a time,
during this action-packed interlude, when some task force of my
command was not fighting a battle. And most of the time, hundreds
of miles apart, separate task forces were fighting separate battles
simultaneously.

Eighth Army fought on Leyte, on Luzon, on Palawan and the Zamboanga peninsula, on Panay and Bohol and Negros, on Mindanao,
Mindoro, and Marinduque, on Cebu and Capul and Samar. And on
a score of smaller islands which, even now, are remembered by most
GIs only as "faraway places with strange-sounding names." These
separate battles—though sometimes bewildering to the troops themselves—were all logical pieces in the jigsaw puzzle of the Philippines
operation.

After the Luzon jobs had been completed our assignment was the
subjugation of the rest of the myriad and (to me) marvelous islands
of the Philippines. It may be difficult to explain my zest for the assign-

ment. Everything about the Philippines made magic for me. I had served there as a young officer, and the lovely place names rang the bell of memory: they were pure music. Davao and Lake Lanao, Parang and Malabang and Iloilo and Cotobato. Pettit Barracks on Zamboanga and old Fort Pikit on Mindanao. My elders had told me the story of the Philippine Insurrection and the several campaigns against the Moro tribes. Surprisingly little has been written about this country's adventures in imperialism, and surprisingly little has been written about the American Army's tedious and difficult campaigns in those early and indifferent days.

Somehow the stream of schoolbook history passed them by—but not me. I remembered hot evenings when veteran officers and enlisted men proudly showed me wounds inflicted by Moro *barongs* and *krises*. The Moslem Moros were warlike and very tough fighters. All of the early Philippines fighting had been tough, with men and mules as transport; and pacification was not completed for a good many years. I remembered boisterous barracks-room songs: the skeptical comment of "The Virgin of Cebu"; the frankly zoological "Monkeys Have No Tails in Zamboanga." When I landed there at Maret Field in the spring of 1945, I saw a Japanese Zero. Its rear protuberance had been shot away. Marine fliers had marked this exhibit with a large-lettered sign. It was a simple confirmation: "THEY HAVE NO TAILS IN ZAMBOANGA."

Many great American military names are indivisible from Philippines history. These great names begin with General Arthur MacArthur, father of my commander. They include General Funston, who captured Aguinaldo, General Harbord, General McCoy, until his recent resignation, head of the Far Eastern Commission, and General Pershing. When General Douglas MacArthur and I visited the island of Jolo in the Sulu Sea, we found that the acting governor was the Moro who had served, many years before, as General Pershing's friend and native interpreter. Governor Tulawe was old in years and wisdom. But now I am ahead of my story.

After Sixth Army landed at Lingayen Gulf there was a heavy concentration there of American troops, American supply, American air and naval support. At times Eighth Army, poised for unknown adventure, felt a wistful identification with Oliver Twist and his porridge; Oliver, you will recall, wanted more. In matters of supply, available shipping, and infantry divisions, we learned to make out with what we had. When we had captured most of the central and southern islands of the Philippines, which was done while the fighting on Luzon still proceeded, General MacArthur sent a memorable message:

"My heartiest commendations for the brilliant execution of the Visayan campaign. This is a model of what a light but aggressive command can accomplish in rapid exploitation."

I considered the message deserved praise for veteran troops and for one of the finest planning and tactical staffs with which any commanding general was ever blessed. Eighth Army had a young staff which was endowed with enterprise and daring. It worked out, intelligently and with mathematical accuracy, the hazards and supply realities of our landings. Never once were its calculations seriously in error. Never once were we forced to resort to the airdrop of supplies because of the failure, or congestion, of seaborne transport.

Eighth Army's first job after my return from Manila was the clearing of the Japanese-controlled shipping lane which ran through a network of islands, large and small, directly south of Luzon. This was not a particularly perilous assignment—the islands generally were lightly held—but it was an important one. From San Bernardino Strait on the east to Lubang on the west there was a three-hundred-and-twenty-five-mile deep-water route which was almost always within sight of land and never beyond range of guns on the green and wooded shores.

None of our convoys had ventured this passage. They reached Luzon by one of two painfully roundabout over-water routes. One led north around the topmost tip of Luzon. The other went south and west from Leyte through Surigao Strait to the Sulu Sea and then six hundred miles north to Manila. Few people realize that the Philippines, north to south, measure more than a thousand miles. Mariners know it. Clearing of this passage meant the saving of hundreds of miles of travel for our supply ships—and the quickening of the whole Philippines campaign.

In the main, these island assaults were made with small units of such divisions as the 24th, the 40th, the Americal. One of the colorful outfits which took part in the enterprise was the 1st Philippine Infantry. This was an American regiment made up of American Filipinos (most of them from California) who had volunteered to fight for the homeland. The regiment was organized as the result of a suggestion by the then President Quezon to President Roosevelt. I used the 1st Philippine Infantry also in the subjugation of Samar, and its record was excellent.

As a matter of fact, by this time I had requested that General Irving be assigned to me as the boss of what we called Eighth Army Area Command. This meant that Fred Irving would command combat activities in Samar as well as supervise military areas behind us. Fred fell heir not only to the 1st Philippine Infantry but to an entirely separate outfit of American Filipinos known as the 1st Philippine Battalion. These troops had sound training. When GHQ requested Spanish-speaking American troops to serve as military police in Manila, Irving recruited them from the 1st Philippine Battalion.

Ten amphibious landings were necessary to wipe out the Japanese positions astride the over-water route south of Luzon. Usually we sent Americans ashore for the quick capture of an island and then moved in native irregulars and guerrillas to serve as garrison troops. In this way we were able to use our combat veterans over and over again. Much of the credit for the speed and efficiency of the enterprise belongs to the motor torpedo squadrons of Seventh Fleet. By day and night raids, by constant surveillance, they disrupted inter-island traffic and blocked evacuation of enemy units to Luzon.

From my headquarters at Telegrafo I took off on February 19, after a morning of staff work, to watch one of the earliest of the landings. Capul is a small island in San Bernardino Strait and it was a small landing—but I wanted to witness it. From my B-17 I could see the PT boats shepherding the slow, wallowing landing craft in a choppy sea. Now they stood off a coastal village and the bombardment started. The enemy was quiescent until our LCMs began to move inshore. Then the defenders' firing began.

Abruptly Chuck Downer, my pilot, asked me a question. I said, "Okay." Down we plunged with all guns firing. We made three runs

over the enemy positions at an altitude of two hundred feet, and at the end of our third run I noticed from the cockpit a shell burst directly below our left wing. It was a burst from a Jap .75, but I am glad to report that my first and only strafing mission, nevertheless, was without crew casualties. I was told later that our rather garish performance encouraged a hesitant wave of landing craft to a quick and successful beaching.

Sixth Army originally had captured the coastal fringes of the island of Mindoro, but fierce fighting continued under Eighth Army auspices. For a time Griz Griswold had his headquarters there, and I landed frequently at the San Juan Airfield. It was often under air attack, and I think Griswold will agree with me that the landing strip could not be classified as a recreation area. Mindoro for many weeks was one of those "calculated risks" which a sensible insurance executive shuns. Too many people were killed there. But Mindoro, throughout the Philippines campaign, was a very important island. It served as a jump-off area for regiments going to Luzon on the north, and to other islands on the south. It was a junction point. The airstrips there, like stoves in an all-night diner, never got cold. And the smell of the burn of landing tires hung over the place always.

Back in Leyte there were, occasionally, lighter moments—for instance, the dedication of the Rinaldo Coe Baseball Field, named for our headquarters commandant who had been killed east of Nasugbu. Joe E. Brown came into Leyte late on a Sunday afternoon, exhausted from a long air flight. I suggested he go to bed. Instead, he insisted upon accompanying me to a hospital I was about to inspect. Joe's jokes and wide smile and honest friendliness accomplished more in the way of therapy for the wounded lads of the Americal Division than a truckload of medicines.

The dedication of the baseball field occurred next day. There were rude bleachers around the diamond, which once had been a part of a swamp which we called Mudville. GIs were perched on every available seat and many sat cross-legged on the ground. The game was about to start. Joe, who had once been a professional baseball player, was on the pitcher's mound. Clovis Byers, armored with a mask and chest protector, was in the catcher's box. I was at bat.

There was great noise among the GIs, but I could not tell whether they were for me or against me. I never found out. Perhaps in pity, but certainly in violation of the rules, Joe gave me four strikes. I whiffed them all. Joe, in the interest of merriment, then paraphrased "Casey at the Bat." It came out this way:

> Oh, somewhere in this favored land the sun is shining bright;
> The band is playing somewhere, and somewhere hearts are light;
> And somewhere men are laughing and little children shout,
> But there is no joy in Mudville, for the mighty Eich struck out.

During the time of the Luzon operations, during the time of the fighting on Mindoro, Eighth Army staff was planning the Victor Operations in the central and southern Philippines. These were designed to clear the enemy from all islands south of Luzon and to furnish a short, protected supply route through southern Philippine waters. The most important island, military-wise, was Mindanao, second largest in the archipelago, and a main enemy fortress. Before starting a full-scale offensive against that target, however, it was decided to seize and occupy Palawan and the Zamboanga peninsula. These are, respectively, the western and eastern boundaries of the three-hundred-mile-wide Sulu Sea. The two-pronged operation was assigned to Jens Doe and the 41st Division.

Palawan was our first strike. Palawan Island is long, narrow, and mountainous. There is no railroad, and roads are few. Population is sparse, and many of the tribes are primitive indeed. Our principal objective was Puerto Princesa, the provincial capital and an old Spanish naval base. The importance of Palawan was its location. From airfields and naval bases on this westernmost edge of the Philippines we could support our own activities and also subject the enemy's principal supply route and communications to continuous attack. It was vital to the future invasion of Borneo and the Netherlands East Indies.

The strike on Palawan was made without serious opposition. Circling the area of Puerto Princesa in my B-17, I watched our troops going ashore. Chuck Downer brought the plane in over the airstrip and the town at treetop level, and I could see little immediate enemy reaction on the ground. It was at Palawan that I later came upon evidence of one of the most brutal Japanese massacres of the war. About a hundred and fifty American soldiers, captured at the time of the American surrender in 1942, had been confined to a stockade there; they worked in labor gangs on airfield construction. During early December of 1944 Japanese naval planes sighted an Allied convoy (it was Kincaid's fleet on the way to Mindoro) and assumed an invasion of Palawan was imminent.

On December 14 the Japanese occupation troops herded the Americans into air-raid shelters they themselves had built. Then the prisoners were saturated with gasoline and blazing torches were thrown into the tunnels. Most of the Americans burned to death; others, trying to escape the flames, were shot down with machine guns and rifles. Eleven men managed to break through the end of one of the tunnels and found themselves on the face of a cliff. They dropped to safety on a beach and were thereafter hidden by friendly natives. They were the only survivors, and one of them told me the whole story. I record for infamy the name of the Japanese unit responsible—131st Airfield Battalion, 4th Flying Division.

Ten days after the Palawan landing I celebrated my fifty-ninth birthday in a blackout aboard the USS *Rocky Mount*. As we moved toward Zamboanga in the darkness, I cut a candled birthday cake— the typical American family celebration in the midst of war made us all a little homesick—and received a friendly greeting card signed by Admiral Royal, General Doe, and all the other senior officers aboard.

Next morning I was on the bridge at seven-fifteen to watch the naval shelling. We had chosen landing beaches several miles west of Zamboanga City in hope of preserving the docks there for our future use. The cruisers were firing six-inch guns, and the destroyers and the destroyer escorts and the rocket-firing LCIs were making life miserable ashore. Just before the first wave of infantrymen landed, two flights of B-24s dropped heavy bombs on the landing beaches. Thirteen minutes later our infantrymen hit the beach; Marine planes and three flights of A-20 planes made strafing flights ahead of them. It was a coordinated job by three arms of our forces and admirable to watch. I went ashore just after noon and found that the 41st was making swift progress. Japanese mountain guns were now laying shells on the beaches.

After the original opposition, the main body of the Japanese retired six miles into the hills. The 41st was to have a difficult job cleaning them out. Our tanks were comparatively useless because of terrain. Roads were mined, and houses and Jap gun emplacements were booby-trapped. I remember seeing a dead American lad inside an abandoned pillbox. He was a souvenir hunter; inside his pockets were the two Japanese medals which had cost him his life. North of Santa Maria the enemy blew up the crown of a tactically important hill. In that one explosion the 163rd Regiment suffered eighty-three casualties. But the stalwarts of the 41st pressed forward and in less than a week were able to begin a series of other Sulu operations, which carried them, island by island, to within twelve or fifteen miles of British North Borneo.

Zamboanga City, third largest municipality of the Philippines, was a shambles. Docks were reasonably intact, but the once beautiful town itself was a ruin. Between Japanese dynamiting and devastation, and our aerial bombardment, the main buildings had become eyeless stone skeletons. There, as before and after, I pondered the cross-purposes of offensive war. Bombardment and bombing so often destroyed buildings, bridges, airports, and roads. Once ashore, in order to live and fight in destroyed country, the infantry and engineers had to build them all over again. And, because of the imperatives of combat, civilians made out for themselves.

After I had spent three days with the task force, the Japanese gave me a farewell salute. I was chugging out to the *Rocky Mount* in the Admiral's barge. Apparently enemy field glasses still accurately observed the harbor. Anyway, a detonator somewhere let loose a naval mine which sent a cascade of water ten stories high. It just missed my boat; after swallowing hard, I found myself intact and went aboard the cruiser. A Navy flying boat picked me up shortly after and took me back to Leyte in very stormy weather.

By the middle of March, Eighth Army was ready for its assault upon the central Philippines. Here, in inland seas once dominated by Japanese Marine and Air, were the rich and comfortable islands of Panay, Negros, Cebu, and Bohol. Before the war, Panay, Negros, and Cebu had been sugar-rich and plantation-rich. Here were beautiful and modern capitals—Iloilo on Panay, Bacolod on Negros, Cebu City. Here were railroads, electric lights, country clubs, and many-bathroomed mansions which borrowed their architecture and interior decoration from Hollywood. Here also, and close at hand, were the nipa huts of the native workers; the cleavage between the rich and the poor has always been deep and readily apparent in the Philippines. Along with Luzon, however, these central islands have been the leaders in education and progressivism.

President Osmeña was a native of Cebu. The prewar governor of Panay (Iloilo province) was the gifted and stubborn Tomás Confesor who was often called the "stormy petrel" of Philippine politics. Confesor, despite Japanese occupation, maintained a free civil government on most of Panay throughout the war; he hid out in the mountains. The guerrilla chief on Panay was Colonel Nacario Peralta, a graduate of the University of the Philippines. He and Confesor were bitter rivals for power, but both faithfully made intelligence reports to Southwest Pacific headquarters. As a matter of fact, Peralta's intelligence network was extensive and efficient.

Panay was invaded March 18. Cebu was invaded March 26. Negros came along three days later. The 40th Division, which had been fighting in Luzon, was charged with the capture of both Panay and western Negros, and, under the skillful direction of Major General Rapp Brush, performed with vigor and intelligence. The 40th embarked at Lingayen Gulf, weathered a heavy storm at sea without the loss of any boats, and made its original landing at Tigbauan, fourteen miles southwest of Iloilo. Colonel Peralta's guerrillas, stiff in starched khaki and resplendent with ornaments, greeted the first assault waves as they waded ashore. Two days later the Americans were at the outskirts of the provincial capital, and expecting a fierce battle for the town.

The morning of March 20 I left Leyte by flying boat and two hours later came down on the water at Tigbauan right beside Admiral Rip Struble's flagship. I went aboard and was met by Struble and Gen-

eral Brush. Just as we were about to go ashore the Fleet intelligence officer brought news that a Navy flier had seen civilians in Iloilo waving American flags and dancing in the streets. Then, for the benefit of the pilot, they had written in large letters in the sand at Iloilo's beach: "Japs Have Left City."

At Brush's headquarters staff officers were skeptical about the reported evacuation because the Japanese had given every indication they intended to match a last-ditch fight to keep possession of the Iloilo docks. I suggested that Struble, Brush, and I take part in the 40th Division's advance and see how far we could get. Our jeeps (Peralta and Colonel Bowen went along) pushed forward with the tank spearhead in the early afternoon. A half-hour later, to our astonishment, we found ourselves in the center of Iloilo and surrounded by a laughing, cheering, flower-throwing city population which seemed to have gone crazy with joy. It was a moving experience which I shall not forget.

Enemy garrison troops, as the result of a panicky, last-minute decision, had fled to the hills. In one instance, they found time to be thorough. At a Japanese military hospital in an Iloilo suburb there were fifty bedridden patients. All fifty of them were given a narcotic injection; then the Japanese set fire to the hospital. A few of the patients escaped cremation by crawling out of the burning building before the narcotic took effect—and that is how I know the story. The Japanese had not been so thorough in other ways. Two-thirds of Iloilo was in ruins, but I was able to inform General MacArthur by radio that the docks were intact and the harbor clear.

Late that afternoon I served as General MacArthur's deputy in pinning the DSC on Colonel Peralta. It was a formal ceremony at his headquarters, and there was a guerrilla brass band to provide the proper musical ruffles. Later I discussed with General Brush plans for the invasion of Negros. This promised to be troublesome. Landing beaches were poor, and the Japanese were there in strength. A key point in any attack must be the six-hundred-and-fifty-foot bridge over the unfordable Bago River. This was a five-span modern steel bridge above a broad and deep declivity. We knew it had been prepared for demolition, and that the engineers of a light task force such as ours did not have the equipment to replace it. If the bridge was destroyed, American troops would be prisoners of the beach for many days and our advance would be seriously delayed.

On the morning of March 29 the 40th Division invaded Negros—which is ten miles across a protected sea channel from Panay. Four hours before the main landing, Lieutenant Aaron A. Hanson and sixty-two men from the 185th Infantry had undertaken a most adventurous expedition. In profound darkness they set out in two boats and came ashore at Patik, a mile and a half below the main landing beaches at Pulupandan. They were afraid the noises of their boat engines might have betrayed their arrival; but they were met only by friendly villagers.

Despite the confusions of night and unknown country, Hanson's group headed speedily inland. At a crossroads they encountered a guerrilla intelligence agent who told them a party of nine Japanese with three oxcarts was moving along the hard-surface highway toward the Bago bridge. It was becoming light. A few minutes later Hanson saw the Japanese and the Japanese saw Hanson. From then on it was a race for the river. The Americans could not open fire, because this would have warned the bridge guards of their proximity. But they moved forward so fast that they intercepted the enemy at the very approaches to the bridge.

The fighting began at once. A quarter of the way across the bridge the platoon was pinned down by intense fire from the far side. The Bago structure had a number of thousand-pound aerial bombs attached to its underbelly. There was an electrical detonator precisely in the center of the bridge. A Japanese soldier was just about to push the plunger which would have blown him and the Americans to Kingdom Come when Private First Class Vintner of the 185th winged him. A time margin of a second or two, and good marksmanship, made the difference between a bridge and no bridge. Tragically enough, the posthumously decorated PFC Vintner was killed just twenty yards farther on.

After a fire fight the Japanese at the far end abandoned their posts. An hour later sixty more Japanese approached the bridge unaware that it was in our hands. When Hanson's bazookas and machine guns

and automatic rifles burst into action, the Japanese fled in disorder, taking their dead and wounded with them. This heroic platoon of the 185th held the bridge until our main force, which hit the beaches at nine-thirty A.M., had passed over the Bago in safety en route to the city of Bacolod.

I was not present at the capture of Bacolod because the 40th Division got there faster than I expected them to. Those daring campaigners tore their own time schedule to ribbons; Bacolod was secured by noon of the second day. On Negros there is a concrete coastal highway, always in sight of the sea, which goes north from Bacolod and encircles half the island. Rapp Brush was convinced the enemy intended to withdraw to the hills, and he let his reconnaissance troops have their head. With intermediate stops for hard fighting they swept around the perimeter of the island in less than a week. Tanks and amphib tractors literally ran their treads off. I had intended to supplement Brush's attack by an airdrop of the 503rd Parachute Infantry, which had made its celebrated jump on Corregidor a fortnight earlier. After a firsthand evaluation of the situation, I decided this maneuver was no longer necessary, and the 503rd came prosaically in by boat.

The Japanese position on Negros was hopeless. To be sure, the enemy fought with tenacity in an inland mountain bastion for many weeks, but the outcome was never in doubt. The Negros campaign highlighted one glaring Japanese deficiency of which we were already cognizant. Enemy commanders rarely had an accurate picture of a battle situation. The reason became clear: their military communications system was primitive and untrustworthy and ridiculously inferior to our highly efficient network of field telephones and field radios.

There were fourteen thousand of the Emperor's soldiers on western Negros. Because of wretched conditions at the beaches, the 40th Division on D-day could put only two battalions ashore. Had the Japanese commander known this, it is conceivable he would have massed forces and utilized his overpowering superiority in numbers to wipe out the Americans on the first or second day. We bet our blue chips he wouldn't, and we were right.

Meanwhile the Americal Division had invaded Cebu. We expected Cebu to be tough. Lieutenant Colonel Jim Cushing, a former American mining engineer, an able and intelligent man, was chief of the Filipino guerrillas on Cebu, and he had been in the bush for three years. Cushing told us there were about thirteen thousand Japs on Cebu and the nearby island of Bohol. As it turned out, he had underestimated enemy strength. Cebu City had been the head-quarters of the Japanese general who commanded both the central Philippines and the big southern island of Mindanao. Originally there had been at Cebu—a central transit point for the Philippines—some twenty-one thousand Japanese. These included airmen, sailors, hospital nurses, and the fancy ladies of the Japanese High Command.

Cebu was rich in agricultural resources, and rich in historical tradition. Magellan, the Portuguese explorer who sailed under Spain's flag, was killed there in 1526 before he could complete his circumnavigation of the globe; he is reputedly buried in the ancient Cebu City cathedral.

The Americal Division hit the island five miles southwest of the Cebu City cathedral four hundred and nineteen years later. I flew over the area and saw that the assault elements were in trouble. Heavy landing craft could not get onto the beaches because of shallow water, so the first wave came ashore in amphtracs (LVTs) with the intention of moving inland in these amphibious vehicles until organized resistance was encountered. However, an intricate pattern of Japanese land mines abruptly halted the first wave by blowing up or damaging half of the advancing amphtracs.

The remaining LVTs halted at the edge of the mine field ashore rather than risk damage by crossing it. Although it had been assumed there would be Japanese defenses on the beaches, the mine field presented a problem that had not been thoroughly explored in pre-invasion planning. There were, of course, mine detectors in the cargoes of the ships offshore, but they were too far back in the landing schedule to be of any immediate value in the situation.

Within a matter of minutes a stalemate developed on the beachhead. The assault forces could not move with safety through the mine field, and the subsequent echelons were pouring ashore steadily, right on schedule. It was a log jam, and serious. The beach offered no cover whatever. Because of that mine field, the power of the Americal's 132nd and 182nd Regiments was held in check for an hour and a half by the cramped dimensions of a strip of beach—not more than fifty yards long and not more than fifty yards deep.

Had the Japanese elected to defend the beachhead with determination, the story of Cebu might have been a different story. Simply by covering the mine field and the water's edge with accurate mortar and machine-gun fire, the Japanese could have inflicted heavy casualties on the crowded-in troops; the Americans had virtually no room in which to maneuver around the obstacles. To be sure, in such an event the ground commanders could have called for gunfire from the warships at sea. With the Japanese close in, this might have been as damaging to the Americal Division as it was to the Japanese. One pessimistic commentator has hazarded the opinion that our troops might have been forced to make a reluctant withdrawal if the enemy had done what the enemy didn't do. The Japanese failed to defend. After an hour and a half, mine-detector crews had been assembled, and they cleared lanes in the mine field and marked them.

When I came in next day by flying boat and went ashore the situation was much improved. Duke Arnold and I chugged toward Cebu City in a jeep and were held up by bomb craters in the road. We were held up by many things; once a bridge was out; another time the road was mined. We shifted from jeep to half-track and back to jeep again, and eventually I got a good look at the Cebu piers. I was cheered to find that there was room for the docking of six Liberty ships at a time. This turned out to be important.

Cebu City itself saddened me. Between enemy destruction and American bombing, a modern capital had been almost completely destroyed. I think it would be accurate to say it was ninety-five per cent destroyed. The profound waste of aerial war is always disturbing; in the Philippines it frequently visited misery on a friendly population.

Between Talisay and Cebu City were several miles of the strongest fortifications I came upon in the South Pacific. They could, in-

deed, have meant death and desolation for the Americal. But the
Japanese, mysteriously, failed to man them. Why? I don't know. All
war is a gamble, and it is always a gamble with the lives of healthy
and promising young men. The Japanese had concentrated their
strength in the rugged country above the capital, where they had
steel-and-concrete strongholds. The one traversable road had been
mined for its entire length with large-size aerial bombs. There were
five hundred caves in the rock and coral hills, and communicating
tunnels and underground command posts. There were regularly
spaced dragon's teeth to impede the progress of tanks.

The Japanese overlooking Cebu City were prepared to fight. From
the high ground they staged night attacks, and, day and night, they
kept our soldiers under artillery and mortar fire. From trenches and
caves and pillboxes, they resisted our assaults stubbornly. The first
battalion of the 182nd Infantry suffered a temporary disaster at a
gloomy and hard-won butte known as Watt Hill.

General Arnold witnessed the tragic drama from his command
post five hundred yards away. Three Sherman tanks were firing
desultorily into caves at the crest of Watt Hill as Company A climbed
the slope. Just as the Americans reached the summit, the whole hill
blew up. The force of the explosion was such that the tanks turned
turtle, and Company A was virtually wiped out. There were a hundred casualties. When Arnold showed me the mined hill a few days
later, all I could see was a coral crater a hundred and fifty yards
wide and the evidences of the landslide which had buried many
infantrymen.

A week after our landing the Japanese were still fighting back
strongly. Now General Arnold asked me to send him Americal's
164th Regiment which had been left behind in Leyte. These troops
arrived by transport the evening of April 9 and immediately began
a night march up the Mananga River. It was Arnold's intention to
put them in the enemy's rear at a place called Babag Ridge. Guided
by guerrillas, the 164th made a wide twenty-seven-mile sweep around
the Japanese without discovery. They traveled for three nights and
remained in concealment during the daylight. This was a sparkling
and successful maneuver. On the morning of the fourth day, the

182nd and 132nd Regiments attacked from the front, and to the consternation of General Manjome Takeo, the 164th attacked from the rear.

To escape encirclement and complete annihilation, the Jap commander now ordered a withdrawal to northern Cebu. His army never fought again as a unified force. Right at this time I was absent from my Leyte headquarters for a week as I launched Eighth Army's Mindanao invasion. There I received delayed reports that the Americal was having a rough time. I set off from Parang to Cebu in a flying boat. When Duke Arnold met me—it was April 19—his face was one big, reassuring smile. I knew then the log jam was broken.

The bitter tenacity of the fighting can be read in the casualty lists. The Americal and attached troops killed 9300 Japanese on Cebu and about 700 more on Bohol and eastern Negros. After the atomic bomb fell, almost 9000 Japanese surrendered on Cebu. They included two lieutenant generals, a major general, and an admiral. Americal suffered 449 men killed in action, 1872 wounded, and 8139 non-battle casualties; these were principally victims of various jungle diseases, but many of them had to be evacuated and replaced.

MINDANAO

By late April I had become one of the Orient's busiest air commuters. The Eighth Army was waging war in many places, and, like a faithful commercial traveler, I tried to visit them all. The airplane was a magic carpet for me. I could rise early, be in the air by seven, take off for a conference with GHQ in Manila, and be back at my desk for a staff conference before sundown. The frequent confusions and contradictions of field reports have always bothered commanders who must make strategic decisions. Because of the airplane, I could whisk out over the green mountains of Leyte, land on Zamboanga, Cebu, Negros—or, later, on one or two of a dozen makeshift grass strips on Mindanao—and investigate the field situation for myself. In the spring of 1945, during a ninety-day period, I was in the air seventy days.

Everyone was worried about the Mindanao campaign, and that included me. Mindanao is the southernmost of the Philippine Islands, and the terrain is bewildering and varied. From its north-to-south extremities the island measures about three hundred miles; at its fattest belt line it measures two hundred and fifty miles from west to east. This, of course, does not include the Zamboanga peninsula, which, for purposes of military planning, was not considered part of Mindanao at all. And with historical and ethnological reasons. The Zamboanga peninsula belongs to the Mindanao mainland, but the mountains between are so steep that the principal contact always has been by boat over a hundred miles of rough water.

Two main roads bisect the island: Highway No. 1, which runs east and south from Parang on Moro Gulf to Digos on Davao Gulf, and the north-south Sayre Highway, which makes junction with Highway No. 1 at Kabacan, a village situated almost exactly at the center of the island. Colonel Dunne, Eighth Army engineer, was pessimistic because the rainy season was close at hand. Colonel Burgess, Eighth Army G-4 and one of the truly fine supply officers of the war, was disturbed about shipping and transport. General MacArthur predicted that after three or four months we would still be fighting around Kabacan. For Mindanao, if one excepted urban communities on the northern and southern seacoasts, was pretty much the same primitive land over which Pershing, Harbord, and Frank R. McCoy had campaigned thirty-odd years before.

We did have considerable information about dispositions of enemy troops, since the guerrilla forces on Mindanao were the most efficient and best organized in the Philippines. They were commanded by Colonel Wendell W. Fertig, an American engineer who had been operating gold mines in the islands when war broke out. Fertig was called to active duty with the Corps of Engineers in early 1942, served on Bataan, and then was sent to Mindanao to direct airfield construction. When the Philippines fell, Fertig took to the bush and became a guerrilla leader. With him were a considerable number of associates, military and civilian, American and Filipino.

I came to know Wendell Fertig very well because of our frequent conferences on the Mindanao planning. He was a slim man with a pleasing manner, but he was fearless and there was iron in his soul. The wives and daughters of his headquarters group moved into the hills around Lake Lanao with their men and did the cooking and nursing. First supplies for the guerrillas were shipped into Mindanao by submarine in February of 1943. From then on supplies came in regularly, initially by submarine and later by airplane and small landing craft. Fertig had been in radio communication with the MacArthur headquarters almost from the first; I had been in the theater long enough to recall that our early receiving equipment was so mediocre that Fertig's messages sometimes had to be beamed to San Francisco and relayed back to us in Australia by a strong California station.

Because of its large area, limited road net, and numerous self-sustaining agricultural areas, Mindanao was ideal for guerrilla operations. The Japanese confined their activities mainly to coastal cities, highways, and waterways, and thus the irregulars were able effectively to control about ninety-five per cent of the island's area. Also, the Mindanao people were warlike; the Americans had not been able to subdue the island and the Sulu archipelago for more than a decade after Aguinaldo's surrender. Fertig's force totaled about twenty-five thousand men. Lack of land communication between separate guerrilla organizations made centralized command a problem, but Fertig, by using a radio network, achieved a degree of unification. As a matter of fact, the guerrillas had taken the offensive early in 1945 and, in an amphibious assault supported only by two small naval craft, had forced the Japanese to evacuate the town of Talisayan on the island's northern coast.

In the beginning, I proposed a direct amphibious assault on Davao Gulf, where we knew there were large concentrations of Japanese. But because of the Okinawa campaign then in progress, the Navy did not feel it could provide protection for such an ambitious expedition. The alternative was a landing at Parang or Malabang on Moro Gulf, which would necessitate a backbreaking overland march. Eighth Army operations were always dependent upon available shipping; if more shipping were available later, it might be possible to complement the overland march from the west with an amphibious assault upon Davao.

General Sibert's X Corps—consisting of the 24th and 31st Divisions —was chosen for the original blow. On April 13 I flew to Mindoro and went aboard Admiral Riggs' flagship, the cruiser *Montpelier*. Next day our convoy sailed. We had just received news of the death of President Roosevelt. Those were strenuous days, and all of us felt things deeply. One of the most impressive ceremonies I have ever witnessed was the memorial service held for the President on the deck of the *Montpelier* as we plowed through alien waters on the way to a new American assault.

Originally we had expected to make our first landing at Malabang. But now we received word from Colonel Fertig that the guerrillas had seized both Malabang town and the airfield there. While we were at sea we completely revised our assault plans. The landing force to be sent to Malabang was reduced to one battalion, and we decided to make our main effort at Parang, seventeen miles down the coast. This would eliminate the reshipping of supplies from Malabang to Parang and hasten our drive inland.

At six-thirty on a bright morning the cruisers and destroyers of the attack forces began an effective bombardment of Parang. The assault waves of 24th Division hit the beaches within thirty seconds of the appointed times. They advanced inland, found all bridges on Highway No. 1 had been destroyed, and waded chest-deep streams to push on toward the east.

The Parang landings were almost without incident. But not quite. General Roscoe B. Woodruff, who had succeeded Irving as commander of the 24th, came ashore and hustled forward as rapidly as possible to catch up with his fast-moving 19th Regimental Combat Team. Striding through high cogan grass, Woody fell neck-deep into a stone-sided Jap "spider hole," and, much to his disgust, had to have first-aid treatment. He was in pain and almost sleepless for two weeks as he pressed ahead by jeep with the 24th Division on its overland trek. Jeep travel on Highway No. 1 was spine-smashing to a well man; it must have been sheer torture for a man with strapped-up ribs.

Woodruff concealed his ills, even smiled amiably when General Sibert—as a jeep companion—complained about the roughness of the road. Woody has told me since that he was haunted by the idea that the medicos would pronounce him unfit for duty and that he would be succeeded in command.

I went ashore at Parang with Sibert at ten A.M. Despite destruction of all bridges, our troops advanced six thousand yards the first day. At the same time Cotabato, ten miles upriver, was bombarded;

it was taken amphibiously the following morning. I went there by landing craft in the afternoon and found the town in ruins but the docks usable. In that day's notations in my diary, I discover this prophetic comment: "Possibility of sending men and supplies up the Mindanao River looks like a good one."

The use of the Mindanao River as a possible supply route had been discussed during the planning of the operation, but the Navy had regarded the prospect with understandable coldness. We had no hard facts about the navigability of the smoky, silty river; information on its currents and shoals simply was not to be had. Once again the Army Amphibian Engineers were to be of tremendous assistance. This time it was one regiment of General Ogden's 3rd Engineer Special Brigade that carried the ball. The entire boat battalion of the regiment traveled under its own power from Lingayen Gulf to Moro Gulf, a distance of a thousand miles. The hundred and twenty-five LCMs arrived, with amazing precision, in Moro Gulf just as the assault forces of the 24th Division arrived by naval escort. It was the kind of timing that no commander in his right mind has any reason to expect.

Immediately reconnaissance units of the Engineers climbed into their amphtracs and explored the river; they reconnoitered as far as the north and south branches without making contact with the enemy, and reported both branches to be navigable. One of General Woodruff's combat teams was proceeding overland toward Kabacan, where Highway No. 1 and the Sayre Highway joined. The Japanese had made no effort to improve Highway No. 1; after three years of disuse the jungle had moved in. It does not take long in a tropical country for abacá (hemp) trees and grass to recapture what men have made. Often, as the 24th moved forward, they found the highway just a tunnel through green vegetation. Only two men had been wounded in the Parang landing, but soon there were many heat prostrations. That section of Mindanao was moist, dank, and insufferably hot.

While Woodruff's 19th RCT advanced along the highway, we hastily re-equipped the shallow-draft craft of the Amphibian Engineers with light and medium artillery, and they carried another combat team of the 24th up the winding, enigmatic river. There hadn't been a military adventure quite like it since Federal gunboats operated on the lower Mississippi during the Civil War. These were, literally, gunboats; even captured Japanese barges were manned and gunned and impressed into the ferry service. The river runs roughly parallel to Highway No. 1, so, with the advantage of walkie-talkie radio contact, the water-transported combat units were able to make shore landings and drive Japanese troops to the woods. And the platoons dumped ashore were also able to maintain a consistent liaison with the overland advance.

Four days after the Parang landing the 19th and 21st Regimental Combat Teams had reached Kabacan. A village named Fort Pikit was the last place upriver which the Army Amphibs could reach; the 21st RCT took off for Kabacan on foot from there. The usefulness of the Mindanao River increased with time. Because of the inadequacies of Highway No. 1, the river became our principal supply line to the interior of the island. The humpty-dumpty overland route was abandoned. The Navy now was willing to carry farther inland, but the shallow-draft Amphib vessels still continued to do most of the job.

Four days after the landing Japanese troops in northern Mindanao were cut off from Japanese troops in the south. Woodruff did not stop at Kabacan to establish a base. The rainy season was already overdue, and he drove the 24th Division relentlessly east toward Davao Gulf. He was happy each day he did not see a raincloud in the sky, because he knew when the rains came his trails would be impassable. Speed was all important.

In the meantime the 31st ("Dixie") Division was on its way from Morotai Island to Parang. This was an outfit which had spent three years in training in Louisiana, Texas, and the Carolinas. In New Guinea and the Netherlands East Indies the division had engaged largely in a static type of fighting. But for six weeks, in anticipation of a war of rapid movement and maneuver, the troops had concentrated on drills for the Mindanao campaign. They had improved their wind, their physiques, their eyesight in darkness, their amphibious expertness, and their marksmanship.

By plan they arrived at Parang some five or six days after the 24th Division went ashore. It is the irony of war that they arrived after the 24th had already begun its war of movement. The 31st Division was just about to begin one of the slowest and most tedious advances —where nature and the Japanese seemed in league—of the whole operation. I had selected the 31st because I had absolute faith in the fighting qualities of Clarence Martin, now its commander. At Buna I had seen him, a staff officer, take command of a combat area and bring it to life. I had watched him "walk out" his own high-tempera-ture malaria, the only time I've seen it done. If Martin had the 31st —that was the outfit for me.

At this point the Japanese were confused, and we knew it. The Japanese had prepared for an attack by sea at Davao Gulf. They were also prepared to meet us at Sarangani Bay, a dozen or so miles away, where, indeed, for a time the Americans had planned to make the first Philippines landing. All big guns were pointed seaward. The Japanese were aware that the Americans were proceeding overland from the west, but the breakdown of communications had left the commanders in a state of utter bewilderment about our exact where-abouts.

Once again, the Jap trouble was the inflexibility of preconceived plans. There were six Japanese airdromes in the vicinity of the city of Davao, which before the war had a population of ninety-three thousand persons. The harbor offered protected anchorages for our fleet. Consequently, and logically, it was assumed we would strike there. Lieutenant General Harada, who commanded the 100th Jap-anese Division and all of its widely scattered and attached troops, had done excellent work in fortifying the area for protection against attack from sea.

Harada continued to believe that our overland thrust was a diver-sion and that a massive amphibious assault was to be made in Davao Gulf. The collapse of the Japanese communication system permitted him to believe that only small forces were advancing overland. At the same time he had been receiving reports from airplane observers that farther to the south large groups of transports and troops were being assembled. They could have been diverted to Davao, but actually they were being readied for the Australian invasion of Borneo, which took place some weeks later.

Harada had his problems, and I was happy to increase them. On April 26 I flew at low level over the middle of Mindanao and saw Woodruff's forces streaming downhill toward Moro Gulf. When I landed at Malabang a little later I was greeted by both General Sibert and the bewhiskered Fertig. Soon Sibert handed me a telegram from Woodruff announcing that he was only ten miles outside Digos and slicing into a Japanese rear that was still lightly defended.

The next morning Digos fell. Only ten days after the original landing the 24th Division had fought its way a hundred and ten miles across the island to the southern sea. Not three or four months—as General MacArthur had predicted—but ten days. It was a remarkable achievement, truly one for the history books. It was the longest sustained land advance of Americans in the Pacific.

General Woodruff wanted to march immediately on Davao City, capital of this rich abacá-growing territory which had been heavily colonized by Japanese civilians twenty-five years before. I debated calling a halt. Thirty thousand enemy troops were estimated to be in the area, and the 24th Division was strung out for fifty miles. But we did have our adversary off balance, and I remembered an earlier statement of General MacArthur's: "Bob, if you get a bloody nose, I'll give you every man I have." I decided to take responsibility for the decision and to go personally into Davao City with Woodruff.

On May 2 General Byers and I landed at the Japanese-built Padada Airfield just outside Digos. We jeeped forward twenty-odd miles to Woodruff's headquarters, which was about five thousand yards outside Davao City in a swamp. In the afternoon we got about halfway to town before being driven back by heavy fire. Early the next morning I crossed the swift tidal Davao River on a shaky footbridge which sometimes was a single plank. Then I walked into Davao City with the infantry. The town had been wrecked. Japanese positions were being gradually liquidated by the 19th Infantry, and I talked with Colonel Jock Clifford who had commanded the same gallant outfit at Hollandia. He was to be killed by one of the last mortar shells fired in the Mindanao campaign.

With the taking of the southern capital, strategic victory on Mindanao was achieved, and General MacArthur announced it. However, there were many hard weeks ahead for the GIs who had no newspapers to tell them that everything was well in hand. The enemy retired to the peaks and hills northwest of Davao City, and it was two months before the 24th could destroy them. The 24th was outnumbered, and I can testify from personal observation to the severity of the hand-to-hand fighting which took place later in the deadly abacá thickets around Mintal and during the advance to Tamogan.

General Martin's 31st Division had followed the 24th east to Kabacan. Prior to the 31st's landing, no orders for its combat employment had been issued. The reasons are understandable: Eighth Army and X Corps were playing a gambler's game. We did not know when—and if—more substantial naval support would be available; we could not be sure of the opposition we would meet; we were determined to improvise until enlightening events made the picture clearer. Many Army commanders, I am sure, would have disapproved this policy; they would have secured every area painstakingly before moving forward. And that is, indeed, the cautious course, and very often the proper course. My staff and I were convinced that the end of Japanese air and sea power in the Philippines warranted a speed of advance that some people might call audacious. There are times for caution, and there are times for audacity. If the 24th had been cautious, it would not have beaten the rainy season to Davao.

Martin's 31st at Kabacan was in a position to reinforce Woodruff if the 24th ran into trouble. With Davao taken, I ordered Martin to turn north up the Sayre Highway to clear the central Mindanao valley. The 31st's immediate objective was the village of Kibawe, and the 124th RCT under Colonel Edward M. Starr, who had performed handsomely in the heavy fighting of the Aitape campaign, pushed forward on a night march to the deep and swift-running Pulangi River..Kibawe lay on the other side.

The Pulangi flows into the Mindanao River, and three American LCMs had worked their way up there to do the ferrying job. It took a whole day for the hard-pressed landing craft to get the advance units across. At sunset Ted Starr's lads started north again on their overland journey.

At this point Sayre Highway (named by the Filipinos for a former American governor-general) was discovered to be something of a fraud. A stretch of thirty miles had never been completed. For ten miles the road proceeded through flat, black river-bottom soil, which baked hard in dry weather and became quagmire in wet weather. This section had been corduroyed, but after three years of neglect the logs had rotted to a pulp. Actually that whole stretch of highway from Kabacan to Kibawe can be best described as a dry-weather road for light traffic only. It could not even accommodate vehicles of medium weight. The first one-quarter-ton truck which essayed the journey bogged down of its own weight two miles below Kibawe.

Lieutenant General Morozumi commanded the 30th Japanese Division in central Mindanao, and, postwar records indicate, claimed for himself command of all Japanese Army and Air Forces on the island by reason of his seniority. I am, of course, in no position to rule upon the legitimacy of his claims. I know only that, unaware of the fact that we had already crossed the Pulangi River, he dispatched one of his infantry battalions toward Kabacan with orders to destroy the American forces there and prevent an advance to the north.

On April 27 a battalion under Lieutenant Colonel R. M. Fowler, having managed the ferry, were proceeding north. It was ten o'clock at night as Fowler's men descended a small hill with the moon over their shoulders. Some of the troops were sullen and some of them were sleepy. When would they bivouac? At that moment they encountered the Japanese force moving south. Automatic weapons fire virtually annihilated the advance American patrol. A terrific all-night fight ensued.

Surprise on both sides plainly had something to do with the fierceness of the engagement. Fowler methodically and coolly brought up and maneuvered his units to meet the repeated Japanese attacks. They continued until daybreak. So fierce was the fighting that many of the enemy were killed after they had penetrated the American

lines. One of the brave men was the Japanese battalion commander who was found dead next morning in our area with a copy of his orders in his clothes. He had led the attack.

There were, of course, Japanese survivors, and, if they returned to their rear elements, they undoubtedly exaggerated the strength of our northern advance. General Martin wrote me recently that he believes that if the American advance had been less rapid—or if Fowler had been held up at the Pulangi—there would have been dire results.

General Martin may well be right. Assuredly, that Japanese battalion would have reached the north shore of the Pulangi, and our ferry service would have met with devastating fire; perhaps, for the time being, there would have been no American crossings. At Kabacan, the axis of the Mindanao road net, we then had inadequate artillery and no heavy equipment of any sort. The results of Fowler's night encounter were more important than the numbers of troops involved might indicate. Certainly a stalemate at the river would have given Morozumi plenty of time to deploy his troops intelligently and to strengthen his defenses. Undoubtedly, he could have made our progress through the gorge country cruel and costly.

The 31st was already in the gorge country and climbing steeply toward the central plateau. There the terrain is deeply slashed by rushing tributaries which flow into the Pulangi. Another battalion passed through Fowler's men and took the lead. Lieutenant Colonel G. D. Williams and his lads ran into two mighty gorges only a mile apart. Originally, wooden bridges, supported by piles twice the height of a tall telephone pole, had spanned the canyons. The Japanese had destroyed the bridges. They hadn't counted on the determination and derring-do of battle-experienced "Pappy" Williams and his gang.

The sides of these gorges seemed almost perpendicular. The Americans left their vehicles behind, slid down the near side of the first gorge, scaled the far side, and went on. At the second gorge there were well-prepared positions manned by two companies of Japanese engineers and other troops. The severity of the defile, the excellent location and organization of the enemy positions, might have convinced an objective observer that the Japanese could hold off a much larger attacking force indefinitely.

Williams wasn't convinced. While he covered the Japanese positions with artillery fire, his rifle units once again slid and stumbled down the near side of a gorge and then valiantly moved up the other side. Near the lip of the precipice they were climbing on hands and knees, using bushes and roots for hand- and toe-holds. Pushing and boosting one another, they emerged on the crest and rushed the Jap entrenchments. Again surprise was a major factor; the defenders had never expected the Americans to make the climb. There was panic among the Japanese; many fled their positions and were overtaken and killed.

Williams pushed on, routing the small and unwisely dispersed units which tried to check his advance. Soon he was out of supporting range of artillery and had only the weapons and ammunition his men carried to argue his case. After they left the gorges behind they traveled through dense rain-forest and could be supplied and fed only by airdrop. They reached the Molita River, which was in the heart of the rain-forest country, and peered apprehensively at the wooded hills on the other side. Now Williams requested air support, and I saw to it that he got it. Marine Corps fliers made a close and splendid air strike. Williams' men forded the river and took the heights.

On May 2 a third battalion of the 124th Infantry caught up with the pacemakers, and the next day Kibawe was ours. Also, to our satisfaction, we captured a small airstrip there where Cubs and—in emergencies—C-47s could land. It was now the assignment of the advance units to hold while strenuous efforts were made to open the road behind them so artillery and vehicles and more troops could be brought up from the rear.

Back in the gorge country the artillerymen and combat engineers worked in daylight and darkness. Brigadier General Tom Hickey, artillery commander, used every expedient to move weapons and equipment. Stout steel cables were stretched across the chasms and fastened to giant trees on the other side. Thus several quarter-ton trucks, a pair of .105 howitzers, a battery of 4.2 mortars, and other

equipment were yanked across space. I recall only one accident. A three-quarter-ton truck dropped seventy feet to the bottom of a chasm. It is still rusting there.

Evacuation of wounded from the front was a serious problem. Day after day the stretcher bearers trudged away from the front, carrying the wounded as delicately as they could, utilizing blessed morphine to minimize the pain. In the end, after the slow trek of many miles, the wounded had the harrowing experience of being strapped to their litters and pulled across the chasms on swaying cables.

The ingenuity of the combat engineers was remarkable. At the first of the gorges, half of a lofty wooden bridge was still standing. The canyon was too wide for a Bailey bridge, but eventually a Bailey bridge was mated to the badly damaged wooden span. Engineers usually insist on a considerable factor of safety; here on this two-piece bridge the factor of safety closely approached zero. Each time a heavy bulldozer set out over the swaying, makeshift trestle everyone held his breath. Would the bulldozer make the far bank, or would it plunge into space? The bridge held.

In one place where it was impossible to construct a Bailey bridge over a ravine forty feet deep and one hundred and ten feet wide, bulldozers took the landscape to pieces. In sixty hours twenty thousand cubic yards of fill were pushed, shoveled, and hauled into the ravine, and then a road was built across it.

"The task," General Martin said, "looked as hopeless as filling the Grand Canyon with a teacup. However, in a matter of days, vehicles and artillery were winched across the fills, and, in a few days more, the gorges were passable. The 106th Engineer Combat Battalion believes it moved more dirt in a shorter time than any other combat battalion in this or any other war."

The campaign throughout was an engineering delirium. Hundreds of by-passes were built, and sixteen Bailey bridges and sixty-five wooden bridges were installed on Sayre Highway. Working continually in isolated places, on day and night shifts, these troops frequently had to drop their tools and pick up their guns to defend themselves against raids by bands of harassing Japanese.

On May 6 the advance elements of the infantry came under heavy
mortar and machine-gun fire from concealed enemy positions astride
the road. Thus began a six-day bloody struggle later known as the
"Battle of Colgan Woods," in honor of Chaplain Thomas A. Colgan.
Father Colgan repeatedly risked his life to bring in wounded men
who lay exposed and helpless, and finally a Japanese bullet—no respecter of the cloth—put an end to his heroic activities. His GIs idol-
ized him.

On May 12 the artillery arrived. Bolstered by artillery, mortars,
and air bombardment, the attack succeeded. The Japanese were annihilated and Sayre Highway was once again open. For the 31st
Division, the picture of the immediate situation was incalculably
brighter. One of the prizes of victory was the Maramag Airstrip.

While fresh troops pressed on, the battered 124th Infantry prepared foxholes and a perimeter for a peaceful night around the airfield. Some tired wag printed a sign on a piece of cardboard which
had been part of a ration carton: "REST CAMP! DO NOT DISTURB!"
Before dawn a Japanese force assaulted the perimeter in a series of
banzai attacks. No one knows the strength of the enemy force, but
seventy-two Japanese dead were lying across and between the foxholes next morning.

That same morning the *Miss Em* came down at Maramag. It was
the first and, I'm pretty sure, the only B-17 to land in that pasture. I,
of course, had no news of the night attack, but I knew that Clarence
Martin, never far behind his troops, was there. I wanted to know
what he needed, what he wanted, how Eighth Army could help.
Martin has written of my visit:

"During the morning the Eighth Army commander landed his
B-17 on the strip. The old war horse had a nose for gunpowder, but
no one knew he could scent it from Leyte, an hour or so away by
plane. Shortly after the three-star general had taken a satisfied look
at the dead enemy, viewed the assortment of weapons collected from
the Japanese, and had congratulated the men, a live Japanese, who
had penetrated to the center of the perimeter and had concealed
himself in the grass, made a break for the woods about a hundred

yards away. The count of dead Japs immediately rose to seventy-three."

On the way back from Maramag I had the opportunity to study the central Mindanao valley. To the north the country broadened out into a rolling grassy plateau flanked by mountains on both sides and cut at intervals by corridors of timber along the courses of transverse rivers. This had once been one hundred and twenty-five miles of grazing country. Now you could see from the air that no cattle wandered there. The Japanese, cut off from supplies, had killed all the cattle, and undisturbed grass grew as high as a piano.

When the rains came, I suspected, the 31st would run into real trouble. And it did. Sayre Highway broke down under the weight of Army vehicles. It became a commonplace then to see water buffalo, as patient and slow-footed as in General McCoy's day, bowing their necks to haul trucks out of the mire. Delaying actions and forays from the hills—there were about seventeen thousand Japanese in that section—added to each day's sodden misery.

General Sibert had predicted confidently that X Corps would be able to supply the 31st Division overland from the base at Parang. Earlier I had expressed my doubts. It was a hundred-and-fifty-mile truck haul from Parang to the upper valley, and over roads already in the process of dissolution. I decided that a new supply base on the northern coast of Mindanao was necessary, and acted at once. This decision later proved to be of great importance to the success of the campaign.

The Eighth Army had been making additional landings in Mindanao as fast as transport became available. I brought in the 162nd Infantry from Zamboanga, and a detachment of the Americal Division. On May 10 I watched from the air the landing of the 108th Regimental Combat Team, 40th Division, at Macajalar Bay. The new supply base was to be located there. This task force later was commanded by Brigadier General Shoe—just recovered from wounds received on Negros. Shoe had gone through the Luzon and Negros fighting as the 40th Division's assistant commander.

The assignment of the 108th was to proceed south from Macajalar and to join up with the 31st. Shoe's determined band started off with speed and dash, but soon they too were struggling with the problems of deep gorges and destroyed bridges. Nevertheless, thirteen days after the landing, Shoe and Martin shook hands as the northern and southern American forces on the Sayre Highway met at the village of Impalutao.

It was raining cats and dogs.

GRAND TOUR

For some time all of us had wondered whether the Navy or General MacArthur would have over-all command of the climactic campaign of the Pacific War—the invasion of Japan. I believe it was in April, during a conference with General MacArthur in Manila, that he told me the Joint Chiefs of Staff had chosen him for the task, and that Eighth Army was to have an important role to play. Then, and later, he expressed his satisfaction with the speed and dash of our troops, and with the cheerful way we accepted very limited shipping and supply, and made out expertly with what we had.

Credit for that, of course, belonged to my planning staff. I realize that the average civilian has little understanding of the intricacies of military supply and, more often than not, little interest. And that the textbook terms in which the Army talks about logistics usually serve to becloud rather than to clarify the issue. So I shall merely say that some Army commanders insist upon as much as sixty days of guaranteed supply before they will undertake an enterprise. This provides insurance against any contingency which may arise. But there can be, under certain circumstances, too much supply—odd as that may sound. I recall one Pacific island invasion in the later stages of the war when so many supply ships hit the beaches that the troops ashore, limited then in number, could not accomplish the dual job of unloading the ships and doing the fighting. They were supplied

232

by air—despite the wealth of cargo in the harbor—for four or five days.

Eighth Army, and Colonel "Tubby" Burgess in particular, made a common-sense approach to the supply problem. We threw logistical textbooks out the window and examined the facts. Large Japanese warships could no longer enter the seas around the Philippines, and we had control of the skies. The submarine danger had lessened, although still a reality, and the deadly threat of attack by suicide enemy aircraft was, of course, omnipresent. Nevertheless, it was plainly evident that our position was much better than that of the stranded Japanese armies in the central and southern Philippines. As a result we decided to conduct our amphibious expeditions on a basis of *fifteen* days' supply instead of sixty. To take care of possible emergencies we maintained floating supply at sea, which in case of dire trouble could be speeded to Cebu, Negros, Zamboanga, or Mindanao.

By the month of May, with the new base functioning at Macajalar Bay, with Woodruff being fed and ammunitioned by sea at Davao, our supply problem was pretty thoroughly licked. We never got into trouble with our unorthodox concept. Our fifteen-day supply proved, in all cases, to be adequate. When Bill Bowen, my operations officer, told me that General Steve Chamberlin at GHQ had described our Mindanao campaign as one of the most brilliant in American annals, I decided that my army had not done too badly. At the same time I knew we were by no means out of the woods.

I kept in touch with the situation by repeated flights to all the combat areas. I watched the 108th make its steep climb from seacoast to plateau. Chuck Downer brought the *Miss Em* in on the airstrip at Del Monte, which is in the rich pineapple country of northern Mindanao. There was nothing dramatic about the landing; the field was adequate and there was no trouble. It was not until the two of us later read newspaper dispatches that we realized ours was the first B-17 to land there since one of Brett's Fortresses settled down out of the sky to take General MacArthur to Australia in 1942. I had absolute faith in my pilot's judgment. On one visit to Clarence Martin, we eased in at Valencia. I wanted to go forward to watch the

fighting around Malaybalay but was told the grass strip there would not take a B-17. Even our Air Force transport C-47s would not risk it. They were landing their cargoes at Valencia; from Valencia the supplies were moved forward by truck, which took an additional four hours.

While I conferred with Martin, Downer took off in the only Cub at the 31st's headquarters. In about fifteen minutes or so he was back. When he reported, as a result of his own survey, that he could safely bring in the *Miss Em* at Malaybalay, I went aloft without the slightest perturbation. We made a beautiful landing, and were home again in Leyte by late afternoon.

The next day we were off on a more eventful visit. Doe's lads of the 41st Division had dug out most of the Japanese on the island of Jolo, and I had promised to pay a formal call on Muhammed Janail Abirir II, Sultan of Jolo and spiritual leader of the three hundred thousand Mohammedans in the Sulu Archipelago. This meant a round trip of approximately a thousand miles in one day, so we departed from Tacloban early. Weather was perfect. The airstrip at Jolo was no La Guardia Field, but, after circling it several times, Downer brought us in without incident. When we returned four and a half hours later, however, the wheels had sunk so far in the soft ground that it was necessary for a pair of tractors to pull the *Miss Em* out on the runway.

Colonel Moroney, thin and hard-bitten commander of the 163rd Infantry, veteran of Sanananda and Biak and other battles, met us, while his soldiers kept back the great crowd of Moro spectators who wanted to surge across the airstrip. First we drove through Jolo City, an ancient and once beautiful town which had been known as the "Jewel of the Sulus," and as the "Shrine City of the Moros." It was in ruins. The Japanese had put it to the torch when American PT boats attacked shipping in the harbor as a preliminary to invasion.

Then we started our drive inland. This was a country of great beauty, of teak and mahogany forests and dark low mountains. I knew the patriarchal Sultan (who had surrendered to Captain Pershing in 1913 at the end of the Moro War) had remained loyal to the United States during the Japanese occupation and had surreptitiously flown the Stars and Stripes at his hideout camp. When Moroney's men came ashore he brought out the tattered old flag.

The Sultan of Jolo—sometimes called the Sultan of Sulu—had once been a wealthy man. The Japanese had stripped him (he told me) of most of his possessions; he keenly felt the loss of a saber presented to him by General Pershing and a rifle presented to him by General Leonard Wood. I was somewhat surprised by the simplicity of his living. Around his compound there was a fine bamboo fence thickly woven to keep out Jap infiltrators. Inside the compound there was a sunken fort where the women could stay in safety while the men manned the barricades. The Sultan's unpretentious house stood on a raised bamboo platform well off the ground.

The Sultan was a gaunt, dignified old man with sunken cheeks. The room where we were received by the Sultan and his *datus* (leaders) seemed to be tapestried on ceilings and walls; I believe now that the tapestries actually were Persian rugs. After some diplomatic talk through interpreters, I presented him with the most modern type of American carbine and a scroll thanking him for his services to the American cause. In his presence I affixed a gold seal with ribbon to the document. I also presented him with a handsome roll of cloth as a tribute to the ladies of his household. The ladies did not appear, but during the visit we glimpsed them peeping out at us from doorways. I was told that the Sultan had eight wives and was, at seventy-two years of age, the recent father of a twenty-sixth son.

After leaving the Sultan we called on Governor Tulawe, Pershing's friend and interpreter. Although both of these ravaged old-timers had been impoverished by the Jap invasion, I noticed that both wore gold buttons inset with diamonds for the formal occasion. At both places my party and I had to take part in an elaborate feast. At each place gifts were presented to us, and it was only international politeness that we should present gifts in return.

This led to what the newspapers might call "My Most Embarrassing Moment." I had known I would meet the Sultan and was prepared, but I had not known I would meet Governor Tulawe. The Governor gave me a *barong* (a heavy knife), a pearl-handled *kris,*

and a spear. Even my own untutored eye could recognize that fine workmanship had gone into them. But I had nothing to give him, and I was heartily ashamed of that failure in diplomacy. On a later visit to Jolo I paid off my obligation.

During this period the 24th Division was pushing north and northwest from Davao and running into stubborn defenses. The days of our swift and roaring advance were now history; as we attempted to move into the hills the Japanese made our progress slow and costly. Davao had been a great naval and air base. Most of the ships and the planes were gone, but there was still ashore an arsenal of naval guns, aerial bombs, submarine mines, and torpedoes. Marines and naval shore units under Admiral Doi had retired to the north of Davao toward Mandog and controlled much of the area east of the Davao River. With their bombs and submarine mines and torpedoes, adapted to land use, they succeeded in mining almost all of the roads and trails which led toward Mandog.

Some of the mines had been installed hastily on the shoulders of the roads and could be spotted by alert observation, but it was a nerve-wracking job for our youngsters and slowed down forward movement to a sedate walk. When Woodruff's troops began absorbing heavy casualties from a pull type of mine which required manipulation by a concealed Jap in the jungle, small flanking patrols were thrust ahead of the main column on either side of the highway. Frequently patrols were able to cut the pull-rope or to flush the manipulator before the mine could be sprung. But in those thickets survival required a wary eye, an agile foot, and a ready weapon.

Woodruff now seemed to have opened Pandora's Box. Many days after the fall of Davao the nearby Libby Airstrip still was in range of Japanese artillery fire, and the Air Forces refused to allow American transport planes to go in. Landing on Padada strip downcoast would have meant a long, time-consuming trip by jeep to Woodruff's headquarters, so on one occasion my staff officers and I decided to fly in over the Japanese lines and land at Libby. To my surprise, Sibert and Woodruff had assembled tanks, anti-aircraft, and artillery at the field to make the landing as safe as possible from enemy attack. Under the circumstances, of course, I would have taken the same precautions to guard my military superior, but it occurred to me that the tanks and artillery would be more useful forward. I was the one at fault. As a result, I stayed away from Davao for the next two or three weeks.

But after that I went there frequently. I had great respect for Woodruff. I had known him in South Carolina when he was with the 77th Division. Later he was sent to England as a corps commander, and Colonel Hugh Cort went along as his chief of staff. For some reason General Eisenhower never gave Woodruff a combat assignment. Woodruff gladly relinquished a corps training command to get a lesser fighting command in the Pacific, and the able Cort (later a brigadier general) came with him. I had told Woodruff as he began his drive across Mindanao, "Let nothing stop you except bullets"; he took me at my word. I knew he was frequently at the front because I had been there with him. I knew he made almost daily flights over the battlefields in an unarmored Cub plane to seek out enemy positions.

The next time the *Miss Em* landed on Libby Airstrip, General Woodruff met me. It was an oven-hot day, one of those days when human flesh threatens to melt and part company with a man's bones. The shadiest place on the field was under a wing of the *Miss Em*. Standing there, I decorated the surprised Woodruff with the Silver Star for bravery, the Air Medal, and the Bronze Star. His ribbons were earned. Later I recommended him to the War Department for the Distinguished Service Medal.

Because of the concentration of Japanese forces, we had anticipated the trouble we ran into around Davao. There was one reasonably pleasant interlude: General Kenneth F. Cramer (assistant commander of the 24th and postwar chief of the Army's National Guard Bureau) led an amphibious expedition to Sarangani Bay and, with exceptionally light American losses, succeeded in wiping out Japanese forces there. But that is the only pleasant thing I can record about the rest of the campaign. The guerrilla forces who were expected to drive down from the north to join us failed to do so; we had to cut our way through to them.

In the meantime the Japanese Army forces had gathered themselves in the foothills around eleven-thousand-foot Mount Apo and

reorganized. A single battalion of the 21st RCT had been sent up the Kibawe Trail to capture and hold Mintal while stronger forces dispersed the Japanese naval units at Mandog. The Kibawe Trail ran along the Talomo River. That lone battalion hung on in Mintal under severe attack and round-the-clock mortar fire. Energetically it attempted to clear out its rear areas, protect its left flank against infiltration, and seize the bluffs along the northeast bank of the Talomo. Its admirable courage was outweighed by the enemy's numerical strength. The 19th, which was supposed to drive west from Mandog to assist, couldn't get there, and it was a considerable time before elements of the 34th Infantry could be shaken loose to join the trapped infantrymen. The fight along the Talomo's bluffs became a slugging match. These enemy troops did not retreat. They fought it out, and they infiltrated every night to kill GIs even in the 34th's rear areas. Some of the most murderous fighting of the campaign took place there after dark. The action was confused and often seemed pointless. After the war, however, it was discovered that Japanese losses around Mintal were extremely heavy. That dazed and frightened night fighting must have seemed to many doughboys like a bad dream, but it ended the desire of Japanese soldiers to fight for Mindanao.

Soon they were in full retreat. The 19th dispersed the naval forces, reached Mintal, and pressed on to Calinan. From Mintal to Calinan our troops progressed through an almost impenetrable thicket of hemp. It is difficult to make clear to Americans, who are used to honest elms, maples, oaks, butternuts, and hickories, the tanglewild which results when cultivated abacá is allowed to run loose for five years. Branches join one another; only specks of sunlight get through. Every hour of the day is dusk.

In the end there was no way to locate Jap defensive and delaying positions except to send a man in with a gun. The casualties among our scouts became staggering. Repeated efforts were made by reconnaissance troops to find a suitable crossing of the Talomo River somewhere near the headwaters. A few men were able to get across a three-hundred-foot canyon and to climb the vertical cliffs; they were compelled to use ropes and a mountain-climbing technique.

This made it evident that a general crossing was impracticable. Our advance toward Tamogan must be made on the left-hand side of the Talomo River.

By this time, some troops of the 24th, moving steadily upland in the temperature of a brick kiln, had wearied. They welcomed the 162nd and elements of the 163rd Infantry Regiments of the 41st Division which I sent forward to take over their sector. Mount Mano had become our main obstacle. An attack plan had already been devised. The 19th would attack on the right, the 162nd in the center, and the 34th on the south flank. But when our troops cautiously approached this stronghold, the remnants of the Japanese force abandoned hope of effective resistance and fled.

Much earlier, X Corps had been convinced by guerrilla information that the Japanese had constructed a road from inland Kibawe to coastal Talomo. After the Sayre Highway had been secured, General Sibert decided to send the 31st Division southeast from Kibawe in order to attack from the rear the Japanese who then faced Woodruff above Davao. I did not believe this was feasible. The way led through trackless forest and wild mountain country. Even the one known road or trail that the guerrillas talked about vanished somewhere east of the Pulangi River. My many flights over Mindanao had convinced me that our job was to drive the Japanese into those barbarous wastes, and that, once they were prisoners of the terrain, we should let them stay there and starve.

I am glad I countermanded Sibert's order. If the men of the 31st Division had continued to drive to the southeast from Kibawe it would have met not only the twenty-two thousand Japanese which the American Army's G-2 said were there, but also a good many of the sixty thousand who actually were there. Our troops killed between thirteen and fourteen thousand Japanese, and more than twenty-three thousand surrendered at war's end. Thousands more, we are sure, died of wounds and sickness or starved in the mountains. Some may be there yet.

Once again I have got ahead of my calendar. Earlier General MacArthur had told me he wanted to see the places where Eighth Army had been fighting. On June 3 I reported in Manila and went aboard

the cruiser *Boise*. After dinner I sat on deck with the Allied commander and watched a beautiful sunset drop into darkness as we
moved sleekly out of Manila Bay. It was General MacArthur's first
trip past ageless Corregidor since his dramatic departure in 1942. He
did the talking, and very good talk it was. He talked about the
desperation of those last days in Luzon. He told me about President
Roosevelt's personal communication which ordered him to Australia,
and of his unwillingness to leave General "Skinny" Wainwright there
on Bataan to struggle to the inevitable end.

The cruiser's first stop was to be in Mindoro, and the second at
Macajalar Bay. Thus we were following the route by which General
MacArthur and his family had escaped from the Philippines. They
had traveled by PT boat and by night from Luzon. At the first dawn
they headed into Mindoro and slept the day. When darkness came
again they were hurried through uncertain and rough water to Macajalar Bay. There, General MacArthur told me, he lived for several
days with his wife and infant son and a few staff officers at Del
Monte (a few miles inland) until airlift was provided from Australia.

When the *Boise* dropped anchor off Agusan in Macajalar Bay,
General MacArthur and I went ashore and started down the Sayre
Highway toward General Martin's headquarters at Malaybalay.
We took one side excursion. General MacArthur wanted to see the
Del Monte Country Club which had sheltered him three years be-
fore. After considerable search we found the site—but only the site.
Bombs had demolished the building; only the foundations, now
overgrown by vegetation, remained to remind one that there once
had been riches and luxury in northern Mindanao. And that, though
man has only a short memory, nature has none.

I had suggested that we go to Malaybalay by air, but General
MacArthur wanted to make the overland trip. All the bridges over
the gorges were now replaced, but I am sure the Allied commander
got a very clear picture of the dreadful terrain with which the 108th
RCT and the 31st Division had wrestled. The road was still a ram-
bling wreck, and—Malaybalay and return—it was a pounding and
spine-cracking ride. There were turnabouts and roundabouts and all

sorts of detours. On the return trip to Agusan the rains, which had taken a holiday, started in again. On several occasions bulldozers pulled out of deep mudholes the jeep in which General MacArthur and I were riding. Traveling time for the hundred-and-twenty-mile trip was then about eight hours, but General MacArthur never once acknowledged physical discomfort. My own teeth were clicking like castanets and my sacroiliac was in painful revolt. There were occasions on makeshift bridges when I put more stock in prayer than in the timbers which supported us. However, nothing happened.

"General MacArthur and I are both lucky," I wrote my wife, "that we are not this moment looking up at the Sayre Highway—with the rain in our faces—from the ground floor of a canyon. What a road!"

The *Boise* sailed that night, and during the next two days we visited Cebu, Negros, and Panay. On two of the islands the fighting was virtually at an end. At Cebu, Duke Arnold took us on a thirty-mile trip while the tactics of that peculiar struggle were discussed. General MacArthur was impressed by the job the Americal Division had done. The next morning we were at Negros. Rapp Brush carried our party of staff officers and correspondents from Bacolod to the mountains east of Silay in captured Japanese motorcars. We made the last lap of the journey by jeep and spent a half-hour at an operations post on an eminence from which we had a view of most of the mile-high battlefield. Fighting was still going on against prepared positions. Because of infiltration, all American and Filipino units there encircled themselves nightly with a complete necklace of barbed wire. It paid off at Negros because the Japanese were inquisitive and brave and committed to murderous enterprise. They were quite willing to accept a cut throat to cut an American throat. The wire made this kind of equalization more difficult. General MacArthur praised Brush's 40th Division troops and decorated three sergeants of the 503rd Parachute Regiment for gallantry.

I remembered a story Bob Shoe told on himself. During the hottest of the fighting on Negros, he was making a trip to the front to look over the situation. His jeep passed through a weary column of the 503rd Parachute which had been relieved after many hours of fighting and was on its way to the rear. General Shoe is completely

free of pretentiousness; he was born honest and friendly. When he stopped for a drink at a spring he spoke to a grimy paratrooper. His question didn't mean anything; it was merely passing the time of day.

"How are things at the front?" Shoe asked cheerfully.

The veteran paratrooper, probably twenty years old, looked at Shoe's clean uniform and his star and his jeep with elaborate boredom and said nothing. Shoe went on to the front and was quite promptly shot. It was a bloody wound, and the stretcher which carried him toward the rear was thoroughly incarnadined. On the way back his stretcher was stopped by a military traffic jam, and he found himself again among the walking 503rd. He saw the same redheaded young PFC he had encountered back at the spring. The PFC was friendly now. He grinned. "General," he said, "how are things at the front?"

In the afternoon General MacArthur and I returned to Bacolod and took off by PT boat for Iloilo. The trip to the island of Panay was through choppy water and at a speed of about fifty miles an hour, which makes for tossing around and occasional wonderment that one is still afloat. I suspected that the Navy lads were giving the older men "the treatment." We bounced and jounced, and the sea-water spray was like wet confetti, but we landed at Iloilo without complaint. As we went ashore General MacArthur remarked that Iloilo had been his first assignment as a second lieutenant, and he pointed out landmarks and changes as we toured the town.

At Iloilo, General MacArthur and I temporarily parted company. He, General Bonner Fellers, Colonel Egeburg, and others were to go on to watch the Australian invasion of Borneo. At one time it had been proposed at GHQ that Eighth Army take over the landings on Borneo and Java after the Philippines campaign was ended. I did not like the idea because I thought there was more important work farther north; but, anyway, British Empire protests about areas of control quickly took care of the matter. The Australians invaded Borneo with Allied naval and air cover. Sometimes I have wondered whether history might have been changed if Eighth Army had eventually captured Java. In that case, the surrender of Japanese weapons would have been made to American troops instead of to Indonesian partisans. Would this have made a difference in the future of Java and Indonesia? Would it have prevented years of anarchy and bloodshed there?

I returned to Leyte by air and for several days was snowed under by administrative work. Then Colonel Coenraad Giebel, as the representative of Queen Wilhelmina and General van Oyen, arrived to pin a Dutch medal on my chest for the work of I Corps the year before in capturing Hollandia. (Colonel Giebel is now Lieutenant General Giebel, chief of Air Staff for the Netherlands.) General Stilwell, Lieutenant General Sir Charles Henry Gairdner of the British Army, and several other visiting officers were my guests at Tacloban at the time and witnessed the simple ceremony.

Naturally I appreciated the thoughtfulness of the Netherlands government and felt that both I Corps and myself were highly honored. But the business of medal giving apparently has its complexities and its amusing side. When Hollandia was taken, I am told, Dutch diplomats approached American military men in Brisbane and asked who had conquered Hollandia. The answer was: General MacArthur. He was decorated as the conqueror of Hollandia. Dutch officers made the same inquiry at Sixth Army headquarters at Finschhafen, and the answer was: General Krueger. General Krueger was decorated. When Van Oyen's representative decorated me, as the task force commander, that rounded out the full circle. General MacArthur, General Krueger, and I have medals which certify each of us to be the conqueror of Hollandia. What could be fairer—or more diplomatic—than that?

That same morning General Stilwell, General Gairdner, and I set out by B-17 for Mindanao. We landed at Del Monte for an hour's conference with Sibert and Martin, and didn't see the sun again for two days. We spent the rest of the rainy day and rainy night with Woodruff at Davao City, and set off the next rainy morning from a muddy airfield for a flight through storms to Zamboanga. I left my guests there and took a flying boat to Jolo. The *Boise* dropped anchor in Jolo harbor about two in the afternoon, and I rejoined General MacArthur, who reported the Borneo expedition completely success-

ful. It was a crowded day. The Sultan and Governor Tulawe came into Jolo to pay their respects to General MacArthur, but he seemed indifferent and preoccupied and cut their visit short. After a tour of the island we went back aboard the *Boise* and headed for Davao City. General Kenney, who now commanded both the Fifth Air Force and the Thirteenth Air Force in the Pacific, was aboard. George and I spent two hours discussing the Philippines campaign and the problems which lay ahead.

That evening General MacArthur talked to us for almost two hours about coming events, and next morning we landed at Davao City. We went as far forward as Mintal, where Jock Clifford and his troops had not yet been able to end their struggle against a stubborn enemy. But we had reason to observe that massive artillery support—now under command of Hugh Cort—was true, accurate, and devastating. It was then that General MacArthur told me he did not believe there were four thousand Japanese left alive on Mindanao; the surrender figures at war's end—twenty-three thousand enemy soldiers—show how wrong he was. That same day we set out for Zamboanga. Jens Doe was on leave in the United States, and Brigadier General Harold Haney, who had led the attack on Palawan, was our host.

I had been at Zambo many times, but General MacArthur had not. Zamboanga City was pretty badly chewed up. Along the principal boulevard there once had been a procession of old and beautiful acacia trees which were now gaunt and torn stumps. Many of the modern buildings were wrecked. I was pleased that General MacArthur could find that Fort Pilar, built long ago by the Spaniards as an outpost against the Moros, was still intact. There was moss growing on the wet stone walls, which were twenty feet thick and rose impressively above the sea wall which held in check the tides of the Sulu Sea. Around that fort, after the Spanish-American War, the Americans constructed Pettit Barracks—a glamorous name to the young officers of General MacArthur's generation and perhaps even more glamorous to mine.

I was proud of the job the 41st Division had accomplished at Zambo when the fighting was done. They laid down their guns and went to work. They cut weeds and they cleaned out debris. They became

good neighbors. The Japanese had refused to allow Catholic Filipinos
—there were a good many in that Moslem area—to worship at the
ancient shrine of Bien Bernido al Virgen del Pilar. The shrine was
about the size of an American sandwich shop, and it was tucked into
a space along a section of the Fort Pilar wall which had fallen into
ruin. GIs of the 41st Signal Company (and I hope my good friend
Cardinal Spellman will note this) went at the work of repair and
finally put up a sign welcoming all nationalities to worship there
again. Before long there were hundreds of burning candles, and the
glory of Pilar's ancient shrine was restored. Methodists, Episcopalians,
Congregationalists, Presbyterians, and lads of no faith at all took part
in that enterprise.

I left General MacArthur at Zamboanga. I knew now what the future held. I would take over-all command of the Philippines on July
1. Sixth Army staff would be retired to plan an invasion of the southern islands of Japan. According to GHQ plan, Sixth Army would in-
vade Kyushu—and hold. General MacArthur told me that Eighth Army
later would make the main blow along with reinforcements which
were still to come from the States or the European theater. Eighth
Army, with most of the armored and paratroop divisions, was to land
and to proceed across the Kanto Plain to capture Yokohama and
Tokyo. General MacArthur's choice of Eighth Army to make the
strike was a great compliment to my men, but I knew the Kanto
Plain—and what a gamble lay ahead.

THE MOUNTAINS OF LUZON

There are many things about the southern Philippines campaign which are worthy of study. American teamwork on the water, in the air, and on the ground was excellent. And, in these modern days of the interdependence of all the services, only teamwork accomplishes the mission. There was a time when the rivalries between the services had a certain usefulness; I am sure the era has vanished. There was a time when the rivalries created what some of my contemporaries called "healthy competition." But in my lifetime I have seen the enmities and suspicions growing out of "healthy competition" sometimes penetrate to the highest level of command. We live now under Damocles' sword, and it is perhaps no exaggeration to say that there may come a day when Americans—military and civilian alike—will either work together or die separately.

Not too long ago a Navy friend who had read a series of articles contributed to the *Saturday Evening Post* wrote generously to me. "One of the finest features of your articles," said the Admiral's letter, "was the absence of any rancor or play-up of the differences of opinion between the various services involved in the Pacific War. I know this was deliberate on your part, having seen the harm that has been done all of us by the overemphasis which has been placed on inter-service frictions."

Well, I had and have no rancor. I disagreed sometimes with the decisions of the Navy, and I disagreed often with the decisions of the Air Force, and there were times when I was not in agreement with all the decisions of my own superiors. But in war—ancient or modern—there must be a certain amount of give and take. Most commanders do their best; all are fallible. Even Stonewall Jackson, the idol of many military historians, was guilty of errors of decision. In our war with the Japanese, particularly in the first years, an impartial judgment must take into account the American insufficiency of weapons and manpower, the lack of firm Intelligence, and the thousands of miles of uncharted sea and unknown land which presented themselves to military planners as possible avenues of advance.

This was not a battle area like Europe, fought over a hundred times, where every river and valley and eminence is known to the textbooks, where the offensive and defensive possibilities of known terrain have been exploited for centuries. The American GIs progressing up a natural valley were retracing the steps of Napoleon's legions, and the rumble of their tanks might have been in an earlier century the roll of Marlborough's drums. When the Americans crossed the Rhine some few may have remembered that Julius Caesar bridged it two thousand years before. But the Southwest Pacific was something else again. Excepting our brief skirmish with Spain, this was a section which had never been the scene of a war between great powers. I have spoken earlier of the inadequacies of maps, of the lack of highways and accurate navigational information. On the enormous island of New Guinea, for example, the white man's influence had penetrated only a few miles inland from the seacoast. Planning a military campaign on the basis of word-of-mouth information and air reconnaissance has its hazards, but a campaign must be planned. Then it must be fought.

I have tried to tell at first hand the story of the Ground Forces, with a natural emphasis on those troops I knew and commanded. This is not because I fail to appreciate the magnificent achievements of the greatest Navy which ever sailed an ocean, or because I fail to appreciate the gallantry and devotion to duty of land-based fighter and bomber pilots, or because I underestimate the intrepid-

ity of our Marine Corps or the expertness of the fine youngsters who manned carrier-based planes. I have concentrated on the story of the ground troops because it has not been adequately told before, and because it is the story I know best.

Every troop movement in the Pacific depended upon the Navy and the Air for success, and I have never met an infantry commander silly enough to deny it. After Pearl Harbor the Navy fought with both arms in slings. It was the unbelievable effrontery of an inferiorly armed American group which turned the Japanese Navy back from Guadalcanal. I knew Admirals Norm Scott and Dan Callaghan, who died there in line of duty; our channel of supply to Australia was never again threatened. The Air Force in those desperate times showed equal fortitude. After the Jap sneak attacks had destroyed most of our fighter planes as they lay in regimented order on the ground at Pearl Harbor and on Nichols and Clark Fields in the Philippines, a few beat-up B-17s with overworked ground crews tried to slow up the Jap advance through Indonesia. It was a lost cause, but day after day pilots and crews kept those bombers in the air. I agree with the eloquent chaplain who prayed one morning:

"God bless these pilots and crews. There is no harder job, Lord, than to continue the attack when defeat seems certain."

Indonesia had been lost and the Antipodes seemed in hazard when General Kenney came to Australia. General MacArthur was already established as the Allied commander. Our fighter planes began to arrive by ship, but it was already evident that the Japanese Zero was superior in maneuverability, and that the Japanese pilots of that time were well trained and highly skilled. Our radar in northern Australia was almost worthless, but on occasion it did provide sufficient warning so our fighters could get in the air in time to fight on fairly even terms with enemy raiders. We were outnumbered five to one. Replacements were easy for the enemy and hard for us.

Great credit is due General Kenney for his unquenchable enthusiasm in the face of odds, and for a brilliant improvisation which helped to equalize an unequal struggle. He adapted the techniques of air combat to meet local conditions. Years before, Kenney had devised the parachute fragmentation bomb, which permits low-altitude attack without injury to the attacking plane. The bomb roused little enthusiasm in Ordnance; nevertheless, Kenney used it with devastating effect against the Japanese when they were advancing—and retreating—along the Kokoda Trail. In the Pacific, also, the inventive George and his associates conceived the scheme of "skip bombing" at sea. The idea was (perhaps too simply stated here) that if a plane got low enough, it could skip a bomb along the water in the same way a boy skips a flat stone across a millpond. The Air Force used this against Japanese vessels with some success—one more weapon in the arsenal.

At the war's beginning, General Marshall had impressed on all ranking Army officers the importance of becoming "air minded." Most of us took his instruction seriously, and I am sure my own record of hours in the air cannot be challenged. But there were times, as the Pacific War went forward, when the infantry began to wonder whether it was not also the obligation of the Air officers to become "ground minded." At Buna our troops were supplied by air transport but were often endangered by American bombing and strafing. At that time I asked Kenney to send over one of his own staff officers (and I said I would house him in my own tent) so the Air could be accurately briefed about our offensives. I never received a reply. When the last Wirraway was shot down, our air reconnaissance ended. I did not take this in good part, and do not yet.

At Biak I had superior tactical support by the Third Attack Group. I have no quarrel with the conception of a strategic air force. But a war cannot be waged in a vacuum, and there must be room enough in any modern conception of war for a tactical air group which intelligently supports ground forces. Major General Paul ("Squeeze") Wurtsmith was the commander of the Thirteenth Air Force, a brave and most efficient officer. At Zamboanga the second wave of his bombers, through some inadvertence, arrived an hour late and dropped their eggs where, by time schedule, the advance elements of the 41st Division were supposed to be located. Fortunately the invading troops had been held up by water and land mines on the beachhead. It was a narrow escape from catastrophe. Brigadier General Tommy White, Wurtsmith's outstanding assistant, was on board the command ship *Rocky Mount* with us, and he quickly straightened matters out.

There were four groups of Marine fliers who, in the interest of the integration of the services, were attached to the Thirteenth Air Force. During the central and southern Philippines campaign I had personal contact with the 12th, 14th, and 32nd Groups, and that was enough to convince me. These fliers had been trained by the Marine Corps with ground troops for the *specific purpose* of supporting ground troops. Their accomplishments were superb in the Zamboanga and Mindanao campaigns. The Marine liaison officers were always in the front lines with the infantry commanders, and they were as familiar with the forward positions as was the infantry. By radio they guided in the planes, and often the target of the strike was no more than three hundred yards ahead of the huddled doughboys.

Colonel Clayton C. Jerome commanded these airmen, and their accurate bombing and strafing earned them the gratitude and friendship of the 24th, 31st, and 41st Infantry Divisions. Nothing comforts a soldier, ankle-deep in mud, faced by a roadblock or fortified strongholds, as much as the sight of bombs wreaking havoc on stubborn enemy positions. It puts heart into him. Jerome's groups received official commendations from me as commander of Eighth Army, from General Sibert as commander of X Corps, from General Woodruff, General Martin, and General Doe. When Colonel Jerome (now General Jerome) came up for promotion after the war, Clovis Byers and I wrote letters to the Marine Corps expressing our admiration for his abilities. Can this be service selfishness?

I had chosen Baguio, a spectacular little city about a hundred and sixty miles north of Manila, for my northern Luzon headquarters. I had been there with my wife twenty-five years before and remembered with pleasure the coolness of the mile-high climate and the wild and breath-taking scenery of the mountain ranges which rise, tier on tier, toward the blue east. Camp John Hay, a permanent mili-

tary installation which had been used as an American rest camp before Philippine independence, is located there, and the town was
once the summer capital. The house I chose for quarters had been
built as the home of the American High Commissioner and now
serves as the summer residence of the American Ambassador to the
Philippines.

For many years a brilliantly engineered scenic highway led from
Manila to Baguio. This was called the Kennon Highway in honor of
its builder, Colonel Lyman W. V. Kennon. Bombings had destroyed
the bridges over the gorges, and Baguio in the summer of 1945 could
be reached only by a longer and more roundabout route. Baguio
itself had suffered gravely, although a group of nuns located there
told me that the Japanese had been gone for three days before the
American bombings began. The airmen, of course, had no way of
knowing that an evacuation had taken place. The High Commissioner's handsome house escaped the general damage. It had been
strafed but not bombed; windows were broken, but machine-gun
bullets had only nicked the walls. Inside, the nara and mahogany
paneling, the chandeliers, mirrors, and mantels were generally intact.

During the Luzon period I was doing three-way commuting between Leyte, Manila, and Baguio, with frequent air trips to the
various fronts where the 6th, 37th, and 32nd Divisions were still
encountering very stubborn resistance from Yamashita's army. After
the steamy heat of Telegrafo and the glittering, brassy sun of Manila,
it was always a happy change when my plane came down at Naguilian Airstrip and I knew that for a day or so I would be cool
again. Naguilian Airstrip was a tiny field in a rugged area without
an adequate runway for a B-17, so we always used a plane smaller
than the *Miss Em* for the Baguio trips. From Naguilian we shifted
to a motorcar for the steep trip up the mountain to the town, and I
shivered in the delightful anticipation of a chilly night's sleep.

Only those who have lived in tropical temperatures month in and
month out can appreciate the pleasure of wearing a sweater to bed,
or the luxury of a climate which demands fires in the grates every
evening. I remember one morning in mid-July of 1945 when I awak-

ened at six. It was dark because the house was entirely surrounded by clouds. Twenty minutes later Baguio was bright and shining as the sun came over the mountains. I wandered around the damp verandas barefooted. The valley was still full of broken clouds that looked like clabbered milk. To the east the ranges rose higher and higher, and everywhere were the tall and beautiful pines for which the region is famous.

The XIV Corps had decided that its most difficult mission in northern Luzon would be the destruction of enemy forces in the Cagayan valley, which lies between the unsurveyed coastal Sierra Madre Mountains on the east and the Cordillera Mountains on the west. As a result, three American divisions, General Beightler's 37th, General Gill's 32nd, and General Hurdis' 6th, had been assigned to the task. Major General Charles Hurdis had succeeded to the command of the 6th Division after General Patrick's death in action. In addition, a guerrilla group under Colonel Russell W. Volckmann was to engage and destroy enemy units in the Cordillera Mountains and press eastward to join up with the advancing Americans. Volckmann's group, known somewhat elaborately as the "United States Army Forces in the Philippines, Northern Luzon," was the only guerrilla outfit in Luzon which functioned as an independent unit.

Only a few main roads traverse this section of the island. Japanese transport suffered heavily from American air attack during the retreat into the mountains; there were no alternate routes for vehicles, and they made easy and profitable targets for our bombers and strafers. Abandoned artillery, tanks, and thousands of wrecked and battered trucks were scattered along Highway No. 4 and Highway No. 5, and bridges were out for miles. This made life miserable for the enemy, but it also confronted our pursuing forces with severe engineering problems and unavoidably slowed down movement.

I started on my first air tour of the northern Luzon fronts on July 6. General Griswold met me at the San Jose Airstrip and we immediately motored through the wildest kind of fighting country to celebrated Balete Pass. It didn't take much imagination, even for a newcomer, to realize what a fine job the 25th Division must have done to win their victory there. The 25th had been relieved, and the 32nd's command post was now located there. I had a long talk with Gill and Horace Harding, his artillery commander. They were pressing on Bontoc, which was the key enemy position in that area, with one regimental combat team fighting north from Baguio.

Griswold had his corps headquarters in the buildings of a Filipino agricultural college outside San Jose. There hadn't been a student there since 1942. The Japanese for several years had found the quarters eminently satisfactory, and so did we. When I saw a movie in San Jose that night and slept in an excellent bed, I'm afraid I arrived in my own mind at the decision that the tussle on Luzon was just about over.

Manila is farther away from northern Luzon than road maps indicate. In one kind of calculation it is two or three hundred miles; in another kind of calculation it is two or three hundred years. Manila, beautiful bright Manila, however crumbled by war, is a cosmopolitan city. But a half-hour plane trip will set you down—away from the main highways—among barbaric tribes. The Igorots around Baguio have been conditioned by the times—one of the most admirable mansions there was built by an American who made a fortune in the nearby gold mines and married an Igorot girl. Their daughter showed me through the house. But at last report the Igorots who come in from the hills still maintain their native market, and are represented, governmentally, by a committee which advises the town council on matters of interest to non-Christians. There are still native peoples in the mountain section who are animists and worship the forces of nature.

We left San Jose the next morning in a C-47. Generals Griswold and Byers and a number of other officers were with me. We came down at Bagabag, in 6th Division territory. General Hurdis met us and we jeeped to the command post of the 63rd Infantry in the mountains northwest of Bagabag on the road to Bontoc. Colonel Everett Yon was full of fight, and the situation looked good: Yon's forward elements were within two hundred yards of the hills overlooking a Japanese stronghold at Kiangan, and he expected to take it within a few hours. There I had my first glimpse of almost naked savages, armed only with spears, who were fighting side by side with our troops. These were the Ifugaos. The tribesmen had come down from their villages and thrown in their lot with us. They were tall, broad-shouldered, splendidly muscled, and despite the cold climate wore only G-strings. They carried deerskin packs. The first one I met, however, indicated by sign language that he wanted a cigarette. Since I don't smoke I couldn't oblige him. Colonel Yon told me that the Ifugaos were excellent fighters; they were also the best of our native scouts.

My next port of call was the headquarters of the 37th Division at Tuguegarao, where my friend General Bob Beightler met me. We proceeded to the command post of the 148th Infantry about fifteen miles to the south, where I had a talk with Colonel Delbert E. Schultz. The 37th controlled the upper section of the Cagayan valley, and in conjunction with the 11th Airborne, which had made a landing at the seaport of Aparri, had seized control of Highway No. 5 shortly before Eighth Army took over. The job of the 37th was to eliminate by-passed Japanese units, a discouraging job indeed. This meant going into sections altogether without roads. The enemy was incapable of offensive action, but the heavy rains aggravated the problem and made it sheer drudgery. The 37th could supply its own troops and evacuate the wounded only by the use of rivers which were often turbulent and unruly. Vehicles with tracks helped on the native trails. Jeeps in the eastern reaches could get nowhere. The object of our offensive campaign was to drive the enemy from the food-producing areas into the Sierra Madre Mountains, where their strength would diminish because of starvation and disease. In retrospect it seems to me that this campaign accomplished little and could have readily been foregone.

The 37th (the Ohio Division) had done a brilliant job in Luzon earlier, and that night at Tuguegarao I listened sympathetically when General Beightler, in the calmest and most measured of words, described his disappointment that his troops had never received proper approbation for their achievements. Pride is important to the morale of combat troops. But this was an old story in the Pacific, where combat units, particularly early in the war, so often were anonymous. Supposedly this censorship was based on security. Actually, of course, the Japanese knew the units we had in any immediate theater, just as we knew theirs. Our policy was ill advised because it is the nature of the American GI to want the home folks to know what his outfit is doing. That evening General Beightler mentioned the fact that the Republican party in Ohio desired him to come back and go into politics. General Beightler was a National Guard officer. In the end he decided to forego politics. He is now a senior major general, Regular Army.

During the next several days I continued to inspect the troops in the field. The headquarters of the 38th Division, which had been assigned the job of cleaning up central Luzon, was on a ridge only about an hour's ride east of Manila. Major General William C. Chase, division commander, met me at Nielson Field, and we made the inspection trip to the front together. From a high hill, Chase and General Bill Spence pointed out to me the Ipo Dam area and other battlefields of the 38th; although the tempo of the fighting was now slowed, two hundred and fifty-nine Japanese were killed between dawn and dusk the day I visited there, and twenty-nine were captured. The 38th and elements of the 43rd Division inflicted appalling losses on the enemy during a six-week period. Some sixty-three hundred Japanese were killed or found dead and more than nine hundred were made prisoners. Much of this slaughter was accomplished by combined artillery fire and aerial attack. Losses of the 38th Division and 43rd Division were small.

That evening at Chase's headquarters I wrote General MacArthur that I had inspected the combat-active divisions on Luzon and found morale very high. My own morale was high. I was convinced that the back of Japanese opposition was broken and that the enemy was incapable of effective resistance. I might not have been so optimistic if I had known that, considerably after the official Japanese capitulation, General Yamashita was to come out of the mountain wildernesses to the northeast of Baguio and surrender forty thousand well-disciplined troops.

Although negotiations with Yamashita for surrender were completed after Eighth Army had relinquished control of Luzon, the
story should be told here. It must be remembered that Japanese
forces at this period had little or no communication with the homeland. On August 7—the day of the fall of the first atomic bomb—an
American pilot was forced to abandon his disabled plane and parachute behind the Japanese lines in northern Luzon. He was picked
up by an enemy patrol the next morning and taken after five days
of forced marches to General Yamashita's headquarters, then southwest of Kiangan.

There he was subjected to vigorous and prolonged interrogation.
He was threatened with physical violence when he steadfastly refused to answer questions. On August 16—the Emperor first offered to capitulate on August 10—the attitude of the Japanese in-
terrogators abruptly changed. The pilot received medical treatment
for his parachute-jump injuries and was extended many small cour-
tesies. The next day the American was guided toward the American
lines; when the Japanese soldiers had gone as far as they dared, they
gave the flier a letter, written by Yamashita himself, which explained
the circumstances of the pilot's capture and commended him for his
military spirit and devotion to duty.

On August 24 the same pilot flew an L-5 liaison plane over the
area in which he had been held and dropped a message of thanks
to General Yamashita and two signal panels of great visibility. The
message, written by General Gill of the 32nd Division, suggested
that if Yamashita were in the mood for surrender negotiations he
should display the two signal panels as evidence of his willingness
to parley. The following morning another pilot found the panels
staked out according to instructions; also on the ground were many
cheering, hand-waving Japanese soldiers, who beckoned the plane
to land. Instead, a second message was dropped. It suggested that
Yamashita send an envoy to the American lines to receive detailed
instructions for his surrender.

Late in the afternoon of August 26 a Japanese captain, carrying
Yamashita's answer, entered the American lines under a flag of truce.
The letter, which was written in English, follows:

GENERAL HEADQUARTERS
IMPERIAL JAPANESE ARMY
IN THE PHILIPPINES

August 25, 1945

TO: General W. H. Gill, Commanding General
Kiangan-Boyombong Area
United States Army in the Philippines

1. I have the honor to acknowledge receipt of your communication addressed to me, dropped by your airplane on August 24th as well as your papers dropped on August 25th in response to our ground signals.

2. I am taking this opportunity to convey to you that order from Imperial Headquarters pertaining to cessation of hostilities was duly received by me on August 20th and that I have immediately issued orders to cease hostilities to all units under my command insofar as communications were possible. I also wish to add to this point the expression of my heartfelt gratitude to you, full cognizant of the sincere efforts and deep concern you have continuously shown with reference to cessation of hostilities as evidenced by various steps and measures you have taken in this connection. To date of writing, however, I have failed to receive order from Imperial Headquarters authorizing me to enter into direct negotiations here in the Philippines with the United States Army concerning the carrying out of the order for cessation of hostilities, but I am of the fond belief that upon receipt of this order, negotiations can be immediately entered into. Presenting my compliments and thanking you for your courteous letter, I remain, yours respectfully,

/s/ T. YAMASHITA

Tomoyuki Yamashita, General, Imperial Japanese Army,
Highest Commander of the Imperial Japanese Army in the Philippines.

This message was the first of a series exchanged between Yamashita and General Gill. The exquisite courtesy of the exchanges probably has for the average reader something of the quality of *Through the Looking-Glass;* these same troops and same commanders had been fighting each other in the same area with no quarter whatever and in a completely barbaric manner. But in the Japanese military character there is a combination of exquisite courtesy and utter savagery, which I understand but am at a loss to explain. I

had met it in 1918–20 during the Siberian adventure—when I first became convinced that the Japanese military intended to dominate Asia.

During the exchange of messages between Yamashita and Gill
the treacherous air currents in that section of Luzon brought about
a plane crash which resulted in the death of the commander of the
127th Infantry. Colonel Merle H. Howe, the onetime schoolteacher
whose blue language appalled rough-spoken top sergeants, the
driving leader who helped make the Buna victory possible, was not
to go home again to his native Middle West. I never knew a more
determined or more courageous fighter.

Eventually an American radio group, escorted by a Japanese safe-
conduct party, moved into Yamashita's headquarters to take over
communications. Details of the surrender were worked out. On the
morning of September 2 General Yamashita and a party of twenty-
one, which included Vice Admiral Okochi ("Highest Commander of
the Japanese Naval Forces in the Philippines"), entered American
lines at Kiangan. The party was escorted to Baguio where the for- ·
mal instrument of the surrender of all Japanese Army and Navy
personnel in the Philippines was signed in my former headquarters.

I was sorry that General Griswold who had directed XIV Corps
operations could not be there to accept Yamashita's sword. But it
was entirely fitting that the 32nd Division should receive the van-
quished enemy. Three years before at Buna they had won the battle
that started the infantry on the jungle road to Tokyo.

General Yamashita was tried for "crimes against humanity" by an
American Military Court in Manila. He was sentenced December
7, 1945, and hanged on February 23, 1946.

JAPAN: PEACEFUL INVASION

When the atomic bomb was dropped on Hiroshima (it was as much a surprise to me as to my newest recruit), I was at my Leyte headquarters. Byers, Bowen, Burgess, and I flew at once to Manila. All of us had been working on plans for the main strike against the Japanese homeland; we then called it "Operation Coronet." A thick document with cardboard covers, once top secret, still slumbers in my files. It is GHQ's basic outline for the conduct of the invasion—the story of what might have happened. Even now it makes interesting reading.

In Manila there was a cheerful atmosphere. General MacArthur told me at once that he believed Japan would surrender as a result of the atomic bombing and because of the prospective entrance of Russia into the Pacific War. (As a matter of fact, the entrance of the Russians, in my opinion, had only nuisance value.) General Mac-Arthur said he had chosen Eighth Army to handle the big push in case of occupation by force, and that he was content to abide by his decision if it were a peaceful occupation.

After August 7 there was a period of watching and waiting and swift redeployment of troops. I heard the news of the atomic bombing of Nagasaki while in a plane over northern Luzon and felt sure capitulation was at hand. For the next two weeks, between plans and changing of plans, there was no rest for the weary. I already had my assignment.

259

I flew into Okinawa from Manila on August 25, 1945, to inspect the two American divisions which were to spearhead Eighth Army's landing in Japan. As I stepped from the plane at Katena strip I felt, perhaps illogically, that the eventful trip from the Philippines had provided a happy omen for our all-important operation. Midway in the journey my plane had been struck by lightning. Yet the engines continued to function smoothly over hundreds of miles of sea. The danger had been real, but we had weathered the passage.

Okinawa, so recently the scene of the Tenth Army's bloody struggle, was now one great armed camp. Even before Japanese capitulation 11th Airborne had been alerted and flown there from Luzon. In just four days the entire division had been moved eight hundred miles. By our plan, 11th Airborne troops would be the first to land in the Tokyo-Yokohama area, to be followed immediately by the 27th Infantry Division, which had been fighting on Okinawa. And there were three hundred magnificent C-54 transport planes assembled to carry them in.

Our approach to the occupation problem had changed sharply as the result of conferences with enemy emissaries at Manila. In the beginning we had intended to supplement the airborne movement with amphibious landings of XI Corps. These troops were to "seize and secure" the Tokyo-Yokohama area. This might have meant fighting with dissident groups and renewed conflict. The new approach was predicated upon the full cooperation of the Japanese government and military. They agreed to all conditions. There would be no forcible disarmament or seizures by Allied personnel. The Japanese government would direct the disarmament of its own forces under our supervision.

This solution, if it proved workable, had obvious advantages. The Emperor's prestige and the Emperor's proclamations could be infinitely more effective than a bullying display of rifles in a land where we were feared and outnumbered. Our occupation was to be gradual. We were assured that the internal police force in Japan proper would maintain law and order until the arrival of Allied forces.

Our gamble was a straightforward one. We wagered that the Japanese meant what they said. Bad weather delayed action for two more days, but at the end of August the northern end of the Pacific had the busiest dark and daylight hours in its history. A tremendous American fleet converged on Tokyo Bay—battleships, aircraft carriers, cruisers, destroyers. There were hundreds of vessels, and most of the Allies were represented. At Okinawa on August 30 the transport planes had been taking off since before dawn. The sky for eight hundred miles was full of noise and traffic.

I took off about six-thirty A.M. for the five-hour ride. Back in the Philippines I had asked General MacArthur to allow me to precede him into Japan by two days, so that I might discover for myself the situation in the Yokohama section. He gave me two hours. This worried me. The safety of the Supreme Commander was my responsibility, and I knew that our airborne troops could not arrive in sufficient numbers to provide adequate protection.

A brisk wind scattered tiny white clouds, and the sky was a gay and unbelievable blue. I had last been in Japan in 1920. As I sped along at two hundred and fifty miles an hour I remembered the legend that if Fujiyama is seen on leave-taking the traveler will come back. I had seen the frosty head of the mountain clearly, but it certainly had never occurred to a young lieutenant colonel that he would return at the head of a conquering army. There below us now was the Kanto Plain, across which—save for the dropping of the atomic bomb—I would have marched my men in an operation which could have been nothing less than a direct assault. In that rolling land of streams and cross-ridges and tunnels, garrisoned by fierce and undefeated soldiers defending their homeland, our casualties could not have been less than one hundred thousand men.

The airplane began to lose altitude. The first landmark I really recognized was the great bronze Buddha of Kamakura, and then, abruptly, we were down at Atsugi Field. From the air, Atsugi Field, with two long runways and scattered hangars and barracks, looked like a deserted Ohio fairgrounds the day after the big show has departed. But at Atsugi the big show was just beginning. The C-54s came in by the clock—one every three minutes—and the policing was so disciplined and efficient that there were no operational casualties.

The Japanese had been ordered to assemble transport to carry us to Yokohama. They had done it, and most of the cars had chauffeurs. Actually, it was a forlorn and decrepit group of sedans and trucks. I conferred unprofitably with a Japanese general named Arisuye. I decided that we would move into Yokohama (about twenty miles) by putting 11th Airborne troops—as many as could be spared from the guarding of Atsugi Field—both in front of and behind General MacArthur.

About two in the afternoon a beautiful plane, *The Bataan*, circled the area and came in for a rubbery landing. The 11th Airborne's military band, determined that a historic event should have its proper musical background, was on hand to give the Allied commander a spirited greeting. General MacArthur ignored the panoply when he appeared at the door of his plane. His shirt was open at the throat and his corncob pipe was in his mouth. As I reported to him he grinned and said, "Bob, this is the payoff."

I thought it was too. But I wasn't quite sure what the payoff would be. We were on foreign soil, and American soldiers were outnumbered thousands to one. As a matter of fact, there had been bitter fighting right there on Atsugi only a few days before. Atsugi was a home base for kamikaze planes, and we could see them lined up, row after silvery row, efficient looking but effectively earthbound. The Japanese Army trusted the kamikaze pilots so little that a military expedition had forcibly removed the propellers from all planes. The air group resisted with arms, and there was fighting, with casualties, before the job could be completed.

Well, we were there now. The gantlet must be run. The Japanese somewhere had found for General MacArthur an American automobile of doubtful vintage; as I stepped into the car with him I was as grim-faced as the troops around me. I had heard about the discipline of the Nipponese people, but I also knew that one undisciplined fanatic with a rifle could turn a peaceful occupation into a punitive expedition. With a roar and a stuttering of motors we started off.

Some indication of the condition of transport in Japan may be discovered from the fact that it took us two hours to go twenty miles. But it was not the snail's-pace tempo or the repeated breakdowns which made the trip memorable. In the hot bright sunlight it seemed like a sequence in a dream fantasy. On both sides of the road there were hundreds of armed Japanese soldiers, and almost all of them stood with their backs toward us. It finally dawned on me that this solid wall of men was there to assist in guarding the Supreme Commander and that the turning away of faces was an obeisance which previously had been accorded only to the Emperor himself.

Nevertheless, I did not draw an easy breath until that journey ended and General MacArthur entered his suite in the New Grand Hotel. At once I established a perimeter defense around the building with five hundred veterans of the 11th Airborne. Before nightfall of the first day the New Grand Hotel was full of newspaper correspondents, GHQ officers, Army, Air Force, and Navy satraps. In fact, it was so full that I found it necessary to scout up other living quarters for myself. I was amused by this beelike swarming at the place of power, and I was not the only one amused. The American Fleet had landed the 4th Marine Regiment on the mainland at the same time our troops were arriving by air. This force came under my command, and I had a merry chat with a veteran Marine officer. I asked about the landings.

"Our first wave," he said, quite without malice, "was made up entirely of admirals trying to get ashore before MacArthur."

The damage and desolation in Yokohama gave us an accurate picture of what we were to find in all the large cities of Japan and a forecast of the occupation's economic difficulties. Only the temple cities of Nara, Kyoto, and Nikko had entirely escaped the wrath of our bombers. In Yokohama some of the largest structures had survived, but we learned that a single fire-bomb raid—on May 29, 1945 —had destroyed eighty per cent of the city. There was almost nothing for sale in the stores—little food, little or no consumer goods of any kind. The people were dressed in rags or rough wartime clothing.

The Eighth Army, of course, had brought along its own rations,

so food was not a problem to our soldiers. But the hard work, the confusions and excitement of the next few days, have burned those days indelibly into my memory.

The formal Japanese surrender took place on September 2, Tokyo time. From the very moment my plane left Luzon I had the eerie feeling that all of us were walking through the pages of history; the ceremony aboard the battleship *Missouri* surely did nothing to dispel this compelling sense of drama. From the steel deck of the *Missouri*, as hot in the sunlight as the top side of a kitchen range, I could see in Tokyo Bay the gleaming might of the greatest armada of all time.

I took my place on deck in the front row of generals and admirals. I watched Foreign Minister Shigemitsu, only a few paces away, sign the surrender terms for the Japanese. I watched General MacArthur and the various Allied representatives as they, in turn, affixed their signatures. Then, smashing the solemn quiet, came the thunder and roar of bombers and fighters as Army and Navy airplanes by the hundreds passed over in sky salute. I stayed aboard for luncheon, the only Army maverick in a herd of seafaring men, and later Admiral Halsey sent me ashore in a destroyer. My escort was a handsome young commander on Halsey's staff. His name was Harold Stassen.

Some of the newspaper correspondents were critical because American troops did not move immediately on Tokyo. But our agreement was that we would not. The Japanese government had undertaken the task of disarming the hundreds of thousands of soldiers in the Tokyo area, and, believe me, I wished them well. This was not a matter of military timidity but of common sense. I wished to avoid any provocation which might lead to needless bloodshed. While the Eighth Army waited it was not idle. And now our waterborne divisions, delayed by a typhoon, began to arrive, 1st Cavalry followed by the Americal Division.

On September 7 I drove to Tokyo to prepare for the Supreme Commander's official assumption of control. The capital was as badly mauled as Yokohama. I went to the American Embassy. One bomb had gone through the roof of the chancellery and there was enough water on the floor to make a wading pool. The furnishings were ruined, but the Embassy itself was intact.

Next day, the 8th, General MacArthur entered Tokyo. Admiral Halsey and I accompanied him on the journey from Yokohama. The distance is about twenty-two miles, and it was a desolate pilgrimage; between the two cities destruction was virtually complete.

It was about noon when we arrived. Troops of the 1st Cavalry Division were drawn up in grim but glittering array within the Embassy grounds. General MacArthur took his place on the terrace and faced the chancellery. The American colors were to be raised over that devastated roof, and the flag was one which had been brought all the way from Washington. It was the banner which had flown over the Capitol on the day of Pearl Harbor. I faced the Supreme Commander and heard the order that was heard round the world:

"General Eichelberger, have our country's flag unfurled, and in Tokyo's sun let it wave in its full glory as a symbol of hope for the oppressed and as a harbinger of victory for the right."

As the flag climbed slowly, gracefully, in Tokyo's sun, as the bell-like crescendos of the bugles rang out, there were many wet eyes in that martial assembly. It was a moment I am not likely to forget. And I shall always remember, as I remembered then the price we paid for that flag raising, the price Americans paid in pain and misery and sadness and heartsickness. The long, cruel struggle was ended, but there were many who would never go home. American casualties in the Pacific War totaled more than three hundred thousand dead and wounded.

The Eighth Army had many occupation jobs, but its first and most urgent one was the succoring and speedy release of Allied war prisoners in Japanese stockades. We arrived prepared for the task. Back on Okinawa "mercy teams" had been organized. They came in with our advance airborne echelons. As a result, American planes swooped over prison camps that very same day to drop food and supplies. Some of our teams rushed inland immediately to seize, before they could be destroyed, the records of the more notorious camps. This was to provide evidence for the future war-crimes trials.

Day after day, Allied prisoners poured into Yokohama on special trains that we had commandeered for rescue missions. They were sick, emaciated, verminous; their clothing was in tatters. We were ready for them with band music, baths, facilities for medical examination, vitamin injections, hot food, and hospital beds. Some would go home by plane; others by hospital ship when strong enough to travel. Perhaps the stolid Japanese themselves had their first lesson in democracy in the Yokohama railroad station. The Japanese have only contempt for a prisoner of war. They stared in amazement when we greeted our wasted comrades in arms with cheers and embraces.

The Eighth Army's teams covered the whole of Japan on these missions of liberation. Allied prisoners of all nationalities were released and processed for evacuation at a rate of a thousand a day. By clearing the camps on the islands of Honshu, Hokkaido, and Shikoku in eighteen days, we far outraced our own most optimistic time schedule. In all, the Eighth Army liberated and evacuated 23,985 persons.

Early in September I was ordered to arrest former Prime Minister Tojo, who had been the leader of the war party. My jail in Yokohama, as time went on, offered hospitality to an imposing list of guests. These included the members of Tojo's cabinet; General Homma, villain of the Bataan death march; Dr. José Laurel, president of the Philippines under Japanese domination, and Jorge Vargas, ambassador to Japan for the same regime. Tokyo Rose was there, and so was Colonel Meissinger, head of the German secret service in Japan, and known as the result of past exploits as the "butcher of Warsaw." Meissinger could—in the phrase of one of the guards—dish it out but he couldn't take it. He was the prison's champion weeper. On my periodic visits I usually found this contemptible fellow in tears.

When my MPs arrived in Tojo's home in Tokyo, the ex-premier shot himself. He used a pistol which had once belonged to an American aviator. I received the news by telephone and directed that an American doctor see him at once. After administering plasma the doctor called me and said—there was no medical center in Tokyo at the time—that Tojo had an even chance of surviving the rough ride to Yokohama. There we could give him a transfusion of whole blood. We were ready for Tojo when he arrived in Yokohama, and he was carried upstairs in the 98th Evacuation Hospital and put to bed. He had not been undressed and his shirt was a sanguinary spectacle. He had aimed at his heart, but the stubborn surface of a rib had thwarted his marksmanship.

Captain Bill Curtis, an Englishman born and raised in Japan, was my interpreter. He told Tojo that I was standing beside his bed, and the closed eyes opened. The ex-prime minister raised his head slightly and attempted a bow.

"I am dying," he said in Japanese. "I am sorry to have given General Eichelberger so much trouble."

"Do you mean tonight," I asked, "or for the last few years?"

"Tonight," he answered. "I want General Eichelberger to have my new saber."

This, perhaps, was an unnecessary gesture, since I already had it in my possession, but it was a symbol of his apology for being a nuisance. That saber has since been presented to a museum in Urbana, Ohio, my home town. At the time it seemed very important to me to keep Tojo alive for trial. A blond American sergeant volunteered to give his blood for a transfusion, and Tojo rallied immediately. Was this procedure illogical? To this day I am not sure. Our expert medical treatment was only a reprieve. Tojo stood trial and was hanged.

That, however, was not until three years later, and after the United States Supreme Court had ruled that it had no power to review the decision of the International Tribunal which condemned Hideki Tojo and six others. The war lords hanged with him at Sugamo Prison were: General Kenji Doihara; former premier Koki Hirota; General Seishiro Itagaki, former war minister; General Heitaro Kimura, chief of Japanese armies in Manchuria; General Iwane Matsui, commander at Nanking during the rapes and butcheries there; and General Akira Muto, chief of staff in the Philippines.

JAPAN: OCCUPATION

It is impossible, this late in a long book, to report in detail the events of our early days in Japan, colorful and melodramatic as many of them were. I was to remain there for three years as head of the Army of Occupation, and it is perhaps of interest that late in 1945 I refused General Eisenhower's deeply appreciated offer to make me Deputy Chief of Staff in Washington, because I wanted to continue in the Japanese post. It seemed to me a job of vital importance.

General Eisenhower's offer was made during a brief leave in the United States. During that time I circumnavigated the world by air, but too swiftly to suit my tourist taste. I returned to Japan by way of Bermuda, the Azores, and Europe. I had an audience with the Pope at Rome and visited Cairo. I spent the night there at the home of General Benny Giles, and Farouk, the King of Egypt, dropped in casually and stayed for hours. It was at Cairo that I picked up General Pat Casey, chief of engineers in the Pacific. Casey had gone to Berlin to attend his daughter's wedding, and, when I saw him, was standing on an airfield trying to thumb his way back to Tokyo. Casey joined the party. I called on General Wavell, who was then Governor-General of India, revisited Shanghai and Peking. When the plane struck the Japanese landfall, I was happy to see Fujiyama once more.

Looking back, I am now impressed by the magnitude of the mission we undertook when American troops landed in Japan. Here, summarized, are some of the things Eighth Army was called upon to do:

1. Establish vast numbers of American soldiers in Japan without provoking combat.

2. Provide housing, clothing, recreation for them.

3. Construct many airfields and thousands of houses for our dependents.

4. Supervise operation of all railroads and ports.

5. Follow through and assure the complete demobilization of the Japanese Army.

6. Crush Japan's war potential by the destruction of ten thousand airplanes, three thousand tanks, ninety thousand fieldpieces, three million items of small arms, and one million tons of explosives.

These things we did, and there were many more. We took charge of the unloading, warehousing, and proper distribution of relief food sent from the United States to succor the starving. We supervised the repatriation of six million Japanese who arrived at home ports from the Emperor's now lost overseas empire. Under our direction, a million displaced Koreans, Ryukyuans, and Chinese, who had served as slave labor, were sent home. And then there were the never-ending and multitudinous duties and responsibilities of our Military Government units, which I shall discuss more fully later.

The Americans found a nation which was on its economic deathbed. Bare chimneys showed where commercial plants had once operated. Not only was a very large percentage of Japan's industry destroyed, but surrender came at a time when the country was entirely geared for war. As a consequence, a Japanese plant which had escaped serious damage still was not prepared for peacetime operation. The vital textile industry was in collapse. Most of the merchant marine was under the sea, and there was almost no food.

Gone with the lost colonies were the oil of Sakhalin, the rice of Korea, the sugar of Formosa. Gone were the fisheries of the Okhotsk Sea, the soybean and iron ore of Manchuria. There was a shortage of all raw materials. But the most critical shortage was coal. Coal production was held up by lack of equipment and skilled manpower, and lack of food for the miners. Increased food production depended on more fertilizer. Fertilizer, in turn, depended on more coal. Only four hundred and fifty thousand tons monthly were being mined in late 1945. The goal for 1950 is forty million tons, or over three million tons monthly. We've made progress there.

Within a few weeks after the flag raising in Tokyo, these Eighth Army outfits had taken over occupation posts in Japan: IX, XI, and XIV Corps, with the 11th Airborne, 1st Cavalry, Americal, 27th, 43rd, 97th, 81st, 77th Divisions and the 112th Cavalry and 158th Regimental Combat Teams. The Sixth Army began to arrive in late September and took positions in southern Honshu, Kyushu, and Shikoku. By late autumn the homeward trek of high-point American combat troops was in full swing, and on December 31 the Sixth Army was deactivated and the Eighth Army took control of all Ground Forces.

During the later years of my stay in Japan the Eighth Army consisted of two corps and four divisions. The 1st Cavalry and 11th Airborne were under IX Corps, and the 24th and 25th Divisions under I Corps. Our peak strength was two hundred and fifty thousand men, and at one time the roster fell as low as fifty thousand; these shifts were largely dependent on defense policies back in the United States, since most of our troops now were not combat men but recruits.

It should be understood that the Eighth Army Command had nothing to do with policy-making in Japan. All directives to the Japanese government were issued by General MacArthur as the spokesman for Supreme Headquarters, the War Department, and the Far Eastern Commission. It was the business of Eighth Army to see that these directives were carried into effect.

It is infrequently mentioned that British Commonwealth forces arrived in the spring of 1946 to share the duties of the occupation in the Kure area. These colorful troops consisted of Aussies, New Zealanders, Punjabi, Sikhs, Gurkhas, the Cameron Highlanders, and other British detachments. Maximum strength was about forty thousand, but this has since been greatly reduced. All ground units were under the operational control of Eighth Army.

One of our sweeping tasks was the apprehension and trial of Japanese war criminals. This required tremendous pick-and-shovel work: examination of mountains of military records, taking of depositions, questioning of countless witnesses. Up until the time I came home, some eight hundred individuals had been tried and convicted of major crimes, and approximately a hundred had been sentenced to be hanged. Thousands of others were brought before provost courts to answer for lesser offenses.

The Eighth Army military commissions conducted these Yokohama trials with scrupulous fairness, and the interests of the defendants were always adequately protected. As commanding general, I reviewed the findings, and it was only rarely that I found occasion to reduce sentences or to quarrel with the commissions' decisions. We were determined that, while the guilty must be punished, the Japanese people would learn from our deeds that a fair trial demanded that even the most malignant rogue be given his full, free day in court.

There were several occasions when, through us, American prisoners were able to fend for Japanese camp guards who had been just and kindly. One American group brought their guards with them to Yokohama to ensure good treatment. And it was my pleasure to befriend a Mr. K. Domoto, who had remained to protect American sick when other camp attendants fled. Mr. Domoto was, I discovered, a graduate of Amherst College and a member of the Psi Upsilon fraternity there. After the war a number of Domoto's former prisoners sent him from America a wristwatch with their names engraved upon it.

The majority of cases, however, showed the Japanese guards and prison commandants to be callous, abusive, and mean in both large and small ways. One example will serve. At a camp in the Japanese mountains, disease-bearing flies became so numerous that Allied prisoners begged for insecticide or some type of trap. The response was to offer one cigarette in exchange for the bodies of each one hundred flies. When the pests began to be delivered in unduly large quantities, the smiling Japanese reduced the bounty to one cigarette for five hundred flies—with the proviso that all must be caught by hand!

Proof of the bitter hostility against Americans is well illustrated by the testimony in one war-crimes case which concerned the beheading

of a sergeant who parachuted from a falling B-29 just six days before
the end of hostilities. The major in charge of the local Kempei-Tei
(secret military police) ordered the flier exposed to a mob of about
eight hundred Japanese. He was tied to a post, and each Japanese
who so desired was allowed to strike the victim with a club. A long
line formed, led by a wrinkled matron of seventy, who struck the
first blow. When the victim became unconscious he was revived with
water and the beating resumed. When the mob had finished, the
sergeant was cut down, hauled to a shrine, and there beheaded by
a Japanese Air Force lieutenant. The case was proved almost entirely
by Japanese witnesses. The Japanese major received a life sentence—
which I considered inadequate.

I was present at the trial of Shin Kojiama, a ship's captain, and saw
there an excellent demonstration of the ability of the War Crimes
Commissions to sift evidence fairly and judiciously. Shin Kojiama
commanded the *Oroyoko Maru*, which transported American prisoners from the Philippines to Japan. On trial with him was the Army
commander of prisoners aboard the vessel. Many of the American
prisoners on the *Oroyoko* had suffocated or died of thirst in the hold.
The accused were provided adequate defense counsel at the expense
of the American government. Dr. Robert Miller, a law professor on
sabbatical leave from Syracuse University, headed the attorneys for
the defense. After prolonged testimony, the commission determined
that the ship's captain should be acquitted because it had not been
proved he had authority to alter the conditions which caused the
deaths, being restricted, by orders, to the operation of the ship. The
commander of the prisoners received the death sentence. My personal observation of this trial reassured me about the care and lack
of prejudice with which all cases were being tried.

As time went on the Japanese themselves became impressed by the
honesty of American military courts. Frequently I received grateful
letters, commending the excellent work of defense attorneys, from
the relatives of men who had been condemned to death. The relatives
appreciated the scrupulous fairness with which the court had examined the evidence before the decision was handed down. In this connection, I am reminded of a story which may shed some light upon

Japanese character. A Mrs. Saito, a cultured and refined gentlewoman, called upon our Chief Defense Counsel in Yokohama and presented him with a handsome cigarette case. When the confounded lawyer asked for a reason, she said she had just read in a Japanese newspaper that her husband had been hanged for a war crime, but that she was grateful to the American defense counsel and to the commission itself for the fairness of the trial. In this particular case, the story had a surprising and a pleasant ending. It developed that another Mr. Saito had been hanged. Mrs. Saito's husband had been given a brief prison sentence. Honor and face come first in Japan. Believing herself to be widowed, Mrs. Saito had nevertheless felt it necessary to conceal her personal grief and express her gratitude for a fair trial.

The Japanese personality is hard for a Westerner to assay. The conscience of the Japanese cannot be plumbed. On January 11, 1948, I received a letter from Tokutaro Suzuki, a quite unimportant young man. He wrote that his conscience required him to confess that he had strangled a fallen American flier.

At the time his crime was committed, Suzuki wrote me, the B-29s were conducting their fire-bombings over Japan and thousands of people were homeless. Suzuki accomplished his own incrimination expertly; he said that a plane had fallen during a raid and that he had approached the wreckage. Several fliers were lying on the ground, and one in particular seemed badly injured. As he approached the man, Suzuki wrote, the crowd called out, demanding that he kill him. Influenced by the vindictiveness of the mob, he stepped forward and choked the injured flier to death. We had no other evidence of this crime except the confession. Suzuki's own story was forwarded to the proper authorities for examination and action.

After the occupation began there was only one instance of a concerted resistance to our troops. Citizens in the community of Yamata, between Tokyo and Yokohama, became annoyed with the visits of Allied soldiers and formed a vigilante association. Unarmed GIs were set upon and assaulted—to warn them and their comrades that they were not welcome in Yamata during their off-duty hours. The climax of this campaign of terrorism came when two Americans, returning

to their barracks, were seized and beaten for two hours. I at once
ordered a show of force, and armored vehicles in battle array cruised
the streets of Yamata for several hours. Members of the mob were
discovered, tried, and sentenced to long confinement.

Two highly publicized riots against the Japanese government were
led or inspired by Communist agitators. The first took place at the
residence of Prime Minister Yoshida. Various Korean dissidents (Korea
was for half a century a Japanese colony, and many Koreans live in
Japan) held a political meeting and then, roused by fiery speakers,
proceeded en masse to the Yoshida Palace to state their woes. Yoshida was ill and could not see them at once. The crowd broke down
the gates and forced the doors of the palace. Japanese police were
totally unable to maintain order, and it was necessary for American
MPs to calm the riot and arrest the leaders of the demonstration.

In April of 1948 it was again necessary to use American troops to
quiet wild Korean outbreaks in the cities of Osaka and Kobe. The
trouble originated in a Japanese government order that Korean
schools in Japan must meet Japanese textbook and language standards, but subsequent investigation disclosed irrefutable proof that
the uprisings were Communist engineered. In Kobe four thousand
Koreans gathered outside the prefectural building where the Governor, the Mayor, and the Chief of Police were holding a conference.
Then some hundred and fifty of the mob entered the building, severed
telephone communications, and held the three officials incommuni-
cado. As the result of the outbreaks, in which twenty-two Japanese
policemen and sixteen Koreans were injured, American soldiers acted
quickly and arrested four hundred of the riot leaders.

At the time, the Kobe-Osaka incidents caused apprehension among
many Japanese officials, who feared widespread Communist disturbances on May Day. Because of prompt action by Eighth Army, however, the temperatures of the troublemakers all over Japan dropped
precipitately, and May Day was as calm as a New England Sunday.

Under the aegis of Supreme Commander Allied Powers (SCAP),
the Japanese had written a new constitution renouncing war and es-
tablishing a democratic form of government. To a considerable ex-
tent, of course, this has been a puppet government, since many of its

pronunciamentos are made at the suggestion of the Supreme Commander and his advisers. Reforms have not always accomplished their full purpose, but they are the law of the land.

I would not attempt to estimate how deeply the democratic spirit is now ingrained in the average Japanese. After all, they have known only feudalism for uncounted centuries. But the Emperor is no longer divine; there are separation of church and state, land redistribution, woman suffrage, free elections—there have been three general elections. Whether or not the average citizen believes in democracy, he now has by fiat those rights which the peoples of democratic nations enjoy: the writ of habeas corpus, freedom of speech, freedom of thought, freedom from fear, equality before the law. And he likes them.

The Eighth Army's Military Government teams wrestled at the grass-roots level with the problem of making SCAP's directives work. We sent a team to every one of the forty-seven Japanese prefectures, which are similar to our states. A typical unit consisted of perhaps seven officers, seven civilians, twenty enlisted men, and fifty educated Japanese. There were also larger regional teams and staff sections at army and corps levels to augment their efforts.

Experts provided agricultural and industrial advice, introduced public health and education and welfare measures, devised practical methods of increasing coal production, supervised—when Japanese nationals were laggard—collection of taxes. But always these advances were accomplished through the Japanese themselves. It was a long way from the high plateau of policy in Tokyo to the governors and mayors—and peasants—in the provinces. The specialty of the Eighth Army lads was follow-through.

Two years ago SCAP ordered enforced rice collections in the rural areas so the starving cities might be fed. Three months before the fiscal year's end, collections by the Japanese government had reached only thirty per cent of the expected total. Then the Military Government teams were sent into action. They needled, cajoled, and pressured the local governments until the farmers' rice was forthcoming. Collections went over the top in six weeks. It was these same lads who were on hand with food and medicine and stretchers in 1947 and

1948 when earthquakes brought suffering and tragedy to many villages and to such cities as Fukui and Kanazawa.

My view of the Japanese situation has always been that the nation brought disaster upon itself and that its people must work out their own salvation. Economically, however, this is at present impossible. Japan was for many years a country which imported raw materials, processed them, and then exported the finished product. This was her place in the Asian orbit. Defeat in the war cost her world markets, resulted in understandable postwar hatreds, and ruined civilian industry. As an occupied country, incapable of self-support, it left her squarely on the back of the United States.

Occupation efforts to revitalize commerce, agriculture, mining, and fishing have shown definite results. We have assisted Japan in obtaining raw materials, and her exports have risen from zero to nearly three-quarters of the average maintained in the years 1930–34. This is at least a good start. Corruption and inefficiency have been dealt heavy blows by the balancing of the Japanese budget and the stabilization of the yen. Since my return to this country many people have asked: "Are the Japanese people friendly to the United States?" They are. During my three years as Army commander I made constant tours of inspection to every corner and cranny of the islands, and I know whereof I speak. When the Eighth Army landed, many of the Japanese expected dire and brutal retribution. We saw few women during those first days; most of them had gone into hiding. Those on the streets had shoved several kimonos into their *mompeis*—wartime trousers—in order to make themselves as unattractive as possible.

The friendly American soldier, with his laughter and fondness for children, became our best ambassador. There were, of course, a few incidents (there are bad apples in any barrel), but former Secretary of War Patterson was right when he said of Eighth Army troops: "They are the best representatives the nation could have. . . . An army of which the American nation can be proud." Laughter did almost as much as the abolition of the secret police to introduce the idea of democracy in Japan. Indeed, the friendship of Japanese bobby-soxers for our soldiers now gives me a rather crooked smile. Once they were fearful; in the end they were so friendly that, in the interests of discipline and ancient Japanese custom and sensibilities, I issued to the troops very positive orders against public demonstrations of affection. It is significant that in a once hostile nation our soldiers, with money in their pockets, may wander unarmed anywhere without the fear of footpads.

The friendship of educated Japanese is based on intelligent self-interest. In their minds there are only two great powers today, Russia and the United States. They are very well aware of the Soviet course in countries occupied by her: the siphoning off of resources, the kidnaping of industrial plants. They have seen what happened in Manchuria, and they know what would have happened if Russia had occupied Japan. They know that in contrast:

1. The Americans have not lived off the country. We have brought in the food to feed our soldiers. We have fed the hungry in the burned-out cities. After five years, Japan still would be a nation of empty stomachs without the regular shipments of American grain to augment the native food supply.

2. By the reparations agreement, certain Japanese plants were taken over. We have not dismantled them and hustled the machinery back to our own country to rust. Instead, many plants have been put in working order and are now enriching the native economy by producing for Japan.

Our honesty and fairness have made a profound impression. Our prestige is enormous. To understand this, one must remember that in two thousand years Japan had never lost a war. Every child, from the cradle, was taught the creed of Japan's invincibility. Yet, after the supposed death blow at Pearl Harbor, after Bataan, after Japan's conquering sweep to the back porch of Australia, the Allies fought their way back. Starting from scratch, America's industrial power produced immense carriers and fleets of battleships, clouds of airplanes and the B-29 bomber, long-range submarines, the marine transport and landing craft to ferry hundreds of thousands of troops to objectives in the Pacific while fighting another major war in Europe. Then came the scientific and industrial miracle which brought about complete submission—the atom bomb. For the Japanese, the Americans are still the giants in the earth.

The phrase "balance of power" is repugnant to many Americans. For them, it has overtones and echoes of the cynical European diplomacy of the nineteenth century. And yet the balance of power did keep the peace in Europe for a good many years. At the moment, because of Russia's intransigence in the United Nations, America's only recourse in the effort to keep the peace in Europe is a balance-of-power policy. The Marshall Plan to bulwark our democratic friends and allies is a part of it. But there is no balance of power in Asia. There, for half a century, a ruthless Japan and a ruthless Russia made the contest a stand-off. Our wartime agreements with the Russians have given them the Kurils, northern Korea and southern Sakhalin, and a dominant position in Manchuria. Thus murky Muscovite dreams of a century and a half have at last become hard fact; czarism is dead, but Stalinism is equally imperialistic.

Chinese Communist armies now have swept over the areas once controlled by Chiang Kai-shek's Nationalist government, and the hammer and sickle throws long shadows over Asia. Militarily speaking, Japan is now a pygmy nation. She could not defend herself against aggression; the defenders would be limited to a few police, armed with pistols. The nation has nothing to offer except manpower and industrial potential. But since we deliberately disarmed the Japanese, we have also—by all the rules of fair play—assumed the obligation of protecting her.

The numerical strength of the Communists is not great in Japan but they have shown political gains. ⌐ ⁊unism always flourishes in a sick economy, and Japan is sick. Her population grows · leaps and bounds; it is now eighty-four million in a small country (approximately the size of California) only seventeen per cent arable. Japan now is a country with an Oriental birth rate and an Occidental death rate. She cannot recover by her own efforts. If the United States should abandon its mission there, the Japanese would have no alternative except to take Russia's eager and outstretched hand. Yet I am sure I am right in saying that ninety-five per cent of the people are anti-Russian and hope to find themselves eventually in a position to be America's friends—or even allies.

Rehabilitation will not be easy, and it will continue to cost money.

But I am confident that much can be accomplished to increase self-support in Japan and to find outlet markets for Japan's industries. Our investment of the blood and suffering of our young men during the Pacific War is far too great to abandon now a victory so dearly won.

Just before I left Japan, Mrs. Eichelberger and I were entertained at luncheon by the Emperor and Empress. The Emperor thanked the Eighth Army for its effective work, and then asked me to assure the American people that he intended to carry out every promise of co-operation made at the time of the surrender.

But the most impressive display of friendship came on sailing day. I was approached at dockside by a tired and worn ricksha man who stammered his gratitude to the Americans. As my ship pulled out, he waved and waved while tears made furrows down his leathery face.

JAPAN: THE FUTURE

I left Japan in the late summer of 1948 and retired from the Army on January 1, 1949. I considered it a privilege to hold a position of authority during three years of the American occupation; it gave me a front-row seat from which to watch one of the most interesting experiments on record: the earnest effort to convert, as speedily as possible, a feudalistic Oriental nation into a modern democracy. It is much too soon to attempt to evaluate the degree of our success. In some things we have failed; the march of the years may quite possibly show that, in others, we have succeeded beyond our expectations.

Whatever the results, it should be said that the experiment was made under world conditions which progressively deteriorated. The first fine promise of unity under the United Nations vanished like morning mists, and both the Assembly and the Security Council became forums for angry and bitter oratory. At some time during this period the men of the Kremlin decided to pursue an aggressive policy, and in many parts of the world we saw a shift of political direction. Statesmen of good will, influenced by the pressure of events, turned their energies to the preservation of freedom where it existed; their often unspoken conviction was that the advance of freedom must wait.

The disarming of Japan and Germany was decided upon by agreement among wartime Allies. It was the first step (at least in the eyes

280

of the Western nations) toward the creation of a peaceful world, the kind of a world for which millions of worn and weary people everywhere were hungry. At the end of the long struggle, even realization of the old dream of outlawry of war did not seem altogether impossible to realistic men. This is the atmosphere in which the democratization of Japan was conceived, and in which it would have thrived. The Japanese took with sober seriousness the provision in their constitution which pledged them to a renunciation of war for all time, and a renunciation of their age-old desire for military domination of Asia.

All of us are familiar with the progressive change in the coloration of international relationships. Even during my service in Japan I saw evidence that Americans were beginning to lose interest in the great experiment. They became alarmed as Soviet imperialism gobbled up the smaller nations of eastern Europe and made them satellite states. Our countermeasures in Europe meant the maintaining of a large military establishment and the outpouring of billions of dollars in treasure. The cost of the "cold war" is one of the American taxpayer's dreariest burdens, and I see no alternative. But it would be fatal for him to lose sight of the importance of Japan.

A few months after my retirement the Department of the Army asked me to return to work at the Pentagon Building as a civilian consultant on the problems of the Far East and Japan. I accepted. In all, I had spent fourteen years working on Far Eastern affairs, but my assignment in Washington taught me many things I would not otherwise have known. The man in the field is on the receiving end; he has no way of knowing about the intricate chess play among departments and bureaus and commissions. I hate red tape, but I learned that a system of checks often prevents irresponsible decisions. I learned, too, that an expert's opinion that an appropriation is necessary does not necessarily convince a congressional committee it is necessary. Those things take time, and, God knows, they take patience. It is a hard lesson to learn, and there are times of emergency when it is a hard lesson to abide by.

Nevertheless, in my position as a consultant, I believe I was privileged to arrive at a factual and unprejudiced point of view. I still

maintain a vigorous correspondence with men in the Far East; I
have talked with most of the technical advisers who have gone back
and forth between the United States and Japan in recent years, and
I have been in a position to read all reports available. Most of the
officials of SCAP summoned to Washington have visited me. Many
Japanese, including members of the Diet, have been sent here on
official missions—to study American educational methods, American
hygiene, and American police procedure—and my office has seemed a
mandatory point of call. This is a matter of personal satisfaction, but
it is more than that. I suspect that I have more understanding of the
changing situation than I would have had if I had continued to live
in Yokohama.

Although there is still a long way to go, real progress has been made
in the rehabilitation of Japan. The diminishing need for United States
assistance provides a yardstick of this progress. In the fiscal year 1949
a total of $507,000,000 was necessary to do the job. In the fiscal year
1950 this fell to $410,000,000, and for 1951 it is expected that Japan
will receive about $250,000,000. The reductions are due, in a large
measure, to the high level of domestic food production and the ex-
pansion of industrial production and exports.

Current food production is now about nine per cent better than the
average of the peacetime years 1930–34. In the last five years nine
hundred thousand acres of wasteland have been brought under cultivation, providing farms for hundreds of thousands of peasants. Some
six thousand Japanese farm advisers have been trained under American agricultural experts, and more than thirty-one thousand farm
cooperative groups have been organized. Today, the acreage under
cultivation on the four sovereign islands of Japan is the highest in
history.

Devastation of plants, inability to finance imports of raw materials,
and the drying up of foreign export markets have made the problems
of industry infinitely more difficult. And yet, progress is being made
there. Production of coal and pig iron, and the manufacture of crude
steel and machinery and chemicals (including fertilizers) are increas-
ingly encouraging. The textile industry, always one of Nippon's main-
stays, is still at low ebb. It is impossible to guess whether or not the

prewar export market for silk and other textiles can be restored. But Japan, because of the inability to import enough raw cotton, cannot, at present, even restore to prewar levels domestic textile consumption. Under the best of circumstances, it will be some time before clothing, rubber and leather footwear, housing materials, paper, soap, can be produced in sufficient quantity to meet the needs of the Japanese people or approach prewar supply.

Yet there are encouraging facts. In 1948 some seventy-five per cent of all imports into Japan were purchased with American funds or transferred to the Japanese from surplus owned by the Army or other American agencies. This proportion was reduced to sixty per cent in 1949, and is expected to fall to forty-three per cent in 1950, and to twenty-six per cent in 1951.

Much credit for the stabilization of Japanese currency belongs to Joseph M. Dodge, a Detroit banker who has served as General MacArthur's financial adviser. Japan now has a balanced budget for the first time since the early 1930's. Government subsidies have been reduced, and there is an increasing transfer of responsibility from the Occupation to the Japanese government and the Japanese people. Since May 1949 at least half of the economic controls then in existence have been eliminated. "In no other nation," said Dodge in his report to Congress, "has so much been accomplished with so little."

The virtually complete destruction of Japan's merchant fleet by the American Navy and American Air has made difficult the restoration of her once great export trade. Nevertheless—and despite the postwar political and economic instability of the Far Eastern area—strides have been made in that direction. In the fiscal year 1948 the value of Japanese commodity exports and invisible earnings totaled $174,000,000. In 1949 it rose to $487,000,000—almost three times the previous year's figure. Despite a temporary slowdown in the early months of 1950 because of the sterling crisis, it is anticipated that exports will rise to $616,000,000 in the fiscal year 1950. In 1951 $800,000,000 is expected.

American attitudes toward the Japanese have been full of contradictions since the war, and sometimes I have found those same contradictions in myself. As a result of my firsthand experiences in Siberia in 1918–20, I have always had a profound distrust of the Japanese

military caste. Throughout the years after World War I, I felt sure that Japanese Army leaders were hell-bent for conquest, and that, if there were no international "incidents," incidents would be provoked. The Japanese civilian, then and now, was something else again. As a matter of fact, it was a group of Japanese civilians in Siberia who warned General Graves, just before he left in April of 1920, that their own Army was planning a *coup d'état* by which they would take possession of eastern Siberia.

I stayed in Vladivostok and saw it happen. The Jap military dreamed up for the world-wide press a story of local enmity, illegality, and anarchy, which demanded occupation and military discipline. Their claims were complete fiction. Vladivostok was a peaceful city. The Japanese military made an unjustified and outrageous seizure of power and mowed down innocent and pacific people with machine guns.

Even then the militarists were operating on a free-wheeling basis and arrogantly ignoring a civilian cabinet at home. When I reported to American Ambassador Roland A. Morris in Tokyo for temporary duty shortly thereafter, he told me that the *coup d'état* had come as an entire surprise to his powerful friends in the Japanese government. They believed the Army's story that an attack by the Russian Reds on Japanese troops had caused the seizure of the city.

This civilian credulity was to bring about a sinister harvest. During the next two decades, despite setbacks and strategic retreats, the militarists steadily tightened their grip on the government of Japan. In the end, they had stifled all opposition and were in complete and fatal control. I cannot explain why the decent and educated people of Japan accepted this situation, any more than I can explain why the people of Germany accepted the mad and diseased rulership of Hitler. I suspect they accepted because, for a hundred complex reasons, they hadn't the fortitude or the energy to resist. After America's triumph, a defeated Japan was converted at once to the gospel that it had followed ill-advised or false leaders.

From the Emperor on down through all elements of Japanese society there has been real cooperation with the Occupation forces. The decision of the Potsdam Conference to retain the Emperor as the nominal ruler of the nation has been a major factor in this cooperation,

and the Potsdam decision (denounced as "appeasement" by some
American critics of the time) has proved itself in practice to be of
the greatest usefulness in carrying out our program. Although the
Emperor is no longer considered divine, his prestige is still enormous.
I remember the story of a street parade in Japan. Communists were
marching and singing, marshals on horseback wore red rags around
their heads. Just then the royal automobile came down the avenue.
One of the noisiest of the demonstrating Communists dropped his red
banner to bow to the Emperor.

The Communist minority is the only group that has failed to give
willing support to our policies. The Potsdam declaration called for
the release from prison of all persons incarcerated for political beliefs.
As a result, some eight thousand Communist leaders bounded out
of prison at the beginning of the Occupation and gained force by
stertorously proclaiming themselves allies of the victorious American troops. When, by direction, we reintroduced unionism, they made
every attempt, and with some success, to infiltrate the unions.

But the Communists have made errors. A considerable group of
Japanese soldiers captured in Manchuria were painstakingly indoc-
trinated in Red training schools and repatriated last summer. They
came home singing the "Internationale" and refusing to speak to their
"fascist-minded" parents. They had been told that they had been de-
tained for years in Siberia because General MacArthur would not
send ships to bring them home; they had been told the Americans
were sending foodstuffs from hungry Japan to the United States. It
did not take them long to learn the real truth and to renounce with
bitterness their allegiance to Stalinism. Enthusiasm for communism
fell to a new low before the end of the summer.

Recent demands by Soviet spokesmen and leaders in the satellite
states for trial of the Emperor before an international tribunal on a
charge of war guilt infuriated many citizens. There is, however, a bit-
terer and deeper wound. Approximately three hundred and seventy
thousand Japanese soldiers seem to have disappeared from the face
of the earth. These are part of the great Kwantung Army which surrendered to the Russians in Manchuria. I suspect that most of these
missing men are now dead or are the faceless automatons, the living

dead, who labor in Russia's mines and forests. Whenever the question of their whereabouts was brought up at the Four Power Council in Tokyo, General Derevyanko, the Russian member, walked out. For weeks Japanese fathers and mothers picketed his handsome residence. Their banners asked: "What has happened to our sons?"

Many Japanese leaders today are apprehensive about the future. Russia and the Chinese Communists control a great section of the Asiatic land mass. The great Russian port of Vladivostok is but four hundred miles west of the island of Hokkaido, Russian-held Sakhalin is separated from Hokkaido only by a narrow strait, and the Russian-held Kuril Islands are so close on the east that the water could be crossed in a rowboat. At the southern border of China, Mao Tse-tung's Red armies stand looking with longing eyes at the raw materials of Burma, Siam, Indo-China, Malaya, and Indonesia. There is reason for apprehension.

If Japan could be captured—either from within or without—for communism, it would be a rich prize for the Soviets. Japan would round out handsomely the economic scheme for a Marxist Asia. Most of Asia is rich in raw materials and poor in industry. The Japanese are the "know-how" people of the Far East. Before and during the war they were able to construct great battleships and carriers, excellent landing craft, clouds of airplanes. Since V-J Day they have manufactured locomotives, and they are the only people of the Far East who can produce electrical machinery.

It is easy enough to envision what would happen in a Kremlin-enslaved Asia. The Japanese are an industrious people with technological skills, a willingness to work, and a tradition of subservience to totalitarian rule. From China and the lands to the south of China would come the ores and raw materials to serve Japan's manpower and heavy industry. From Japan there would go out the arms and processed goods which might make communism impregnable in the Far East.

The Japanese are apprehensive about the future because they are not sure what the policy of the United States will be. They are fully aware of the world hazards implicit in the cold war between Russia and the West. They suspect that, should the cold war become a fighting war, many Americans would clamor for the evacuation of our troops with the slogan, "Let the Japs defend themselves." This, at the moment, they are quite unable to do. The announcement that Russia has achieved an atomic bomb of its own (or, at least, an atomic explosion) is not calculated to assuage Japan's worries.

It seems to me that the Japan we completely disarmed is entitled to a clear statement of our intentions. Before such a statement can be made, a good many rank-and-file Americans must face a situation not too pleasant to face. Japan is vitally important to our defenses and to the preservation of democratic society everywhere. Because a friendly Japan is now vital to our interests, I can find little altruism in the money we now spend to fortify and improve Japan's economy. Why fool ourselves with pious talk? We have served a high purpose, to be sure, but it is useless to pretend that, at the same time, we have not served our own interests, and the interests of such other nations as Canada, Australia, New Zealand, the Philippines, and Indonesia.

All of them, whether or not they are cooperating in our economic program, hope to keep Japan out of the arms of the Russian bear. But how? There are only two ways: we must be prepared to defend Japan, or Japan must be armed so that she can defend herself. There are no other possibilities. I believe I was one of the first to point out in the public prints that because we had disarmed Japan and given her a "Made-in-America" constitution, we had also assumed the obligation to protect her against aggressors. General MacArthur, in his New Year's message for 1950, affirmed in his own luxurious prose the right of any country to defend its shores if attacked. Secretary of State Acheson has echoed this sentiment in several public statements.

These sentiments are all very well, but the fact is that Japan has nothing with which to defend herself except a few thousand pistols carried by the police. I know, because it was under my supervision that guns and munitions were carried far out to sea and deposited there. Americans must make up their minds, and very quickly, whether they will maintain the present Occupation forces or begin arming from our own arsenals a Japanese constabulary which might in time evolve into a standing army.

Recently there has been a great deal of talk about a peace treaty with Japan. General MacArthur has been widely quoted as favoring the project. The question came up at a British Commonwealth conference in January, according to the press, and there was no unanimity of opinion. Several usually well-informed commentators have stated recently that our State Department favors a peace treaty while the Department of Defense opposes early negotiations on the ground of American security. Certainly any peace treaty based on a neutrality agreement with Russia would have no value. As President Truman has pointed out, the Reds have kept none of the promises made at Potsdam.

It seems to me unfortunate that the treaty question should have arisen during the present crisis in Europe and Asia. From the viewpoint of the United States, we already have under the SCAP system the very security we might only *hope* to get under a treaty. It is easy to sympathize with the sentiments of General MacArthur when he says, in effect, "The Japanese deserve a peace treaty"; but the world situation is shaky and explosive and major shifts in policy (or so it seems to me) should be undertaken with the greatest caution.

The present military occupation was created under international agreements to which all the Allied nations, including Russia, subscribed, and its legality cannot be challenged. The original agreements provided that all Occupation troops—whatever their nationality—would come under General MacArthur's command. The Russians, however, refused to send any troops into Japan, and the British Commonwealth Occupation Forces have now shrunk to a roster of about twenty-five hundred men. Nevertheless, under the SCAP system, the Yokosuka Naval Base, the various air bases, the four infantry divisions of Eighth Army, are directly under General MacArthur's control and provide an automatic security for Japan which would be gravely threatened by our withdrawal.

The time will come, of course, when we must turn Japan loose to make her way in a disturbed and turbulent world, but the time is not yet. The rehabilitation of that shattered nation has made progress, but it is by no means a completed job. Japan, like England, can never be self-sufficient; nothing less than the restoration of her right to build and use her own shipping, and the restoration of her import and export trade, will solve her financial problem. For most of her citizens life is hard at the present time. Prices are high and wages buy only the sheer necessities of existence.

Many intelligent Japanese leaders who sought a peace treaty a year or so ago have had their enthusiasm chilled by the frosty winds blowing in from Siberia. Russia is an ancient enemy. Rearmament—even if permitted by the Allied powers—would put an intolerable burden upon an already hard-pressed economy. A good many of these leaders prefer to avoid the issue of rearmament. They are quite satisfied that, for a reasonable interval, the Americans should continue to man the bastions and meet the payroll.

Whatever the outcome of high-level negotiations about the future of Japan, it seems to me of the first importance that a forthright statement of policy should be made by our government. It will hearten the wondering Japanese, it will warn the Soviet, and it will make our position clear to all the world. The statement can be brief: "We will consider aggression against Japan as we would consider aggression against our own territorial limits. If aggression occurs, we will fight."

Japan's security and our own are now indivisible.

POSTSCRIPTUM

The concluding chapter of this book was written before the Communist aggression in Korea. After sober reflection, I have changed it in no way. The future will prove or disprove the validity of a point of view.

July 10, 1950

UNI

ORGANIC REGIMENTS OF DIVISIONS
IN THE PACIFIC (EIGHTH ARMY)

Americal Division
132nd Infantry Regiment
164th Infantry Regiment
182nd Infantry Regiment

1st Cavalry Division
5th Cavalry Regiment
12th Cavalry Regiment
7th Cavalry Regiment
8th Cavalry Regiment

6th Infantry Division
1st Infantry Regiment
20th Infantry Regiment
63rd Infantry Regiment

7th Infantry Division
17th Infantry Regiment
32nd Infantry Regiment
184th Infantry Regiment

11th Airborne Division
187th Glider Infantry Regiment
188th Parachute Infantry Regiment
511th Parachute Infantry Regiment

24th Infantry Division
19th Infantry Regiment
21st Infantry Regiment
34th Infantry Regiment

25th Infantry Division
27th Infantry Regiment
35th Infantry Regiment
161st Infantry Regiment

27th Infantry Division
105th Infantry Regiment
106th Infantry Regiment
165th Infantry Regiment

31st Infantry Division
124th Infantry Regiment
155th Infantry Regiment
167th Infantry Regiment

32nd Infantry Division
126th Infantry Regiment
127th Infantry Regiment
128th Infantry Regiment

33rd Infantry Division
123rd Infantry Regiment
130th Infantry Regiment
136th Infantry Regiment

37th Infantry Division
129th Infantry Regiment
145th Infantry Regiment
148th Infantry Regiment

38th Infantry Division
149th Infantry Regiment
151st Infantry Regiment
152nd Infantry Regiment

40th Infantry Division
108th Infantry Regiment
160th Infantry Regiment
185th Infantry Regiment

291

41st Infantry Division
162nd Infantry Regiment
163rd Infantry Regiment
186th Infantry Regiment

43rd Infantry Division
103rd Infantry Regiment
169th Infantry Regiment
172nd Infantry Regiment

77th Infantry Division
305th Infantry Regiment
306th Infantry Regiment
307th Infantry Regiment

81st Infantry Division
321st Infantry Regiment
322nd Infantry Regiment
323rd Infantry Regiment

93rd Infantry Division
25th Infantry Regiment
368th Infantry Regiment
369th Infantry Regiment

96th Infantry Division
381st Infantry Regiment
382nd Infantry Regiment
383rd Infantry Regiment

97th Infantry Division
303rd Infantry Regiment
386th Infantry Regiment
387th Infantry Regiment

98th Infantry Division
389th Infantry Regiment
390th Infantry Regiment
391st Infantry Regiment

INDEX

INDEX

ARMED FORCES

GENERAL INDEX

Inada, Maj. Gen., 119
Indo-China, 9, 169, 186
Indonesia, 243, 248
Invasion of Japan, *see* Japan, invasion
Ipo Dam (Luzon), 255
Irving, Frederick A., 104, 107-109, 173, 203, 219
Itagaki, Seishiro, 267

Janail Abirir II, Muhammed, 234-35, 244
Jannarone, John R., 160
Japan: constitution, 274-75, 287; currency stabilization, 276, 283; defense, 278, 287-89; disarmament, 269, 280, 287, 289; economic status, 269, 276, 287; food, 282; industry, 269-70, 276, 279, 282-83, 286, 289; invasion, plans for, 166, 232, 245, 259, 260; merchant fleet, 269, 283, 289; occupation of, 107, 164, 260 ff; peace treaty, 288, 289; surrender, 255-58, 259, 264; relations with US, 272-74, 276-79, 282, 284-85, 286-87.
Japan, Armed Forces: military character, xii-xiv, xxii, 119, 257-58, 283-84; preparation, 18-19, 72, 90, 113, 114, 136, 150, 163, 211; tactics, 24, 69-70, 114-15, 118-19, 153, 169-70, 189, 195, 213-14, 222
— Air Forces, 9, 37-38, 120, 163, 166, 167, 171, 186, 225, 248
— Army: 8-9, 10, 12-13, 52-53, 61, 73, 105, 122, 140, 143, 146, 151-53, 178-180, 181, 187, 225-26, 233, 237-39; troop surrender, 101, 181, 215, 239, 244, 255-58; *see also* Casualties
— Naval Forces, 8-9, 89, 120, 169, 171, 186, 197, 233, 248
Japanese High Command, xii, 119
Jautefa Bay (Dutch New Guinea), 109
Java, 9, 242-43
Jerome, Clayton C., 250
Jeune, P. C., 133
Johnson, Nelson, 78, 81, 82
Joint Chiefs of Staff, 5, 90, 101, 167-68, 232
Jolly, Eustis A., 180
Jolo (Sulu Arch.), 201, 234-36, 243-44; City, 234; Sultan of, *see* Janail Abirir II
Jones, Carey, 81-82
Jones, G. A. A., 160

Kabacan (Mindanao), 217, 220-21, 224-226
Kamakura (Honshu), 261

Kamikaze planes, 184, 262
Kanazawa (Honshu), 276
Kanto Plain (Honshu), 245, 261
Kapa Kapa Trail (Papua), 12, 13, 23, 56, 93
Katena Airstrip (Okinawa), 260
Kavieng (New Ireland), 126
Keele, Charles C., 74-75
Kempei-Tei, 272
Kemper Military School, xii
Kenney, George, xv, 6, 11, 12, 13, 14, 21, 34-35, 76, 89, 106, 159, 170, 171, 176-177, 187, 244, 248-49
Kennon Highway (Luzon), 251
Kennon, Lyman W. V., 251
Kiangan (Luzon), 253, 256-58
Kibawe (Mindanao), 224-25, 227, 239; Trail, 238
Killerton, Cape, *see* Cape Killerton
Kimura, Heitaro, 267
Kincaid, Thomas C., 164, 177, 206
King, Edward L., xv
King, Ernest J., 165, 168, 169
Kiriwina I. (Trobriand Is.), 90-91
Kitazona, Maj. Gen., 119-20
Kitchener, Lord Horatio Herbert, 81
Knudsen, William S., 79
Kobe (Honshu), 274
Kojiama, Shin, 272
Kokoda Trail (Papua), 13, 19, 33, 56, 62, 249
Kolchak, Alexander V., xiii
Korea, 278; riots in, 274
Korim Bay (Biak), 151
Krueger, Walter, 71, 98, 106-107, 122, 138, 144, 156-57, 174-75, 243
Kueker, Earl E., 148-49
Kuper Range (NE New Guinea), 92
Kure (Honshu), 270
Kuril Is., 278, 286
Kurita, Bunji, 169, 184
Kuroda, Shigenori, 170
Kuzume, Col., 143, 146, 150, 151, 153
Kwantung Army, 170, 285
Kyoto (Honshu), 263
Kyushu (Japan), 245, 270

Lae (NE New Guinea), 23-24, 75, 76, 89, 92, 94, 95, 103
Laguna de Bay (Luzon), 198
Lake Lanao (Mindanao), 217
Lake Sentani (Dutch New Guinea), 102, 109, 110, 138, 156, 158
Lake Taal (Luzon), 189
Lanao, Lake, *see* Lake Lanao
Launcelot, Sgt., 130-32

Google

WAKE

A

MARSHALL
ISLANDS

AUSTRALIA

SYDNEY

MELBOURNE

NEW ZEALAND

§235   STATUTE MILES ⟶ ◉
SAN FRAN

MIDWAY

PEARL HARBOR ○

HAWAII

C   I   F   I   C

O   C   E   A

PACIFIC
THEATER,
1942

Black areas indicate territories
occupied by the Japanese

Lightning Source UK Ltd.
Milton Keynes UK
UKHW022309070223
416656UK00016B/198